STRATEGIC

PROSPECTS FOR

HRM

Shaun Tyson gained a BA and Ph.D. from London University (Goldsmiths and LSE), where he studied social sciences. Following experience with the Ministry of Labour, he spent 11 years as personnel manager first with the Thorn Group of companies and then with the Bestobell Group. For four years he was a lecturer in personnel management at the Civil Service College. In 1979 he joined Cranfield School of Management where he is now professor of HRM, director of the Human Resource Research Centre, and dean of the Faculty of Management. He has published 13 books and over 50 articles and papers on HRM and has acted as consultant to a range of public- and private-sector organisations both in the UK and overseas. He is a fellow of the IPD and a member of the British Psychological Society, the British Academy of Management, and the Association Française de Gestion des Ressources Humaines.

The Institute of Personnel and Development is the leading publisher of books and reports for personnel and training professionals and students and for all those concerned with the effective management and development of people at work. For full details of all our titles please telephone the Publishing Department on 0181 263 3387.

STRATEGIC PROSPECTS FOR HRM

edited by
Shaun Tyson

INSTITUTE OF PERSONNEL AND DEVELOPMENT

Design by Paperweight
Typeset by The Comp-Room, Aylesbury
Printed in Great Britain by
Short Run Press, Exeter

British Library Cataloguing in Publication Data
A catalogue record for this book is available from the British Library

ISBN 0-85292-578-6

The views expressed in this book are the authors' own and may not necessarily reflect those of the IPD.

**INSTITUTE OF PERSONNEL
AND DEVELOPMENT**

IPD House, Camp Road, London SW19 4UX
Tel: 0181 971 9000   Fax: 0181 263 3333
Registered office as above. Registered Charity No. 1038333
A company limited by guarantee. Registered in England No. 2931892

CONTENTS

CONTRIBUTORS

Chris Brewster is professor of European HRM at Cranfield School of Management. He joined Cranfield 10 years ago following extensive experience in trade unions, government, specialist magazines, personnel management, and consultancy. He is a prolific author of books and articles. He has also taught and provided consultancy services to major organisations around the world.

Cary Cooper is professor of organisational psychology at the Manchester School of Management, University of Manchester Institute of Science and Technology (UMIST). He is the author of over 70 books and has written over 250 articles for academic journals. A frequent contributor to national newspapers, TV, and radio, he is editor-in-chief of the *Journal of Organizational Behavior* and co-editor of the medical journal, *Stress Medicine*. He is also a fellow of the British Psychological Society and of the Royal Society of Arts. He is currently working on two books for the IPD: *Stress and the Law* (with Jill Earnshaw) and *The HR Aspects of Mergers and Acquisitions* (with Dr Sue Cartwright).

Alan Fell is managing director of human resources and organisation consultancies at the Alexander Consulting Group, and is a visiting fellow at Cranfield University School of Management. He has extensive experience in working with companies to develop greater effectiveness to meet their client and customer requirements and to integrate business objectives. His client responsibilities lie primarily with top team strategy and organisational change, strategic business development and planning and, of course, the evaluation of human resource strategies. A well-known lecturer and speaker, he is also the author, with S. Tyson, of *Evaluating the Personnel Function* (2nd rev. edn 1992), a major contribution to the design of practical personnel strategies.

Peter Herriot has recently been appointed associate director of the Institute for Employment Studies, having previously worked as director of research, Sundridge Park Management Centre. He is also visiting professor at the City University Business School and the University of Surrey. His main interest is in the management of careers by organisations and individuals, and the changes in progress in the nature of the employment relationship. He is co-author with Carole Pemberton of *Competitive Advantage through Diversity* (1994) and *New Deals: The revolution in managerial careers* (1995). He contributes regularly to academic and professional journals, and is a fellow of the IPD and the British Psychological Society.

Andrew Kakabadse is professor of international management development at Cranfield School of Management and director of the Cranfield Centre for International Management Development. He acts as a consultant to numerous multinational organisations and has recently completed a major world study of chief executives and top executive teams. He has written over 70 articles and published 14 books, including the best-selling *Politics of Management*. He holds positions on the boards of several companies and is external examiner to a number of universities. He is the editor of the *Journal of Management Development*, the outgoing editor of the *Journal of Managerial Psychology*, and associate editor of the *Leadership and Organisation Development Journal*.

Alistair Mant is chairman of the Socio-Technical Strategy Group, an association of executives, researchers, and consultants interested in organisational transformation and blunder-avoidance driven by socio-technical (human factors) research. He has a worldwide practice in leadership development and spends a third of each year working with public- and private-sector clients in Australia (his home country). He has worked in business (mainly IBM), academia (Manchester Business School and South Bank University), and research-based consultancy (Tavistock Institute). His books include *The Dynamics of Management Education* (1981) and *Leaders We Deserve* (1983).

Mick Marchington is professor of HRM at the Manchester School of Management, University of Manchester Institute of Science and Technology (UMIST), where he has worked since the mid-1980s. He has written widely on employee relations and HRM, specialising in employee involvement, workplace industrial relations, HRM in retailing, and more recently on the links between HRM and total quality management. He is currently chief examiner for the IPD and has played a major part in the redesign of the professional education scheme.

Andrew Mayo is a consultant in people and organisation development, operating internationally. A B.Sc. in chemical engineering and an M.Sc. in management, he has worked for nearly 30 years in major international organisations, leaving his last post as director of human resource development for the ICL Group in October 1995. He is a Fellow of the IPD and also of the Royal Society of Arts. He is the author of *Managing Careers: Strategies for organisations* (1991) and co-author, with Elizabeth Lank, of *The Power of Learning* (1994), both published by the IPD. He is a frequent speaker at business schools and public seminars.

Keith Sisson is director of the Industrial Relations Research Unit of the Warwick Business School. Before taking up this post he was labour secretary of the Newspaper Publishers Association. The founding editor of the *Human Resource Management Journal*, he is also the author of *Negotiating in Practice* (IPM 1977), *Industrial Relations in Fleet Street* (1975), and *The Management of Collective Bargaining* (1987). In 1989 he edited *Personnel Management*, a collection of specialist contributions. He is at present investigating developments in pay and working time, as well as the management of industrial relations in multinational companies.

Barbara White is lecturer in psychology at the University of Liverpool, where she teaches final-year and Masters students organisational psychology and organisational behaviour. An MA and Ph.D. in organisational psychology from the Manchester School of Management, University of Manchester Institute of Science and Technology (UMIST), she specialises in women's career development (in 1992 she published a book, *Women's Career Development: A study of high-flyers*). She has presented a series of conference papers and published several articles on the subject.

Editor's acknowledgements

I wish to acknowledge with thanks the various permissions for quotations from other works; the unstinting efforts of the commissioning editor, Matthew Reisz; and the help of the secretarial and administrative staff at our contributors' organisations in producing the typescripts.

PREFACE

This book originates from the mixture of curiosity and apprehension we have for our future as a new century and a new millennium dawn. The general mood of uncertainty is fed by a coalescence of concerns: the end of the old power blocks, demographic shifts, global trading, the strategic use of IT, and rising popular expectations, for example. Both the positive and the negative trends cause us to pause and to wonder what these changes mean. The management of people at work is changing in response to these general economic, social, and technological factors. New types of organisation are emerging, there are new ways of using the labour market, new employee relationships, new occupations and new policies to achieve competitive advantage through people management.

The end of the millennium has a powerful symbolic effect on the imagination. It can be perceived as a full stop in history. However, so much of what is said and done at work is dependent on our history and culture that we must be careful not to assume that there is no continuity. Any forecast of the future must be rooted firmly in an understanding of the present. The approach we have adopted here is therefore to examine current issues in order to foresee the changes and the trends to come. Given that we wish the text to be issues-driven, we had first to identify the current and future issues on which to base our analysis.

Most definitions of human resource management (HRM) place the management of human resources at the centre of the business strategy. How organisations use their people resources to achieve their objectives must be the critical matter to ponder when considering the contribution this function can make – and we have naturally taken this to be the starting-point.

The overall changes to work are chief amongst the drivers for change in HRM. The shifts in demographic patterns, the new knowledge-based occupations, and the changing orientations to work provide us with one aspect to the new working environment which is emerging. Of equal importance, new organisation structures and new approaches to corporate governance offer the other side to the scene-setting. From these new structures and the labour market strategies that accompany them new employee relations approaches have been emerging. The diversity that characterises British industrial relations means that there are a number of different scenarios we can predict, each with significant implications for the human resource policies pursued. Underpinning all our understanding of HRM is our appreciation of how people think and behave in response to different policies. All HRM is predicated upon the assumptions about what actions employees are likely to take in response to external and internal influences. The study of organisation behaviour thus is the key to the HRM field.

For management, leadership abilities and the capacity to create stakeholder value are perhaps the most tested abilities. By comparing Japanese and European approaches to these qualities we are able to move away from the old assumptions about styles of management, and to see where management development and organisation development can contribute. The end of the career concept, the move towards multiple careers, and the focus on the psychological contract are now part of everyday organisational life. How management in the future can retain the motivation and the commitment of employees must be a concern. Organisations now trade globally, and the multicultural aspects to all our societies imply that HRM will become more and more concerned with managing diversity. Consequently, how to create multinational management teams and how to cope with cultural differences within the work force are policy issues.

Measuring HRM performance has long been regarded as essential if HRM is to have strategic prospects, but has equally long been regarded as a task fraught with methodological difficulties. For the future, there will be little chance of creating new human resource strategies that gain the support of management unless evaluation techniques are more developed.

These topics are dealt with in the book by acknowledged experts, each of whom has a substantial research and publications record in the field. They are able to bring to their chapters a clear insight from which the future scenario for HRM may be constructed. Of course, no one is blessed (or cursed) with powers of divination. This is not a book devoted to clairvoyancy. What we hope our readers will see we have done is to analyse current trends, set out the arguments, and offer an informed judgement of how these trends will develop as we move into the next century.

Shaun Tyson
Cranfield 1995

CHAPTER ONE

Human Resource and Business Strategy

Shaun Tyson

The closing years of the twentieth century have been distinguished to a remarkable degree by institutional review in the face of unpredictable change. Any consensus over the role and purpose of social or governmental institutions broke down in the long years of Conservative governments after 1979. Expressed in various ways, the basis for this review seems to be a challenge to existing values and economic practices. In this book we are engaged in a similar *fin de siècle* review of human resource management (HRM) as a set of practices, activities and philosophies designed to manage the employment relationship. Our review takes the form of a critical examination of the constituent parts of the field and a debate on where we see this field moving as the new century dawns.

The need to take stock in order to see what, if any, progress has been achieved and to look forward to the next century is only partly prompted by the coming millennium. A felt need for change seems to pervade all our old institutions: the monarchy, Parliament, the law, education, health care and the ethics of business itself have all been called into question in the 1990s. Perhaps behind the questions, often of a practical nature about regulation, or how much profit should be retained by privatised utilities, are more fundamental uncertainties concerning the nature of our society, which are brought into sharper relief by the ambiguity surrounding the UK's relationships with the European Union. One is reminded of the general feelings that surfaced at the end of the nineteenth century:

> The late Victorians, though incapable of coping with their own distress, were beginning to be aware of it.
>
> Trevelyan (1946:579).

A century of new ideas has not solved all the old problems. Management as a distinct occupation grew in this century and is now separated from ownership. Whilst bringing specialist independent expertise to bear on organisational problems, the solutions in the first half of the century centred on formalising as many of the human work processes as possible. Technical systems were organised to maximise efficiency, but were perceived to be alienating (Blauner 1964) and susceptible to manipulation (Miller and Rice 1967) as workers sought to push back the frontiers of control (Fox 1974; Edwards and Scullion 1982).

Following Bendix (1959) we can see that management ideologies can be construed as an index of social structure. From the early days of Taylorism throughout the attempt to bring industrial conflict under the control of the broad social interest, to industry-level attempts to conduct collective bargaining, and now to legal regulation and local-level bargaining, there has been a growing bureaucratisation of work. The rules of work have been used in the legitimation of managerial roles, thereby shifting managerial roles into impersonal, formal relationships with workpeople (Nichols 1969; Fox 1974). The last quarter of this century has seen many attempts to change this trend, with the reduction of massive organisational hierarchies through de-layering, devolved structures, and through the trend towards various forms of 'empowerment' and gainsharing. Small is beautiful again, flexibility is much valued, and tailor-made products and services are prized.

Gospel (1992) has argued convincingly that labour and product markets have been important independent variables affecting HRM, and that corporate strategies, organisation structures, the quality of management, investment in new technology, and the division of labour have all influenced British labour management decisions through historical traditions and institutional structures. He goes on to place failure by management squarely on failures to develop sufficiently well-organised internal labour markets – arguing in a sense for a greater bureaucratisation of work rather than in favour of a growing reliance on the secondary labour market, in which subcontracting, casual, temporary, and other forms of employment contract can be formed as a flexible sourcing strategy (Atkinson 1985). The alternatives presented by this debate offer two views of HRM (Tyson 1995): the hard contract based on transaction costs, where companies are organised as markets; and the soft contract based on socialisation and values, where companies are organised as hierarchies. (See also Williamson 1973.) The combination of the hard and soft contracts, with contrasting stable v casual, insecure employment, has consequences for our society. Moves to flex the labour market are reminiscent of nineteenth-century approaches towards employment. If there are now two nations – the 'haves' and the 'have-nots' – how will the 'have-nots' become incorporated into our society? Trade union roles in defending workers' interests have diminished, and trade unions now have to choose between adopting a 'quality of working life' strategy, a 'Friendly Society' strategy, and integrating their work with a more pluralist form of HRM, according to Guest (1995).

However, capital now moves relatively freely around the world, and business strategies are set less in the context of particular societal needs, and more in the arena of global competition. The societal implications for independently orchestrated business strategies have not yet been fully explored. There is a large literature on the causes of HRM. Now it is time for us to consider the consequences.

In this chapter, human resource strategies will be examined as responses to new business strategies and to changes in the planning environment. The consequences of these changes, it is argued, are new ways of organising work and a changed HRM function. The chapter seeks to examine the strategic options currently available to firms in the UK, and to reveal the inadequacies of the present strategic stance in HRM in the face of the likely future challenges. Many organisations are already responding to these challenges and have reviewed the place of HRM in the creation and operation of business strategies – using the concept of HRM as a shorthand for the whole range of line and personnel function activities designed to manage the employment relationship. In examining what to do, those concerned with integrating HRM within organisational or business strategies will be reframing the activity in a new organisational and societal role.

Business and human resource strategy – definitional problems

Business strategy has been studied as a method for obtaining a competitive advantage – for example through the generic strategies of cost leadership, or differentiation or focus on one of these two in a niche market (Porter 1980). To Miles and Snow (1978) business strategy was best defined as a broad organisational approach, with 'defender', 'prospector', 'analyser', and 'reactor' organisations each taking a particular strategic stance according to their position in the market-place.

None of these rather simple classifications of strategy is entirely satisfactory (Bowman 1992). Apart from the difficulty most researchers have noted in applying these taxonomies to real companies, where often there is a mixture of strategies, such as companies seeking to compete on a basis of cost and of quality, the neat formulations proposed do not match the speed of change and complexity of organisations that offer a range of products and services, and that compete simultaneously in a variety of markets. Product and service life-cycles are now rapidly traversed; new technology and instant communication result in immediate reactions from competitors. Competition for some goods and such services as cars, white goods, electrical equipment, airline travel, and financial services is increasingly international. Different products or services have to be sold with many different market-places in mind, therefore. Early formulations of strategy tended to reify organisations, presuming that 'the organisation' could act with one voice, with all the key players accepting without argument an agreed definition of what should happen.

A further, major criticism derives from the failure of the complex corporate planning approaches, so favoured in the 1960s and 1970s (Mintzberg 1994). As Mintzberg puts it, amongst the key false assumptions about strategic planning is the fallacious belief that the analytical planning approaches, necessary because the corporate planning models required a disaggregation of the issues for planning purposes, would produce synthesis. Objectives, budgets, strategies, and programmes did not link together in practice in the way the early writers such as Ansoff seemed to believe. Three further fallacious assumptions are also shown to be behind strategic planning: that strategists can be detached from managers; that strategy is or should be driven by hard data rather than intuition; and that the context in which planning occurs is sufficiently stable to allow reliable forecasts to be made.

Increasingly therefore strategy is theorised as a human process. Strategies are seen as 'emergent', not necessarily pre-set and carefully calculated; a difference is seen to exist between intended and realised strategy; and strategy may be seen as an output from complex decision-making processes (Johnson 1992; Hampden-Turner 1990). Although these interpersonal processes are themselves common to behaviour amongst all groups of people, what makes these especially significant is the strategic use of power amongst the dominant coalition to achieve personal aims which have become organisational aims (Kakabadse 1983, 1991).

Whereas there may be a lingering doubt that strategies have sufficient permanence or general acceptance within organisations to be anything more than just a set of vague, probably incoherent, plans to achieve a very broad organisational aim, business strategies do have sufficient general recognition for the phrase to be used by senior managers. Although in some cases the strategies could be reduced to the objective to survive and provide income and status for those with organisational power, there is ample empirical evidence that managers do strive to reach generally agreed goals. There is evidence of written strategies used as a touchstone for guiding action. Even if one accepts that talk of strategies by those at the top may be prompted by a desire to legitimise their status and the power to obtain their own ends, the very power play of life at the top necessitates strategies for achieving goals. That those in such senior positions use strategy for their own career benefit may be true, but far from invalidating the notion of strategy, this provides a sound reason for its existence.

In view of the potential confusion, some definitions are in order. Business strategy may be defined as 'the attempt by those who control an organisation to find ways to position their business/organisation objectives so that they can exploit the planning environment, and make the optimum use of capital and human assets'. This definition stresses two important elements in strategy: the need to respond and to place the organisation in the most favourable position possible in an increasingly uncertain environment, and the need to make use of the strengths of the organisation in exploiting any opportunities available. Strategy is not static: it changes in response to external threats as well as to internal pressures. Although strategy is usually perceived as relating to the long term, there is no logical or empirical reason for making this assumption or, at least, for regarding the planning horizon as fixed, for example, at five years or more.

Although military theorists such as von Clausewitz and Moltke argued to the contrary, the merging of the tactical, day-to-day operations and the strategy perceived to be best for the organisation is quite normal. Tactics in a military sense was about achieving success in a battle, whereas strategy was concerned with the overall conduct of the campaign. This idea gained ground in the nineteenth century, when war was used as an instrument of national policy. However, for commercial organisations, failure in the short term means there will be no long term for the organisation; it was John Maynard Keynes who commented 'in the long run we are all dead' (*Collected Writings IV*, 1971). The speeding up of everyday life through technology and greater awareness of the interrelationships between events and actions has moved modern organisations to a more immediate approach. In retail and the service sector, and consequently in the manufacturers that supply them, there is constant pressure for change, inimical of long-range strategy. The end of long-range corporate planning has dealt a blow to the perception that strategy concerns solely the long term.

Along with the conception of the long-range planning approach, there was a belief that detailed functional plans should be prepared to support the corporate plan. 'Corporate strategies' are sometimes differentiated from 'business strategies'. Corporate strategy is seen as the overall strategy related to the portfolio of business interests, whereas business strategy is the term used to describe intentions relating to particular products, services, or at the level of the strategic business unit (SBU). Functional plans would therefore be prepared at local (company, SBU) level and at corporate or group level. There is evidence to support that this happens, but not in the neat simplistic way advocated in textbooks.

All the evidence from both surveys and case-studies shows that human resource strategies do not exist in all organisations (Storey 1992; Brewster and Hegewisch 1994), and that there is a significant gap between theory and practice in the related human resource planning activity (Rothwell 1995). Brewster and Hegewisch claim there are around 50 per cent of companies with a written HR strategy in the UK. Unfortunately, there is no agreement on what an HR strategy is. In particular, the differences between HR strategies and policies is not clear, and companies may therefore be reporting the existence of policies in such areas as recruitment, training, development and rewards. The difficulties of defining industrial relations strategies are outlined by Thurley and Wood (1983), who go on to show how even at an empirical level there is such enormous diversity that generalisation is impossible. These variations include differences according to size, industry sector, and ownership. Amongst the problems noted by Rothwell and accepted by the main surveys in this field are the problems of understanding the complex interpersonal processes where strategy is formed. There are also evidently social desirability effects in survey responses, as uncovered by Marginson *et al* (1988): in their survey 84 per cent of UK employers claimed to have an overall employee policy and 50 per cent a written policy – but most managers could not describe it. There are therefore strong possibilities for misreporting due, for example, to the social desirability of claiming to have a policy as opposed to the embarrassment of stating that the management of people at work is left to chance.

When defining human resource strategy we are incorporating policies and practices, and the overall philosophies of management (if any exist) espoused by the company/organisation. We recognise that these may vary at corporate, group and company/unit level. Human resource strategy can be defined as a set of ideas, policies, and practices that management adopts in order to achieve a people management objective.

A study of 30 high-performing UK-owned organisations revealed three distinct approaches to strategy formation (Tyson 1995). Companies mostly adopted flexible approaches to strategy formation, seeking to create flexible responsive structures and policies so that they could respond to any future challenges. There was also some evidence of formal long-range planning, but this was only in capital-intensive businesses such as mining or where there was a technical need for long-time horizons, as in the nuclear industry. Also apparent were 'attributional' strategies, ie strategies that were really *ex post facto* rationalisations of a stream of managerial decisions.

Human resource strategies as functionally supportive sets of plans did exist, but were very much draft documents, constantly up for revision, and were framed to reinterpret organisational or business/corporate strategies into people management objectives, with all the implications for policies and practices. There were some formal planning processes, especially in regard to succession planning and management development, but otherwise the planning approach supported Purcell's (1989) idea that human resource strategies are typically 'downstream' (second- or third-order strategies) from first-order business or corporate strategies. A review of human resource strategy documents shows certain commonalities:

- a review of external influences. These include the political (eg what the effects of a government change will be, or European institutional arrangements); the economic (inflation, interest rate, unemployment, pay prospects); and the social (demographic, marital, crime and other trends)
- technical and social (the impact of new technology on work, communications etc) and any specific legislative trends or changes anticipated – for example the Employment Rights and Disability Act or the European directive on atypical workers may be cited
- an examination of the main business trends as they are likely to affect human resources in particular – expansion, contraction, and any collaborative arrangements
- the examination in turn of each main policy area, in order to analyse the impact of external and business change on, for example
    employee resourcing
    employee relations
    rewards
    health and safety
    training and development
    performance management
- a description of the prospects for the type of service from the specialist

human resource function. Relationships with line management, the expertise required in the function, and the way the function should operate in the future are dealt with here.

The amount of emphasis on each of these topics varies considerably according, for example, to whether there is trade union recognition on any or all of the sites covered, the effects of legislation on any specific industry, and the organisation's stance on such issues as equal opportunities. There is also an overall 'flavour' to the strategy emanating from the organisation's philosophy of management. The espoused values generate particular emphases on such policy areas as rewards, seen for example in a move towards single status, and employee relations, through for example methods of employee involvement. Human resource strategy documents often explicitly state what the values are, and how the management process should reflect these values.

From this description we can see that human resource strategy is concerned with integration, as Baird and Meshoulam (1988) put it, of both an internal 'fit' of strategy to policies, and an external 'fit' between the organisation and its environment. HRM reinterprets business strategy into human resource policies, whilst also seeking to maintain a coherent management philosophy. Human resource strategy is therefore the object of strain and pressure. The process of creating a strategy is one in which attempts are made to reconcile the various pressures, with varying degrees of success. The first stage in creating strategy is typically to scan the political, economic, social, and technological environment where the organisation operates.

Changes in the planning environment

Any observer of managerial thought in the last quarter of the twentieth century would notice the effects of a move to the political right that has now shifted the grounds on which any debate about social philosophy and management ideology takes place.

The characteristics of the new philosophy are an acceptance that private-sector ownership, even if mixed with some public ownership, is the norm, and that the collapse of socialist systems is taken as proof of capitalism's inevitable march forward. The related conceptions made managerial prerogatives paramount, and a belief in a unitary frame of reference became the received wisdom. Along with this ideology comes a belief in individually directed policies rather than collectivist ones. The objectives for this philosophy placed efficiency goals as the key to organisational survival, so value for money and shareholder value became the priority, rather than harmony or broader social goals. The philosophy espoused could, of course, be justified on Benthamite utilitarian grounds, as a means by which the greatest happiness will be achieved for the greatest number of people; however, there seems to be no necessary connection between managerialism with its efficiency goals and the public good without some method for redistributing wealth. At the heart of the debate on the kind of European Union which should be created is the unresolved question of whom the market is created for. If, in fact, it is for the people of Europe, then the legislation contained in the Social Chapter would have a purpose.

The economic changes in the planning environment have stimulated a new approach to management. Large-scale unemployment at around 20 million people in the European Union has come from industrial structure changes. The collapse of the older industries such as mining, heavy engineering, and shipbuilding has been matched by a rise in the more efficient newer industries, where occupations based on knowledge have been created, along with semi-skilled assembly work and a variety of service industry jobs, many of which are to be found within small organisations — around 27 per cent of those employed work for firms with fewer than 20 employees. Many of the new jobs are part-time or are based on non-standard contractual relationships. Using proportions of the working population, there are around 24 per cent employed part-time, 3.6 per cent on temporary contracts, and approximately 12 per cent self-employed (*D.E. Gazette*, July 1994). In addition, there are many people with what amounts to casual work (even at managerial level); and short-term contracts have become more popular. The restructuring process has resulted in many functions such as IT, accountancy, training and management services being outsourced. Outsourcing is a preferred option now for many manufacturers seeking reduced labour costs.

The economic aims for the changes were clear: European and global competition have had to be met by a constant pressure to reduce costs and, in the 1990s recession, to concentrate on core business. The expansionist 1980s were a time when human resource solutions were attempted during organisation development activities. In the 1990s recession, structural change has not been so easily supported by the human resource function. The aim has been to strip out costs, form flatter structures more responsive to market needs, and to change processes rather than to build up strong cultures or elaborate human resource systems. This has been a time to return to the core business, to expand through alliances and joint ventures. The economic case for change may have been generally accepted by working people, but of itself such a case does not justify the means. The unpopularity of the Conservative Government (for example in opinion polls and in the local elections of May 1995) has derived from the absence of a social or moral mandate. The laudable aims of inflation reduction, efficiency in public spending, and free trade in markets have not been enough without a social purpose.

The social changes that have accompanied economic structural change have reinforced the sense that new directions are being taken. Demographic trends have changed the age distribution of the workforce. The current prediction is that the number of people aged over 90 will double by 2001, and there will be a significant increase in all ages over 35. These changes coincide with changes in family structure which have become more noticeable – 20 per cent of families in the UK now consist of one parent, mainly single mothers, who gain 64 per cent of their income from state benefits, and there are increasing numbers of single-person households. More than half of the working population are women, and women are forming a higher proportion of young people in higher education than ever before. There are increasing numbers of young people taking various kinds of higher education courses, as a consequence of which fewer than half of 16–18-year-olds are in the labour force. Ethnic minorities are an increasing proportion of the workforce, which is one reason why employers are turning their minds to how to manage increasing diversity at work.

The trade union and industrial relations trends represent a backcloth of turbulence and change. The law has entered industrial and commercial life through a constant legislative stream. Within the Thatcher years (1979–90) there was an express government policy to reduce trade union power by 'giving the power back to individuals' and by removing the protection that unions had enjoyed during industrial action, through allowing claims for damages under the common law (except for a limited range of cases). Trade union membership fell steadily throughout the 1980s; it is reduced now to approximately one-third of the workforce as members. Unions have also been under financial pressures (Willman *et al* 1992). More and more firms have derecognised unions, more mergers between unions have occurred and an attempt has been made at strategic reorientation by the larger unions. Local-level bargaining has become widespread, and changes to the large public-sector organisations has also tended to push more decision-making down to the SBU level, including industrial negotiations (Millward 1994). Alternative models for managing industrial relations are present, acting as exemplars and stimulating new approaches, whether Japanese, North American or European models (Wickens 1987; Brewster and Hegewisch 1994). Amongst the institutional pressures for change in the UK are movements towards more joint consultation, sponsored by Brussels, the felt need for improved communication and supervision, employee involvement and gainsharing. However, one could argue that it is really the various effects of legislative pressure and labour market changes (including occupational changes) that have had the most important influence on industrial relations. Reduction in trade union membership derives from changed employment patterns, more women at work and the end of the large factory complexes of the mid-twentieth century. Reductions in militancy come from high levels of unemployment and difficulty in mounting quick responses to management provocation whilst remaining within the law.

New information technology and robots, the TQM movement, new production methods such as JIT, and the significance of logistics to all business have also stimulated changes to working life. Most of these changes come from outside the human resource function (Clark 1993) but have had a profound effect on the management of people, through new occupations, increased teamwork, new organisation structures and the linked concepts of empowerment, teambuilding, continuous learning and employee involvement schemes. The idea of 'corporate citizenship' and the ultimate flexible worker comes to mind, where employees are seen to be entirely at the service of their customers, both external and internal. It is not surprising that books such as *The Managed Heart* (Hochschild 1983) and *The Fifth Discipline* (Senge 1990) have had such an impact on organisation development.

There is a curious contrast here between rhetoric and reality (Storey 1992; Blyton and Turnbull 1992). In spite of the talk about greater employee commitment, all the anecdotal evidence and much of our own experience point to the increasingly instrumental attachment to work exhibited by employees. If anything, lifestyles are changing to give a greater emphasis to home and family and to more personal values. Personal development is meant for all, not just the rich few. 'Self-actualisation' is now often seen to be achieved through a better balance between home and work. The capacity through new technology to work at home blurs the distinction but also caters for the felt need to make more personal choices, to be in control of one's own time and one's own destiny. Dual career issues have also forced couples to rethink their personal strategies for coping with home, children, work, money, and family relations. The demands for elder care and care in the community for the sick force such a re-evaluation also. Lifestyle includes 'workstyle', and in so doing alters both.

The debate on HRM

The debate about whether 'human resource management' represented a new way of 'doing' personnel management, expressed in the notion that HRM represented a new paradigm, came to the fore in the 1980s. Yet this was really a continuation of the long-standing debate on the inherent ambiguity surrounding this particular specialist managerial occupation. Changes in job title over the past century, from the 'welfare secretaries' of the 1890s, to the labour officers, employment officers, personnel officers, personnel managers and on to the human resource managers of the present day do not represent a long march of steady progress into the strategic decision-making caucus of the organisation.

Throughout the history of this occupation those working in it have been subject to self-doubt, to being undermined by line managers, and to being challenged about their contribution to the business (Hunter 1957; Niven 1967). There is an ambiguity cycle:

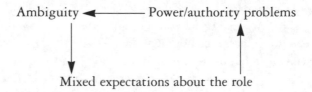

Ambiguity ◄——————— Power/authority problems

Mixed expectations about the role

This is where mixed and uncertain expectations concerning the way personnel specialists are expected to behave result in line managers' being unwilling to accord personnel specialists the authority they desire. One reason for the ambiguity is that there are different models of personnel management, each model representing different perceptions of the personnel function's main purpose (Tyson and Fell 1992).

These models vary between organisations and within large organisations, and change over time. The three models Tyson and Fell delineated were the 'architect model', a business manager model with a strong strategic orientation; the 'contracts manager' model, which sought to maintain the industrial relations systems and procedures in order to sustain or create harmony; and the 'clerk of works' model, aimed at providing a basic administrative service to line managers. Uncertainty about what the function can or should do has therefore strengthened the view that personnel management is not central to business concerns. Recent criticisms have fuelled questions about the legitimacy of the function by arguing that personnel management does not serve organisational goals (Fernie *et al* 1994).

Ambiguity partly accounts for the failures of earlier, prescriptive models of HRM. One feature of the self-doubt is the distinction between the rhetoric of personnel work and the reality of personnel roles. Personnel specialists have to face up to the reality that, in spite of their claims to professional status, and in opposition to their cherished beliefs about a humanitarian mission, what line manager colleagues often value most is the delivery of an efficient administrative service, with as little 'interference' in the running of the business as possible (Watson 1977; Ritzer and Trice 1969). The debate on HRM has to be seen in this context, therefore. Even such models as that produced by Beer *et al* (1984) failed to show the saliency of business strategy for HRM, and made no mention of customers amongst the major stakeholders.

A series of major studies during the early 1980s sought to build more positive and more accurate frameworks for understanding HRM. Using a contingency approach, Ackermann (1986) and Jackson, Schuler, and Rivero (1989) delineated the factors influencing HRM and examined policies in different contexts. Similarly, Hendry and Pettigrew (1992) researched the strategic orientation within HRM and set out the factors that influenced the strategic direction. The findings from these studies confirmed that organisation size, structure, and employee relations traditions influenced the role and function of HRM. Strategic orientation was affected by the maturity of the organisation, the difficulty of the business environment, the complexity of the business, and the firm's rate of growth.

A further range of studies have examined the question of 'fit' between human resource strategy and business strategy (Lengnick-Hall and Lengnick-Hall 1988). HRM's effectiveness has, it is argued, been shown to depend upon the integration of the human resource with the business strategy, especially through the process integration activities found in the work of the personnel department (Guest 1995). This latter point is well made by Storey (1992), who demonstrates from his extensive case-study work that the strategic integration of HRM arises from HRM's managing the change process. In essence both Guest and Storey are showing how HRM contributes through implementing strategy. This accords with Purcell's (1989) view that HR strategy is second- or third-order strategy, downstream from the main strategic decision-making undertaken by marketing and finance functions.

In an attempt to discover what contribution was made by those working in the HRM function, Tyson (1995) undertook a 30-company case-study research project looking at high-performing organisations, which was followed up by a further survey (sponsored by the IPD) of 61 high-performing and 61 low-performing companies. Amongst the findings was the significance of flexible strategies for these major corporations, who saw a benefit in avoiding rigid long-range plans. All these companies also ranked management development high on their strategic agenda and adopted strategic policy levers in employee development, organisation design and employee relations in order to fit their human resource strategies to their business strategies. Although there were similarities, there were also many striking differences between these companies, which should reinforce the cautious counsel not to generalise about HRM. For example, there were significant differences between centralised and highly decentralised organisation forms, between different industry sectors, and between the recently privatised businesses (which constituted around one third of the sample) and the rest. In the survey, personnel departments in leading companies were more involved in developing business strategy than those in trailing companies, and in these leading companies personnel departments were more able to predict change. From the evidence the role of human resource directors at divisional level may be as strategic as the role of human resource directors in the centre, given highly devolved structures.

A number of conclusions may be drawn from this brief summary of recent research into HRM. The debate about whether HRM represents a new management paradigm seems sterile now. There have always been different ways of doing personnel management, new models have always been added to old, but there will always be a variety of approaches according to the many internal factors, and to changes in the business environment.

A number of factors have emerged in the last two decades which have focused attention on managing the human resource as a main competitive advantage. This points to the significance of contexts for understanding HRM, and shows up the weaknesses of prescriptive accounts. The changing economic circumstances, labour markets, industrial structure and international competition affect companies in different ways. Similarly, new political ideologies influence management ideologies. The internal context is equally important, therefore. This includes the management philosophy and organisation structure, and the size, history, and culture of the firm. From the case-study research we know that there are enormous differences, for example, between Marks and Spencer and other retailers, such as those that are part of the Kingfisher Group; between pharmaceutical companies such as Glaxo and Zeneca; or between leisure/hotel companies such as Scottish and Newcastle, and Forte. The list could go on. Some companies, such as BAT, are a mixture of cultures whereas others, such as British Airways and BT, are working hard to create one strong culture based on shared values.

The last 20 years have witnessed transformational change for HRM. Even as the case-study research was being completed, ICI was splitting into two, Scottish and Newcastle had purchased the Chef and Brewer chain, and a year later Glaxo had bought Wellcome; indeed there were changes taking place in all industry sectors besides those in that particular study. One has only to reflect on change in financial services, with mergers between building societies, the takeover of the Midland Bank by Hong Kong Shanghai Bank, and the collapse and subsequent purchase of Barings to be aware that there is no stability in the commercial environment. In his chapter on organisation structure, Keith Sisson discusses some of the effects of this period of transformational change (Chapter 3). For HRM, the reduction in head office departments and the outsourcing of many traditional human resource activities (such as recruitment, training and reward restructuring) have potentially long-term consequences.

Nevertheless, there is evidence that in the 1980s and early 1990s human resource functions played a strategic role in high-performing businesses. This has centred around positioning the business in a flexible stance, able to move quickly into new configurations as business opportunities arise, integrating the human resource function as a process within line management and within strategy formation, and using human resource policy areas in employee relations, sourcing, development, and organisation design to push business strategies forward.

The evaluation of HRM remains a problem. Most of the policy areas are difficult to evaluate because they are not subject to the classic cost benefit approach. However, as Andrew Mayo shows in Chapter 9, there are now more and more attempts to find ways to evaluate HRM activity as a contribution to corporate performance. The continuing problems arising from the ambiguity of the personnel management role will only be resolved when HRM is understood through analytical models that account for its dynamic nature, and after a general theory has been agreed on which to base our discussion of its value.

Such a general theory is likely to be found by understanding the integration of HRM, and by accounting for the different levels of analysis at which it can be studied (Tyson 1995). It is argued that the strategic role for HRM therefore consists in translating societal-level variables and their effects into organisations' strategies and policies, whilst also managing the needs of organisation members.

Human resource strategies and the organisational consequences

The process of strategy formation is a process by which societal-level influences are translated into organisation-level responses, which in the case of human resource strategies requires a further adaption to both organisation-level variables and to the needs and expectations of organisation members (Tyson 1995). It is argued that the process by which this adaption occurs involves the use of the symbolic order to manage the meanings in the organisation.

Salaman (1992) suggests that there are three different types of strategy, these being cultural, structural and personnel systems strategies. We would prefer to differentiate between on the one hand overall human resource strategies developed to implement a change, eg those seeking to achieve transformational change within an organisation, which may for example be aimed at organisational renewal, and on the other hand specific human resource strategies used in support of a business strategy, which seek transactional change (Burke and Litwin 1992). The first group includes cultural, values, organisation development, and change management strategies, which seek therefore to change what happens within organisations *as a whole*. By contrast, transactional change strategies seek to alter the way things are done within the organisation that are aimed at securing *particular* sources of competitive advantage. These will be shaped by the ideology or philosophy of management, as for example the Japanese corporate approach, which until recently was centred on a 'lifetime employment' philosophy, the clan style of large Japanese corporations, and the 'soft' as distinct from the 'hard' contract. Table 1.1 shows the strategic typologies proposed.

Cultural strategies were evident in the major change programmes adopted when organisations sought to adapt in the mid-1980s. The recently privatised businesses in the UK are good examples of companies that have tried to relaunch themselves. Change programmes such as the British Airways 'winning for customers' initiative attempted to create entrepreneurial cultures amongst the newly privatised utilities, and are good examples of transformational change. All such programmes used integrated strategies to inculcate new values and new cultures. The changes to organisation structure can hardly be described as 'strategies', but the reorientation towards business processes, combined with flatter structures, pioneered by companies such as Carlson's Scandinavian Air Services over a decade ago, were intended to transform the organisations concerned by adopting a more 'organic', post-modernist approach (Burns and Stalker 1961).

Table 1.1

Broad strategies
Objectives: transformational change – changes to what happens.
Aimed at: organisational renewal.
Subjects: organisation development, change management, culture, values.
Examples: British Airways, BT.

Specific strategies
Objectives: transactional change – changes to procedures, systems, processes.
Aimed at: particular sources of competitive advantage.

Subjects: employee sourcing   ⎫   Differentiated according
                employee development ⎬   to management ideologies
                employee relations   ⎭   eg 'hard' *v* 'soft' contracting.

Examples: revised employment contracts, total compensation approaches, new forms of consultation.

The creation of specific human resource strategies to obtain a competitive advantage is the *raison d'être* of HRM. Such strategies are not produced in a vacuum but arise from specific business needs within an organisation's ideology. We have already outlined the two extremes of 'hard' and 'soft' contracting. The move towards hard contracting is a good example of how societal-level change is translated into an organisation-level response. The hard contract represents a shift towards a market-driven perspective, found for example in the reorganisation of the National Health Service, the shift towards matrix and network organisation structures, and the increased use of outsourcing, franchising and joint ventures.

Clearly, changes to strategies and to detailed policies are necessary in order to initiate cultural and structural change. However, cultural and structural changes come from an organisation-wide response to the markets, usually led by the CEO and the top team, with all the functional strategies supporting – in short, there has to be an integrated organisation strategy in place to achieve the objectives, but this is different from the strategies that will actually effect the process of change. These transformational change strategies are the process strategies to move the thinking, the values, and the culture of the organisation into a different direction. Central to the notion that there needs to be a fit between the two types of strategy in order to achieve the business strategy objectives is the notion of 'fit' between the functional strategies and those seeking to effect the change process. The capacity to fit process strategies to functional role was shown by Guest to be an important criterion of human resource effectiveness (Guest and Peccei 1994). Similarly, the capacity to fit internally and externally oriented strategies was claimed to be a source of superior organisational performance (Miles and Snow 1994; Baird and Meshoulam 1988).

Specific HR strategies developed to assist business strategies include sourcing strategies, which seek through new contractual forms to make the best use of the labour markets. Increasingly, people are appointed to achieve tasks rather than jobs. Now there are shifting clusters of tasks, replacing the hitherto conveniently fixed collection which used to be called jobs (Bridges 1995). Competency-based approaches to sourcing are already more in tune with strategic plans that have identified the competencies on which the company is to compete. The flexibility to be had from short-term contracts, casual labour, outsourcing, and subcontracting to suppliers (who themselves may subcontract further) has to be balanced against the long-term loss of skills and future capacities in the business. Changes to the labour market mean there is a continuing need for managements to develop people with diverse backgrounds; and there are also the perhaps more demanding expectations of a labour force who offer knowledge and creativity rather than muscle power and loyalty.

At a time when the career concept has collapsed, employee development strategies are amongst the most significant strategic levers (Tyson 1995; Fox 1991). For 'learning organisations' to be able to regenerate themselves they need development policies to be built into the company's ethos. This strategic significance derives from a coincidence of needs: for personal development, to achieve personal growth and satisfaction; for increasing the range of skills, to improve employee flexibility; and for learning as a tool in organisation development, to assist the organisation to change. Management development and fast-track schemes have continued through the 1990s recession, indicating the value accorded to a strong management cadre in order for a company to compete effectively.

Development strategies are also significant, as Peter Herriot points out, as a means of retaining commitment at a time when there are few promotion opportunities in hard-contracting organisations. At the same time, employee development strategies have become customer-oriented (whether relating to internal or to external customers) through 360° appraisal policies and competency approaches.

Employee relations strategies now concentrate on single-table or single-union bargaining, using the combination of policies in rewards, communications, and employee involvement to achieve flexibility and individual or team responsibility for quality standards. So far trade unions in the UK have been on the defensive. Employers' strategies for pushing bargaining down to the lowest level possible have been aided by changes to organisation structure, and seem to be successful, even in the National Health Service (the UK's largest employer), and are in any case compatible with a tradition of local-level influence already present in British industrial relations and now exercised by local full-time officials.

Performance-based pay and team rewards, broad salary-banding, and total compensation schemes are all policy options available for the achievement of a flexible, committed workforce, and for employer control of costs. The difficulties in maintaining traditional job evaluation schemes in the face of these changes (tasks rather than jobs, broadbanded scales, maximum horizontal flexibility etc) demonstrate the problems of creating a coherent policy package to support the strategy.

What are the consequences for HRM of these strategies? The flexibility strategies of the 1980s may have been created from the necessity of operating in a highly uncertain environment, but no new certainties have emerged in the 1990s – if anything, the world looks more subject to unpredictable change. Flexibility has its price. What happens if the core skills disappear? What does an organisation/company represent or stand for any longer?

There is now a new division of labour. Work teams are now the focus of policies, and we can see the emergence of the autonomy of the skilled worker, able to trade his or her skills in a wide market. Flexibility policies have encouraged the emphasis on tasks, teams, and costs. Employers are now no longer tied to an outdated career concept; the new division of labour supports the hard contract. However, without careers to manage and without a large internal labour market to control, the sourcing strategies can equally well be managed by senior line management. Smaller human resource functions at the centre seem now to be the norm. For example, Lloyds Bank has devolved all its human resource activity to its regions and divisions, and BP has similarly reduced a large central function to a handful of experts at the centre. Devolved strategic business units require devolved structures, with devolved powers to boards and unit managers. New models of the personnel function have consequently emerged. Personnel management has been redefined as a service business and markets its policies (the 'products' – recruitment, appraisal, reward policies, systems etc) to customers (line managers) and to the consumers of policies (employees). The function uses service agreements with line management to establish boundaries of authority and responsibility, and typically operates in small teams of consultants.

New approaches to employee relations have at their heart communication practice changes. These may involve joint consultation or employee involvement, which require strong leadership from line management. No longer is HRM the sole guardian of complex national agreements. Line managers are instead using their own role and their supervisors to draw people together locally. The strategic-level work for human resources here is to create strategies and involvement structures, as well as to train people to operate effectively within these new structures. Reward strategies through gainsharing, flexible benefits and total compensation approaches still require central direction or control. High-level direction is necessary for responding to the questions now arising, such as 'Do we need occupational pension schemes when there are no careers', 'How can we manage the total costs of employment more effectively', 'How can we mix individual performance-based pay with team rewards?'

The globalisation of business and European-wide trading call for international management teams, multicultural employment, suppliers, and the strategic use of logistics and information technology. Matrix structures are complex enough, but when these operate across Europe the complexities of cultural and working practice differences are multiplied. Management development is more frequently now in a European context, expatriate reward strategies have to be developed, and the working practices of different countries accommodated. The recent European directive on joint consultation, although it did not apply to the UK, nevertheless has been adopted by companies with a significant continental European workforce, including Marks and Spencer, United Biscuits, P&O, and ICI.

The stress of change and the problems within our anomic society require a powerful HRM response in traditional welfare, counselling, and personal assistance roles. Personal development and individually directed rewards also put the human resource specialist in the personal advisor role. This split in the roles of HRM between strategic-level direction and personal counselling seems to represent the real division of the role. The question is therefore whether HRM as a special management approach was a phenomenon of the optimistic 1980s. What we should expect in future for

HRM will be dependent upon how new societal trends are translated into organisations, and how changes to structures and to the nature of corporate governance affect senior management roles.

The future scenario for HRM

Whatever the future for HRM as an occupation, it is the broad social and economic circumstances that hold the key to future prosperity and future well-being. From the analysis so far, the degree of change that has occurred in the 1980s and 1990s means we must be cautious when making predictions. We have also noted that there have been fundamental reviews of all our major political and social institutions in these last decades of the twentieth century. What can we therefore predict about HRM in the next century?

The society into which we are heading is one that shows increasing signs of disintegration. Paradoxically, however, as societies move nearer and nearer to the abyss, the pressure for cohesion in the face of chaos also grows. As all the indices move up to danger levels, whether suicide rates, divorce rates, crime rates, racial attacks, bankruptcies, homelessness, or poverty, there is a reaction that moves society towards a changed state of affairs. The nostalgic search for a social identity goes hand in hand with a search for a personal identity. Search for regional nationalisms in Wales, Scotland, Ireland, and elsewhere may well be fuelled by old conflicts, but such searches represent the yearning to belong to a social unit which is comprehensible and has shared values and a shared history. Similarly, the search for racial ancestors by those whose origins were in Africa, India, or the Caribbean is not mere escapism. On the contrary, the important ingredient is the desire for self-worth, for the representation of a personal identity where there is respect, cultural richness, and a sharing of meanings.

The changes to occupations and to organisations during the last decades of the twentieth century have been so fundamental that it is impossible for working people at whatever level to find their identity in the organisation any more. These hitherto defining structures no longer provide a basis for making judgements about self or others. The instability is accompanied by a further paradox: the work organisation since early this century has been presented as the main source of social status and economic standing. 'Organisation Man' as Whyte described him (it was invariably a 'him') built an ideology in which organisational and personal values were believed to be in ultimate harmony. Organisation men belonged to the organisation – 'They are the ones of our middle class who have left home, spiritually as well as physically, to take the vows of organisation life, and it is they who are the mind and soul of our great self-perpetuating institutions' (Whyte 1957:3). Much of today's social instability arises because organisations have ceased to be a source of stability. The way such an existence was shattered by the rollercoaster boom-bust economy of the 1970s and 1980s, and the consequences for executive redundancy, are fresh in the memory of surviving employees (Doherty and Tyson 1993). The end to permanent employment and the spread of casual work up organisations have dealt a fatal blow to organisation man – or woman (Sampson 1995).

Yet, if we accept that governments wish to be less involved, and that in the UK there will be a reformulation of the welfare state, we cannot look to the government to foster a sense of identity, or to replace the organisation as a source of status and personal self-worth. Trade unions are equally unable to offer much more than a minimal relationship to working people, especially when the latter cease to be working. Local communities, in spite of Etzioni's exhortations, do not seem able to fill the vacuum, partly because high-rise apartments, commuter villages, and modern life do not encourage long-term local relationships. Apart from those with a religious vocation, there seems nowhere else to turn but to the work organisation.

Economic instability underlies social instability. There are a number of fundamental problems with the British economy that arise from the failure of many of our businesses to be competitive in the long run, and from the threats to employment and to our standard of living from newly developed countries, especially those in the Pacific Rim. Whereas a change in political direction within the UK may produce a move back to the left, in particular to a strengthening of employment rights and statutory works councils, to improve British economic performance requires a long-term investment shift towards industry, which needs to be able to recruit, train, and develop the highest levels of talent available. Unfortunately, the competitive threats put considerable strain on employment policies and practices. Without offering careers, without a reliable national technical training system, without the ability to afford the best reward policies, and locked into short-term planning horizons, UK companies are not best placed to counter the Far East threat, or to compete effectively with strong European or North American economies. The low wage, flexible workforce strategy which, it is claimed, has attracted investment to the UK is also unlikely to be effective against the opportunities in East European labour markets.

Economic problems also undermine the move towards more employee involvement, better communication policies, and 'empowerment'. Massive inequalities in the distribution of wealth, whereby chief executives can be receiving (with share options) 20 times or more the wages of shop-floor workers (compared with a ratio of around seven times more in Japan, for example), cannot be overcome whilst there are modest economic growth rates and shareholder pressure for dividends without major pay reductions for senior staff – itself demotivating and unacceptable. Yet in the words of the American Society for HRM, from its research, 'in the midst of this period of stable growth, income inequality is sapping the American sense of well-being' (Society for Human Resource Management 1994:9).

The dangers for a society fragmented by the changes of the last quarter-century come from the polarisation of working people into the employed, who will be either full-time employees working flexibly or part-time and casual staff, and the unemployed, who will be a mixture of those who have dropped out, those who are too old (in the eyes of prospective employers), the unskilled, and the incapable. However, as Alistair Mant reminds us in Chapter 2, there are also other groupings, including the self-employed. This group, which includes the skilled artisans who have moved around since the Middle Ages as carpenters, bricklayers, stonemasons, and now as electricians, plumbers, drivers, and technicians are adding new mixes of skills. The flexible self-employed person combines many of the old craft skills. Similarly, there are new occupations within the information technology field as well as the 'mosaic' career which combines many different occupations. A mixture of employment and self-employment also seems to be more common.

New strategic responses

Political initiatives are essential to solve the dangerous problems outlined in this chapter. The political will emerges as the desire for cohesion strengthens from a recognition of the problems ahead. Amongst the societal changes inevitable is a redefinition of the welfare state and of the roles to be played by the various parts of the system. This is likely to require a greater burden of the costs for care falling on organisations and employees – either through statutory elder care, health care and child care policies for organisations, or through tax changes, with some statutory regulation. Portable pensions and private health care would increase in this scenario.

To support fundamental shifts to responsibility one might also expect a politically sponsored shift in societal values, enhancing in particular community values – those of sharing, caring, helping, neighbourliness and community responsibility – at the expense of individualism, personal wealth, and an instrumental approach to relationships. Community values are, after all, in line with environmental concerns and the need to combat crime, as well as the economic need to shift the burden for care away from the state.

One consequence of these changes will be a newly formulated corporation. The political initiatives outlined above can only be achieved if there is strong corporate support. Corporate governance issues are now high on the agenda for change. The Cadbury committee and the Greenbury committee have both presaged changes to the responsibilities of directors, the ethical position of senior managers, and the need for a balanced representation of stakeholder interests. As a European company statute eventually emerges there will no doubt be a further need to reassess these interests. Shareholders in particular might be expected to have more rights to information. If the European Union is able to deliver a new reality out of the European dream, the conditions for a new-look corporation will be ideal. The concept of social responsibility fits neatly into the wider sharing of information, consultation, and the need to manage through a consensus of interests.

New organisation forms are already emerging, in what has been termed a 'post-modernist' approach. This implies greater flexibility and responsiveness. However, responses to markets will in future have to be accompanied by responses to internal organisation needs. Such responsiveness is integral to the role of HRM. New technology offers a number of ways in which responsiveness may be achieved, and the evaluation of all policies is made easier by the use of information technology, as Andrew Mayo shows (see Chapter 9).

The inadequacies of operating a hard contract are revealed in the de-skilling of the enterprise and the loss of core competencies but, equally, reliance on a soft contract is also problematic, as witness the difficulties IBM experienced: having a strong internal culture and a massive structure was inimical to quick, responsive, entrepreneurial flair. Given the move towards hard contracting in the 1980s, it is unlikely that organisations can simply reverse the trend and achieve a strong normative commitment from employees. What seems to offer the best way forward is an emphasis on a process strategy. This means the accent would go on to transformational change policies, directed at employees themselves, rather than at changing purely to meet market needs. Changing what happens to people at work is implied here, rather than just changing the way things are done. There is evidence for this in a recent study of international businesses, 'Champions for Change' (1994), which found that CEOs believed transformation to be a regenerative process, not a one-time event, and that the new leadership challenge is to engage the entire organisation in continuous regeneration. The participants, ranging from AT&T, Siemens AG, Daimler-Benz AG, Fiat, British Airways, and other large companies had worldwide responsibilities and reflected the need for change in all developed economies.

The societal role for HRM is to engage employees in this change process. The human resource strategies are essentially concerned with integrating people into society, through participation in wealth creation, service to the community via the corporation's involvement, and through taking responsibility for one's own work. An essential component of such policies will be to smooth out the effects of product market changes. This would require larger employers to adopt the Japanese style of using employees on whatever work the company can get, retaining the majority on a version of the soft contract whilst (as now) using subcontractors or the hard contract for the remainder. The societal role proposed here would be possible only if the corporate governance issues outlined earlier have been addressed, otherwise the degree of change and the uncertainty in the environment would not permit the use of the soft contract in this way, which requires a reassessment of investment and shareholder interests, and a new approach by banks and financial institutions.

HRM as a function of all management work provides opportunities for integration – through more economic participation, reduced wealth disparities, creating equal opportunities, and racial harmony. At a personal level it will become central to the need to create a new value set. From the developmental actions of managers and their attentiveness to the problems of surviving in modern life should come increased interpersonal sensitivity and an appreciation of the relationship between mental and physical well-being. None of this will be possible without political stability and economic growth. Nor will political and economic solutions be effective without changes to the way we manage the human resource.

The symbiotic relationship thus described is the rationale for this book. The intention here is to present each author's vision of the present and the future in the critically important areas in HRM. No one can predict with precision what the future may hold, but we can make explicit the choices we face, and our own best estimates of where our future rests. Inevitably, there is no general agreement on what that future will be; however, there is in the pages that follow a realistic assessment of what HRM can and does contribute to our lives as we approach the next millennium.

References

ACKERMANN, K-F, (1986), 'A contingency model of HRM strategy. Empirical research findings reconsidered', *Management Forum*, Vol. 6, pp65–83.

ATKINSON, J, (1985), 'Flexibility: Planning for an uncertain future', *Manpower Policy and Practice*, 1, summer, pp25–30.

BAIRD, C, AND MESHOULAM, I, (1988), 'Managing two fits of strategic human resource management', *Academy of Management Review*, Vol. 13, No. 1, pp116–18.

BEER, M, SPENCER, B, LAWRENCE, P, R, QUIN MILLS, D, AND WALTON, R, E, (1984), *Managing Human Assets*, New York, Free Press.

BENDIX, R, (1959) 'Industrialization, ideologies and social structure', *American Sociological Review*, 24, pp613–23.

BLAUNER, R, (1964), *Alienation and Freedom: The factory worker and his industry*, Chicago, University of Chicago Press.

BLYTON, P, AND TURNBULL, P, (eds), (1992), *Reassessing Human Resource Management*, London, Sage.

BOWMAN, C, (1992), 'Interpreting competitive strategy', in D. Faulkner and G. Johnson (eds), *The Challenge of Strategic Management*, London, Kogan Page.

BREWSTER C, AND HEGEWISCH, A, (1994), *Policy and Practice in European Human Resource Management*, London, Routledge.

BRIDGES, W, (1995), *How to Prosper in a Work Place without Jobs*, London, Nicholas Brealey.

BURKE, W, W, AND LITWIN, G, H, (1992), 'A causal model of organisation performance and change', *Journal of Management*, Vol. 18, No. 3, pp525–45.

BURNS, T, AND STALKER, G, M, (1961), *The Management of Innovation*, London, Tavistock.

CLARK, J, (1993), (ed.), *Human Resource Management and Technical Change*, London, Sage.

DOHERTY, N, AND TYSON, S, (1993), *Executive Redundancy and Outplacement*, London, Kogan Page.

EDWARDS, P, AND SCULLION, H, (1982), *The Social Organization of Industrial Conflict*, Oxford, Basil Blackwell.

FERNIE, S, METCALF, D, AND WOODLAND, S, (1994), 'Does HRM boost employee–management relations?', *LSE Working Papers*, 548.

Fox, A, (1974), *Beyond Contract: Work, power and trust relations*, London, Faber.

Fox, A, (1991), *A Sociology of Work in Industry*, Oxford, Collier-Macmillan.

Gospel, H, F, (1992), *Markets, Firms and the Management of Labour in Modern Britain*, Cambridge, Cambridge University Press.

Guest, D, (1995), 'Human resource management, trade unions and industrial relations', in J. Storey (ed.), *Human Resource Management*, London, Routledge.

Guest, D, and Peccei, R, (1994), 'The nature and causes of effective HRM', *British Journal of Industrial Relations*, 32:2, pp219–42.

Hampden-Turner, C, (1990), *Charting the Corporate Mind*, New York/London, The Free Press/Collier-Macmillan.

Hendry, C, and Pettigrew, A, (1992), 'Patterns of strategic change in the development of human resource management', *British Journal of Management*, Vol.3, No.3, September, pp137–56.

Hochschild, A, R, (1983), *The Managed Heart*, University of California Press.

Hunter, G, (1957), *The Role of the Personnel Officer*, London, Institute of Personnel Management.

Jackson, S, E, Schuler, R, S, and Rivero, J, C, (1989), 'Organizational characteristics as predictors of personnel practices', *Personnel Psychology*, pp727–86.

Johnson, G, (1992), 'Managing strategic change: strategic culture and action', in D. Faulkner and G. Johnson (eds), *The Challenge of Strategic Management*, London, Kogan Page.

Kakabadse, A, (1983), *The Politics of Management*, Aldershot, Gower.

Kakabadse, A, (1991), *The Wealth Creators*, London, Kogan Page.

Lengnick-Hall, C, A, and Lengnick-Hall, M, L, (1988), 'A perspective on business strategy and human resource strategy interdependence', *Academy of Management Review*, Vol. 13, No. 3, pp454–70.

Marginson, P, Edwards, P, K, Martin, R, Sisson, K, and Purcell, J, (1988), *Beyond the Workplace*, Oxford, Blackwell.

Miles, R, E, and Snow, C, C, (1978), *Organizational Strategy, Structure and Process*, New York, McGraw-Hill.

Miles, R, E, and Snow, C, C, (1994), *Fit, Failure and the Hall of Fame*, New York, Free Press.

Miller, E, J, and Rice, A, K, (1967), *Systems of Organisation: the control of task and sentient boundaries*, London, Tavistock.

MILLWARD, N, (1994), *The New Industrial Relations*, London, Policy Studies Institute.

MINTZBERG, H, (1994), *The Rise and Fall of Strategic Planning*, Hemel Hempstead, Prentice Hall.

NICHOLS, T, (1969), *Ownership, Control and Ideology*, London, George Allen and Unwin.

NIVEN, M, (1967), *Personnel Management 1913–1963*, London, Institute of Personnel Management.

PORTER, M, (1980), *Competitive Strategy*, New York, The Free Press/Macmillan.

PURCELL, J, (1989), 'The impact of corporate strategy on human resource management' in J. Storey (ed.), *New Perspectives on Human Resource Management*, London, Routledge.

READY, D, (1994), *Champions for Change: A global report on leading business transformation*, International Consortium for Executive Development Research and Gemini Consulting.

RITZER, G, AND TRICE, H, M, (1969), *An Occupation in Conflict: A study of the personnel manager*, Cornell University.

ROTHWELL, S, (1995), 'Human Resource Planning', in J. Storey (ed.), *Human Resource Management: A critical text*, London, Routledge, pp167–202.

SALAMAN, G, (1992), *Human Resource Strategies*, London, Sage Publications.

SAMPSON, A, (1995), *Company Man – The Rise and Fall of Corporate Life*, Glasgow, Harper Collins.

SENGE, P, M, (1990), *The Fifth Discipline*, London, Random House.

SOCIETY FOR HUMAN RESOURCE MANAGEMENT, (1994), *Human Resource Forecast 1995*, Institute of Industrial Relations, UCLA.

STOREY, J, (1992), *Developments in the Management of Human Resources*, Oxford, Blackwell.

THURLEY, K, AND WOOD, S, (eds), (1983), *Industrial Relations and Management Strategy*, Cambridge, Cambridge University Press.

TREVELYAN, G, M, (1946), *English Social History*, London, Longmans, Green & Company.

TYSON, S, (1995), *Human Resource Strategy: Towards a general theory of human resource management*, London, Pitman.

TYSON, S, AND FELL, A, (1992), *Evaluating the Personnel Function*, 2nd Edition, Cheltenham, Stanley Thornes.

WATSON, T, J, (1977), *The Personnel Managers*, London, Routledge and Kegan Paul.

WHYTE, W, H, (1957), *The Organization Man*, London, Jonathan Cape.

WICKENS, P, (1987), *The Road to Nissan*, London, Macmillan Press.

WILLIAMSON, O, E, (1973), 'Markets and hierarchies: some elementary considerations', *American Economic Review*, LXIII, pp316–25.

WILLMAN, P, MORRIS, T, AND ASTON, B, (1992), *Union business: Trade union organisation and financial reform in the Thatcher years*, Cambridge, Cambridge University Press.

CHAPTER TWO

Changing Work Roles

Alistair Mant

They [the poor] sit in front of their television for hours on end, complaining about their poverty and not growing vegetables when they could do so easily and cheaply . . . [laughter]. Opposition members of this house would do well to stop laughing and encourage people who are feeling the pinch . . . whether due to unemployment or to other reasons – to go out and take an allotment.[1]

Toby Jessel MP

One of the most important aspects of coping with change is that individual employees should take responsibility for their own continuing professional development . . . their goal should be to remain employable in the face of changing technology, flatter organisations and demand for new skills . . . job security was no longer linked to an organisation, but relied on individuals selling their experience and talents to different employers.[2]

People Management

Change is less pervasive than it may seem. Women are still overwhelmingly responsible for their traditional work. They simply do more of other kinds of work as well. Where the goal of most employers throughout the world is to get the work of one full-time male done by one part-time female at a fraction of the cost, talk of the new liberation from toil can sound offensive.[3]

R. E. Pahl

Introduction

The world of work is changing – that much is clear – and it is probably changing more drastically than at any time this century. The three, contrasted, quotations above give a flavour of the changes from a more or less Western European point of view. Equally drastic changes in the developing world lie beyond the scope of this chapter. There is, as Professor Ray Pahl has acutely pointed out, a 'future of work industry' that tends to the ethnocentric and deterministic, as though the whole world *should* dance to our economic tunes, and as though the painful and damaging impact of fashionable economic orthodoxies on people's lives is inevitable.[4]

We have to be sensible about changes to work. There are a number of probably inevitable deep-wave global changes taking place, changes that are truly irresistible and that it would therefore be foolish to attempt to resist. On the other hand, it would be stupid to assume that we can do nothing to diminish the deleterious impact on individuals, families, and communities of changes that suit increasingly privileged minorities only and nobody else at all. Clearly, government has a key role to play here but the human resource profession, if it has serious pretensions to be a profession, should also have a significant part to play in altering for the good that which can be altered. Strategic management, after all, is always concerned with distinguishing between what can and ought to be changed and, on the other hand, what must be accommodated to.

The managers who need to keep a cool, clear (strategic) head through all this are themselves under unprecedented stress. Pahl, who edited the seminal *On Work – Historical, comparative and theoretical approaches* (1989), has now reviewed the last 30 years of observations on managerial status, behaviour, and morale. The outcome is a book published in 1995 entitled *After Success – Fin de siècle anxiety and identity*.[5] It seems that managers and their spouses (usually wives) are much as before, except for greatly heightened anxiety and disillusionment. They have become, in the jargon, an 'anxious class'. Robert Reich, one of the keenest observers of the US scene, says, 'The coming political battle will be for the soul of the anxious class.'[6] Scase and Goffee in *The Reluctant Manager* echo Pahl's findings of 30 years ago about the perceived impotence of individual managers in the face of economic orthodoxy and entrenched managerial cultures; they report that managers are, as never before, working long hours to demonstrate their indispensability.[7] This does not suggest that managers in general and human resource managers in particular are likely to be able to shape the world of work; it is more likely that they are being shaped by it.

This chapter begins with the historical context. We neglect this at our peril: if we don't understand the past, we are doomed to repeat it. What follows makes no pretence to survey the whole field of work – that would require a whole book. The aim is to pick out a few significant themes and examples in order to suggest in which direction the wind might be blowing. The hope is that human resource management really can, by understanding current events, have a strategic impact on events in the future.

The historical context

The most obvious contemporary shift is the decline of the collective mass worker in Western industrial societies and, in particular, the decline of the numbers of sole male breadwinners. If we view this change historically, we see that the years between the late eighteenth century and the mid-twentieth century saw the emergence of the male breadwinner as the sole or principal provider for families. The current decline in male full-time employment presents itself as a 'change'. In reality, it is the end of an atypical period of 200 years or so and marks the return of the old pattern of irregular employment and concealed unemployment, as described by E. P. Thompson.[8]

The problem of 'unemployment' now is that the networks of familial and community support that looked after indigent, part-time, or casual workers and their families in the eighteenth century have now largely gone. In general, the state has stepped in to provide for the very poor or unemployed, but there are big differences from country to country in how the responsibility for the provision of employment and for unemployment are shared between the state and employing firms. It is at the join between the state and the employer that the HRM 'profession' stands.

Malcolmson comments that even as late as the eighteenth century 'In most households an adequate subsistence depended on a complex of various forms of task work and wage labour; regular, full-time employment at a single job was not the norm.'[9] Most of an individual's work was done in and for the household. The viability of the household was the crucial priority in life and the work of all its members had to be co-ordinated to achieve that end. Very often women were the main money-earners, either by selling produce at market or by the manufacture of textile goods at home.

The disappearance of local self-support networks has not been universal throughout Europe. Hungary, for example, industrialised relatively late and many of the co-operative peasant traditions linger on in local communities in the form of house-building combines and other forms of communal work exchange. Nor is the tradition dead in Britain. The Demos think-tank has published a pamphlet called *The Common Sense of Community* which points out the various ways that traditional habits of community collaboration could be revived in modern Britain, using core schools as local 'hubs' for school clusters and tying in family centres, the use of open spaces, housing associations, local forums and so on.[10] These kinds of initiatives produce work and new work roles; the challenge is to create the enabling infrastructure.

The idea that one should obtain most, if not all, of one's material wants as a consumer by spending earnings from employment emerged for the first time in the nineteenth century. This change created a new social category – the *unemployed*. E. P. Thompson, writing on the so-called Protestant work ethic, pointed out that even the American working class made the transition to industrial society uneasily, the transition involving as it did 'new disciplines, new incentives, and a new human nature upon which these incentives could bite effectively'. American and British workers fought against this new discipline of employment; now they demand it as a right.

> Employment has shifted from being a burden to be resisted to a necessity that cannot be forgone.[11]

Once employment came to be regarded as the only kind of work that really counted, because survival now depended on having an income, then unemployment became synonymous with poverty (see Toby Jessel's wonderful strictures on the poor, above, and his nostalgic reversion to the myth of eighteenth-century agricultural self-sufficiency).

The meaning of 'work'

Most dictionaries define work as something like 'effort directed to an end'. This broad definition disposes of the idea that work and employment are always or necessarily the same thing. Work outside employment

> may be exhausting or exhilarating; it may be done under conditions of oppressive exploitation or it may be voluntary work hard to distinguish from play. Some of the most demanding work outside employment, such as child care, can also be remunerated when done for others; so clearly it is not the nature of the task that matters most in determining whether or not it is to be financially rewarded and whether it is to count as 'work', but rather the social relations in which the task is embedded. Again, in the production of goods and services it is not always financial considerations that determine whether we have, for example, home-made or bought jam. Technological developments allow us to produce more and different goods and services in the home, but it does not necessarily follow that we have the money, time or inclination to do so. There are many questions relating to unpaid work and how this relates to employment. Work outside employment can only increase relative to paid employment if, overall, people have sufficient time and financial resources. The lifestyle of the gentleman is possible only if it is based on unearned income based on profits or rents. The divisions of labour in work outside employment cannot be divorced from

the divisions based on remunerated work. Those quasi-Utopians who seek work outside employment as an alternative to remunerated work must consider the financial implications of what they advocate.[12]

Some writers have defined the concept of work much more narrowly. As recently as 1958, Robert Dubin, in a widely used US textbook, defined work as 'continuous employment in the production of goods and services, for remuneration'.[13]

The distinction between work, broadly defined, and employment work becomes crucial when we come to examine the meaning of the term 'human resource management' (HRM). We have to ask whose human resources, managed by whom, on behalf of whom? Outsourced, de-layered, downsized people are still members of the national skill pool, available for other forms of work – ie resources.

Any cool analysis of the human resource function in modern business over the last 10 years or so would suggest that the true primary task has been to minimise the political outfall from the human consequences of cost-cutting (ie headcount reduction). Whether this can be regarded as a 'strategy' is open to question. C. K. Prahalad has pointed out that by acquiescing in and facilitating widespread downsizing, the human resource function simply reflects the strategic short-sightedness of general management.[14] He pointed out that new technology applications and the emergence of new markets are daily opening up the possibility for scores of completely new work roles in newly emerging fields all around the world. The problem is that in order to create new work, corporations need to anticipate change, position themselves early in nascent fields, and plan for long-term investment in innovation. The cheap, easy, and short-term option is to 'stick to your knitting' and squeeze profit from continuous downsizing. For too many European firms, Prahalad argues, that has been the preferred option – once the 'outplacement' bill has been paid and the compensation package agreed, the individual ex-employee is on his or her own. This cannot be viewed, in his opinion, as a true 'HR strategy'; rather it is the inevitable outcome of the absence of a true business development strategy.

The psychological need for work

It is clear that enforced and unfocused idleness is damaging for human morale. People need to be engaged, at best collaboratively, in the manipulation of materials or circumstances towards valued ends. This is hardly surprising. It is not so long ago that we were hunter-gatherers. The work of getting food, by one means or another, led directly to one of life's most pleasurable sensations – a full belly. To do the job efficiently and skilfully, to general approbation, must have been a source of high social esteem in hunting bands and, later, in settled agricultural communities. We are *Homo habilis* as well as *Homo sapiens*, and we need to be useful to our fellow human beings.

Maslow's hierarchy of human needs embraces both the survival and social approval aspects of these premonetary forms of work.[15] The modern urban drug addict, in desperate need of a 'fix' also has *work* to do – getting the wherewithal (usually by theft) for new drug supplies. That, in his or her eyes, is the basis for survival and the mugging he or she carries out is merely 'effort directed to an end'.

The question is in how much work do we need to engage in order to satisfy our need to be productive and skilful? In England in particular the pastoral myth of Merrie England, promoted by a literary élite, tended to romanticise country life and rural work. The fact was that agricultural labour was always hard and pre-industrial attitudes to repetitive work were not much different from those of factory workers today. As Pahl comments, 'There was no pre-industrial age of satisfying work.'[16] Even artists in Renaissance workshops relied mostly on commissions as jobbing craftsmen, producing long runs of standard altar pieces or mass-produced routine pictures for export. It is unlikely that the craftsmen of fourteenth-century Florentine workshops were that much more contented than their agricultural counterparts.

In a seminal collection of essays Elliott Jaques pointed out that

> the normal person seeks not only to work, but to work at a level of responsibility that taxes his capacity to the full. Man is a problem-solving animal and must make continuous use of his mental and physical apparatus. Not to be able to work at full capacity is restrictive, depressing, and finally persecuting. The avoidance of work at full capacity, or the acceptance of underemployment, is symptomatic of emotional disturbance.

In the same place Jaques drew distinctions between

> *Employment work*, in which the object is essentially determined by an employer who has to approve work output and decide to continue the employment (in the last ten years or so, most big employment bureaucracies have decided to discontinue the employment of very substantial numbers of 'human resources'. Generally, the chairmen of those organisations have continued to intone the ritual message 'Our employees are our most important asset!').

Creative work, in which the object arises from the internal world and is produced initially for an internal audience. This type of work is wholly symbolic and the work itself touches upon and derives from the deepest layers of the mind, unaided by any objective or concrete point of reference.

Running a business, where the main task is to discover the object of the work by exploring consumer needs to be satisfied. Understanding the market is the hallmark of a successful business. There is an external reference but it is not given by instruction; discovering it calls for a particular sensitivity to the needs of others. Running a (smallish) business is an intermediate state; there is an external framework, but it requires symbolic work to discover it.[17]

This psychological analysis of the nature of work and its satisfactions throws some light on current developments. The amount of employment work available is diminishing steadily and the pressures on those remaining in employment are increasing. In the USA the average number of employees per company increased until the 1970s. Since then it has been decreasing, especially in manufacturing. In the 1950s, 33 per cent of all US workers were employed in manufacturing. By the 1960s the number of manufacturing jobs had dropped to 30 per cent, and by the 1980s to 20 per cent. Peter Drucker estimates that employment in manufacturing is going to continue dropping to less than 12 per cent of the US workforce in the next decade.

In the 1980s US firms eliminated 20 per cent of their employees and tripled investment in information technology. The investment generally preceded the downsizing. Charles Handy pointed out back in 1989 that the remaining 'core' full-time employees were working much harder (probably too hard for the sake of their marriages and other personal relationships, although for greatly enhanced earnings) and that the great mass of the occasionally contracted were employed too fitfully for any personal sense of well-being (or for the good of their marriages and other relationships). He also alerted us to the fact that over the last 150 years the annual working time in the industrialised countries has fallen steadily: from around 3,000 hours to between 1,400 and 1,800 hours.[18]

Leaving aside 'true' artists, traditionally unmindful of wealth, the ideal work state for psychological health and well-being might be engagement in essentially creative business. In recent years about 50 thriving firms have emerged in Britain specialising in the production of computer games. Some of the founders of these firms have become millionaires very quickly because they are gifted and have positioned themselves intelligently in a new and expanding market-place. Furthermore, these firms collectively represent a 'cluster' in Michael Porter's terms: they compete with one another but together they constitute a national economic asset.

How this came about overreaches the scope of this chapter, but it has been suggested that the far-sightedness of Sir Clive Sinclair 20 years ago was an important contributory factor. Sir Clive kept making what seemed to be short-term business blunders, but he seeded the means for cheap and easy computer programming into a whole generation of enthusiasts. That generation has become the benefactor of the computer games explosion. Governments could learn from this how to target long-term technical, commercial, and human resource investment. (The Japanese approach to this is touched on below.)

Charles Hampden-Turner points out that in the quickly developing East most students do not want impressive management traineeships or salary packages: they want to be where the technology *action* is.[19] The preferred employers in Malaysia, for example, are Intel, Hewlett-Packard and Motorola, because all the students want to work on the most sophisticated, complex and knowledge-intensive jobs. These are the 'horizontal' technologies – the ones that involve the greatest contribution to developments in parallel fields. At the leading edge, new technology and new applications are enhancing the quality of work for the most able and best trained. The picture for the vast mass of work roles is somewhat different.

The impact of new technology on work roles

John Child has commented that business managers still appeal to the 'ideology of market-driven technological determinism'.[20] The goal of management is the achievement of work flexibility in the production of goods and services by the elimination of direct labour, by subcontracting, by the use of 'polyvalence' (that is, maintaining core workers who are able to perform a range of tasks which cut across or extend traditional skill and job boundaries), and, finally, the degradation of jobs. The new flexible firm is characterised by a core of polyvalent ('empowered') workers and a periphery of subcontractors, outworkers, and (mostly) female part-time workers.

The impact of this on work roles is evident. To take one obvious example, the introduction of electronic point-of-sale (EPOS) systems at supermarket checkouts has reduced the intellectual demands on those who work at the checkout and increased control over them. Even more significantly, the information that EPOS systems provide on sales profiles and stock levels permits routine programming (eg automatic reorder routines) of decisions that used to tax the judgement even of quite senior buyers.

Similarly, new information reduces the reliance of store general managers on the judgement of department and section managers. (It is said that cool-weather systems rolling in from the south-east of England accurately predict the sales levels of lettuces in supermarkets throughout the country. The store manager may well be 'empowered' but there is actually little technical or professional judgement for him or her to exercise. All that is left is the management of ambience, and that calls for somewhat different skills.) Much the same kind of thing has happened to front-of-bank staff: telephone banking and depersonalised automated telling machine (ATM) outlets are taking over.

Who is responsible for HRM?

The familiar view, bolstered by the pretensions of 'professional' personnel bodies in for example the UK and the USA, is that HRM is entirely a matter for organisations themselves. Once individuals join the 'strength' or the 'labour force' of an organisation they take on the identity of employee and shelve for the time being the status of citizen. Only if the employer transgresses a law will the individual, as a citizen, be able to claim redress, for discrimination, for example, or unfair dismissal.

In the UK, the state has generally been reluctant to legislate for workers' democratic rights within the firm. Even now the EU Social Chapter is unacceptable to the present British government, partly because of its provisions on the payment of a minimum wage. The UK wants, apparently, to be a low-wage economy in order to maximise labour flexibility (and uncertainty) in order to attract inward investment by foreign manufacturers. This means that a substantial proportion of work roles created will be characterised by low pay and uncertain conditions. The distinguished American social planner, Professor Peter Marris, has pointed out how large employer organisations, in order to maximise their global freedom of action, seek to assert control over labour markets by creating a buffer zone of subcontractors.[21] The firm thus avoids social commitments whilst exporting uncertainty to the least well-off in society.

This, Marris argues, is a chain reaction. The overworked 'core' executives of big firms make their contractors compete fiercely for work, at thin margins. The contractors have to work long hours to prepare and contest bids, parallel to their productive core activities. The individual contributors who serve the contractors are in turn similarly squeezed and, frequently, are paid for their services long in arrears. At the end of the chain the stresses are severe and the uncertainty may be close to intolerable. We can assume that some of the costs of these pressures are borne by those with least resources to withstand them – the families of the least powerful people in the contracting/competing chain.

Much has been written about the new 'freedoms' of outsourced ex-employees of big firms. These people, compared with their previous existences, are spending a disproportionate amount of otherwise creative time in fighting to win work. In terms of Jaques' analysis of the need for productive work, this represents a severe degradation. The International Labour Organisation (ILO) estimates that job stress costs the UK up to 10 per cent of GNP a year, and time off work for stress-related illness has increased by 500 per cent since the 1950s.

In the 'caring' professions similar stresses and strains are clearly at work: between 1990 and 1992, for example, 153 nurses in UK hospitals killed themselves. Although it is impossible to establish causes with any certainty, the Department of Health was sufficiently concerned about this to call together the leaders of the relevant professional associations to discuss what might be done to reduce stress for nurses working under extreme pressure. The causes of stress in the health field appear to be similar to those described above – what health service (employer) trusts call 'multi-skilling' and what the health service unions describe as 'de-skilling'. A typical example would be the replacement of a permanent night floor sister grade with part-time 'night nurse practitioners'. It saves money, because management can employ fewer qualified staff and at a lower cost, but it destroys the continuity and professional attachment within what is essentially a *vocation* as well as a job. At the same time, any claim to vocation or 'professionalism' in management work is also stripped away.

Clearly there is an ethical issue here, but even if these kinds of changes in the structure of work are viewed quite pragmatically, suicide is an expensive business. So too is the cost of hospital pilferage encouraged by the loss of permanent staff with a sense of ownership and continuity of system understanding and recognition, and their replacement with cheaper but less committed and less knowledgeable part-time contractors.

Even for those still within the corporate embrace there is an absence in Britain of those rights and reassurances that flow from the various forms of 'industrial democracy' to be found on the Continent. In 1995 the EU directive on European works councils was greeted with some suspicion by a few big British firms on the grounds that pan-European unions might be placed in a position to interfere with international executive decisions. Against a background of general employee insecurity the absence of statutory works councils in Britain means there is no 'legislature', through representation, to give the employee the sense that his or her voice will be heard by higher management. Work roles are becoming increasingly insecure and the individual employee is entirely at the mercy of the employer.

If there is a dispute, it will probably be dealt with by external tribunals, not by the firm's appeals procedures. In Britain Glacier Metal has been one of the few companies to devise and operate a fully fledged home-grown system of industrial democracy. It was based, as in the British constitutional structure, on the separation of powers between the executive (the management), the legislature (the works council) and the judiciary (the independent appeals procedure). As a series of important books and studies have shown, it worked outstandingly well. The Glacier 'representative system' not only incorporated union power, it also demonstrated management's preparedness to create, modify, and take ultimate responsibility for a constitutional framework for work relations. Except for a few isolated instances, Glacier was probably the last British gasp of a major company-directed constitutional framework for regulating work and work relations. Traditionally, the HR profession in the UK has paid little attention to this aspect of work management. This was a source of some irritation and frustration to the late Lord Wilfred Brown, the principal architect of the Glacier arrangements.[22]

In the USA deregulation of labour markets has created vast numbers of low-paid and, frequently, part-time jobs in the service sector – which have largely become the preserve of women. Many unskilled American men would much rather 'work' in the escalating black economy of drugs and street crime, where the rewards are higher and the image more 'manly' than in unskilled, low-paid, service-sector employment. The USA's huge prison population consists predominantly of these uneducated men caught in the informal economy. In 1986, 26 per cent of black male dropouts were in prison. Thus the export of uncertainty by corporations feeds into enormous social and economic costs downstream. If the numbers of adult American men aged between 25 and 54 who declare themselves economically inactive are added back into the unemployment statistics, the 'official' 5 per cent unemployment average over the 1980s rises to over 12 per cent.

All this suggests that the new 'flexible' work roles which have emerged in the 1980s and 1990s have hidden costs. Will Hutton's best-selling book *The State We're In* delineated the new so-called 30/30/40 society in the UK – a society in which some 40 per cent of citizens are increasingly secure, wealthy and *privileged* (full-time employees, successful self-employed, part-timers with five years' continuity in their work).[23] This group includes most of the 31 per cent of the workforce still represented by trade unions. It is increasingly buying its way out of civil society and is resentful of the costs of the underclass. The extreme form of this, so far, is to be found in the USA, where hatred of big government symbolises the resentment and fearfulness of this privileged, but overworked, class.

Hutton designates a further 30 per cent as *marginalised* or insecure – people with insecure, subcontracted, part-time or intermittent casual work. The final 30 per cent is the positively *disadvantaged* – the four million people who are out of work, including those who do not receive benefit or have not looked for work and who do not therefore count as unemployed. Britain has the most deregulated labour market in Europe as well as the highest divorce rate; some commentators see a link between these two facts.

In the 65 years up until the First World War the UK economy was characterised by price stability, deregulated labour markets, an absence of a strong trade union movement, minimal state spending, balanced budgets, no employee protection or welfare system – in fact, all of the conditions desired and increasingly enjoyed by employers today. Yet the period saw violent oscillations of unemployment from virtually nil to over 10 per cent. *Laissez-faire* labour markets in Europe were both unstable and inefficient and helped to give rise to both fascism and communism. In the end, short-term economic benefit for corporations turned out to be costly for society.

In the UK, and particularly in the USA, we have now returned to a somewhat similar situation to that prevailing at the turn of the century. Senior management, although they experience a heightened uncertainty, enjoy a greater freedom of action than they have done at any time since then. 'Management has never been so powerful, or so unaccountable', according to Chris Haskins, the chief executive of Northern Foods and a notable critic of modern corporate ethics. 'Business isn't naturally democratic; the early owner-managers were all autocrats. Capitalism has really failed to achieve accountability.'[24]

In Germany, with a different twentieth-century tradition, the so-called social market economy has tended to smooth out the effects of economic cycles. The Germans are not immune from international economic effects, but the entire economy, as opposed to individual firms, seems to have a buffer zone against violent fluctuations. A good example of German government/industry collaboration is the *Kurzarbeit* system – a fund into which employers and employees pay 2.5 per cent of salary and to which employers can apply in lean years for help with the wage bill. This helps them to keep valuable experience in the firm for six, 12 or even 24 months. (Hampden-Turner cites the case of Intel's 'credit union' in its Chinese operation. The union was originally financed from the company's shop, which saves employees from having to leave the factory site. As the credit union grew it bought shares in medium- and low-tech local companies. Any employee who cannot keep up in the 'learning race' is outplaced in a lower-tech company, thus preserving the principle of employer/employee reciprocity.[25])

In Britain, by contrast, firms are able to 'off-hire' quickly and efficiently (in economic terms) when trouble strikes, because of flexible labour laws and short notice periods. This has the effect of transferring labour costs from firms' accounts to the government. Drastic reductions in disposable income lead to a fall in demand, thus further affecting business confidence and causing further job losses. The government loses out on all counts: corporation and income tax receipts fall, and the bill for unemployment benefits rises. Government deficits rise and calls for cuts in spending and for tax increases generally follow. In industry, skilled employees are lost, order books become volatile, and investment is cut at just the point in the economic cycle when the Germans are reinvesting for the next cycle.

We have to remember that there was a kind of consensus about the relationship between big firms and the state in both the USA and the UK after the Second World War. Big firms such as IBM and General Electric were not legally obliged to supply elaborate welfare systems for their employees. Anthony Sampson quotes Gerald Czarneki of IBM:

> (The big firms) created a kind of balancing act with governments . . . who supported big business as a kind of quid pro quo for looking after their employees' welfare.[26]

That balancing act, or consensus, has now largely disappeared.

The purpose of this brief tour around the role of government in HRM is to pose a question about the role of the personnel or human resource profession in Britain. In other countries, such as Germany, it is made easier for firms to sustain long-term reciprocal relationships with workers. In the Netherlands, for example, the government has decreed that all new posts in the public sector should be limited to a 32-hour week. That was a bold and fascinating experiment in long-term reciprocity. As it happens, between 1983 and 1991 there was a 30 per cent rise in employment in the Netherlands and a 13 per cent reduction in hours worked per person. Similarly there is a growing interest in work-sharing on the Continent – an interest not shared in Britain. The French government led the way in the early 1980s by encouraging firms and unions to agree 'solidarity contracts' (involving early retirement, wage restraint, new jobs for the young and different working-time flexibility options) and backed this up with a decree reducing the length of the statutory working week. This became part of a broader five-year law in 1993 with incentives for companies and unions to reduce working hours, cut pay, and recruit new staff. In Belgium, legislation in 1983 required new public-sector recruits to work for 80 per cent of normal time and at 80 per cent of pay for their first year.

Typical emergent work roles

The 'radically flat organisation' created by downsizing, de-layering, and technology is spawning new kinds of work roles. Research at Cornell University has identified a new breed of highly skilled 'technical workers'. The old distinction of blue- and white-collar makes no sense in relation to this group. They

> often wear white collars, carry briefcases, conduct relatively sophisticated scientific and mathematic analysis, and speak with an educated flair. They also use tools and instruments, work with their hands, make objects, repair equipment and occasionally get dirty. They range from medical technologists to paralegals, from 'test-and-pay' technicians to the person who hooked up the PC in your office'.[27]

Together with professionals such as accountants, scientists, and engineers (whom they increasingly resemble), the new-style technical workers are expected to constitute 20 per cent of the US workforce by the year 2000. Included in this group is a range of relatively new professional/technical roles – air traffic controllers, nuclear technicians, broadcast engineers, and materials scientists. It should be noted that information technology, in one form or another, determines all these roles.

Other emergent work roles are concerned with human services – what the Americans call 'nurturant service workers'. Demographics rather than technology largely determine these roles – home health care providers, licensed massage therapists, counselling psychologists, and even 'personal trainers' for the seriously rich. With relative wealth comes the chance to farm out service work and to pamper oneself. There is every indication that these new kinds of work will continue to spread from the USA to other relatively wealthy societies.

These new kinds of 'workers' are managed differently, which means that managerial work roles are changing accordingly. The old idea of being a 'professional manager' holds little attraction to a highly specialised professionalised workforce, whose loyalty is as much to the profession or speciality as to the employer. A microcomputer support specialist, for example, reads trade magazines, goes to trade shows, collects vendor information and pieces together what is going on in the field in order to integrate it with the needs of the organisation. He or she scrambles to stay on top of constant change. The new manager is more like a co-ordinator and negotiator than an exerciser of clearly laid-down authority. He or she (women may have superior skills here) has to make deals in order to put together optimal teams, deals with other organisations to develop jointly new products, deals to obtain resources for less cost from inside or outside one's own firm, deals to eke out a modest profit as more and more product markets act like commodity businesses, driven by other similar deal-makers.

Women's work roles

It is clear that women are supplanting men in many junior or routine work roles, if not in higher-order professional and managerial work. Much of this, as noted above, is low-paid and part-time work. This is one reason why women, working flexibly, are replacing expensive (usually older) male workers. New research by Professor Lynne Murray at the Cambridge Market Research Council (MRC) makes it clear that although such women may be being exploited, part-time work particularly suits young women with children.[28] The evidence is that, in most cases, better attachments are made with infants if the mother is engaged for part of her time out of the home. If she stays at home all the time, in conditions of relative poverty and inadequate support, the situation is likely to become claustrophobic, with severe psychic costs to both mother and infant, with a loss of adult/worker identity and status in the outside world. If she works full time, attachment is likely to be incomplete and the mother may well be badgered by feelings of frustration and guilt. The case for exploitation of the female part-timer can be made, but it is clearly a two-way street.

Similar considerations apply to the growth in home-working, again principally on the part of women. Hakim's 1981 study showed that home-working jobs are very diverse: they are spread across all industry groups and most of the 15 main occupational groups. Even more striking is the fact that as many as four-fifths of all home-workers turned out to be owner-occupiers and relatively well educated. Only a quarter of Hakim's sample reported that the home-based job was the main or usual job. Home-workers were in excellent health, suffered very few accidents, and only about 5 per cent expressed dissatisfaction with their work. The explanation for this may be that while the absolute rewards from part-time home-work are low, the marginal utility is high. Two-thirds of the female home-workers studied (excluding childminders) added their wages to the income of a 'core' or permanent worker/partner.

> The component wages provided by the female partner may be based on more than one part-time job and similarly, the chief earner may be moon-lighting with a second, weekend or evening job. One of the most signifi-cant developments in the distribution of work . . . is that money-generating jobs are being clustered in *work-rich households* leading to a privileged 'middle class' with a relatively comfortable standard of living. Such house-holds with multiple contacts in the labour market and the sphere of employment are better placed to find further employment for their off-spring as they leave school and, for a time, seek to add their wages to their natal family income.[29]

These kinds of female workers, part-timers, home-workers, and the like remain exposed to exploitation. To quote Angela Coyle, 'employers' strate-gies for reducing their wage bills have developed to an art form. The secret is to employ a lot of people for a short time, rather than to employ a few for longer' – to avoid National Insurance contributions, tea and lunch breaks, and so on.[30] (Since 1979, the poorest 10 per cent of women part-time workers have seen their average earnings fall by 4 per cent.)

A recent study of female workers in the insurance business suggests that the first wave of office automation did have the effect of de-skilling cleri-cal jobs. The emergence of computer-linked multiactivity jobs means that unskilled clerical work has been largely eliminated. In its place has come high pressure and decentralised work done by married, well-educated (mostly white) women who are paid on a piece-rate basis. Productivity is very high but 'the new jobs in the insurance industry may be not only dead-end, but also boring, stressful and deeply unsatisfying. Whereas the factory socialised production, the new technologies are paving the way for an organisation of work that is extraordinarily isolating'. Cheap though it is, this is nonetheless a high-quality workforce. 'For women at the bottom of the clerical hierarchy, jobs are simply disappearing.'[31] For all these women, the HRM profession can have little significance.

At higher levels we are beginning to see a substantial increase in the numbers of women entering the professions – particularly in medicine and family law. These are fields where women's natural gifts ought to confer advantages to them over many males. The same argument ought to apply to managerial work in business and industry, but the penetration of women into these roles is still marginal. Some recent studies even suggest that there has been a diminution in the numbers of women at the highest corporate level. A study of the 'glass ceiling' in 11 of the biggest Australian firms has indicated that so pervasive was the locker-room ethos of the corporate boardroom that outstanding women were voluntarily removing themselves from the race.[32] Their reasoning was that the male behaviour was merely childish (though sometimes dangerously so) and they (the women) had better things to do with their lives and careers.

In an important paper published in 1994 Charles Hampden-Turner pointed out how the familar male biases of US, British, and Australian firms are inimical to success in the new multicultural, strategic-alliance based global business system.[33] Women are, by contrast, naturally collaborative and, furthermore, highly attentive to detail. These characteristics are often used to explain the success of female-dominated mass-assembly operations. In his *Work and the Nature of Man* Fred Herzberg paid much attention to the so-called 'dissatisfiers' associated with monotony and boredom.[34] Ronco and Peattie, who studied highly satisfied workers, discovered that whereas challenge, intellectual stimulation, variety, personalisation of work, meaning, and autonomy are all important (as Herzberg pointed out), a surprising number of workers apparently need – and enjoy – occasional repetition and monotony. They cite as the archetype a fisherman who insisted on baiting all his own hooks (hundreds of them) while his crew looked on.[35]

In management women naturally approach work in a way that has some affinity with Asian manager/entrepreneurs. This was captured nicely by the remark of a senior Australian manager in the study referred to above: 'The trouble with women (managers) is, they don't give putts!'[36] To the unitiated in golf, this means that a chap might well relieve you of the nerve-wracking need to sink a tricky three-foot putt ('That's a gimme!') on the understanding that you may well do the same for him at some future date. It is a form of male-bonding reciprocity, based on bending the rules. The point is, however, players don't give putts in the US Open either, or in any professional or benchmarked international competition. Asian businessmen don't give putts when it comes to work standards and quality, and certainly not until trust has been built up over years and years of shared social interaction and strategic alliance-building. Women are good at that kind of bridge-building too, though uncompromising on the important details.

Hampden-Turner suggests that the characteristic weaknesses of US business – a universalistic and rigid reliance on tough, legally binding rules (as in gridiron football), a mania for analysis of discrete facts, items, tasks, 'the bottom line' and numbers (what might be referred to as the trees rather than the wood), an overemphasis on individual rights, motivators, capacities, rewards and punishments and, finally, an absolute reliance on measured performance as the basis for all status – could be softened or enriched by an influx of women, whose social culture in the USA is somewhat different from the above.[37] In fact, their social culture is somewhat similar to Asian cultures in some respects.

Hampden-Turner and Trompenaars suggest that the female side of US culture displays the opposite values – the capacity to deal in a particularistic and accurate way with each situation, an ability to integrate and synthesise into meaningful patterns (what you might call the woods rather than the trees), a preference for the communitarian values of co-operation and service and, finally, a leaning to ascribed status, based on earned, long-term respect rather than short-term performance. If this is what Asian business is good at and what, arguably, Anglo-Saxon business needs to move towards, why don't women move more readily into senior management roles? Part of the answer, Hampden-Turner and Trompenaars argue, is that those women who compete in the USA for these roles have absorbed, or adapted to, the prevailing male culture. US female executives even outscore senior men on some of the variables, such as the insistence that day-to-day achievement be the sole basis of status.[38]

Hampden-Turner and his colleagues have something important to say not just about the new work roles of female managers but also about the way that all senior managers need to behave in the future. They do not argue that particularism, integration, communitarianism, and ascribed status are always or necessarily preferable to universalism, analysis, individualism, and achieved status, merely that the latter values dominate our business cultures to an extent that may be damaging our capacity to compete internationally. It might be valuable to examine the extent to which the human resource field too has been captured by this lopsided view of the values associated with work.[39]

The psychological contract

All of the changes in work and work roles noted above add up to a renegotiation of the 'psychological contract' between employer and employee that was first described by Ed Schein.[40] Herriot (and others) has drawn attention to the profound shift in the formal and technical aspects of employee contracts and also the deeper and more powerful 'basic assumption' level of interrupted dependence and premature fight. (This is explored further in Chapter 7 of this book.) Within that implicit contract are embedded three kinds of individual expectations and needs:

1. The need for equity and justice – that employees will be treated fairly and honestly and that information and explanation about changes will always be provided.
2. The desire for security and relative certainty – that employees can expect, in return for their loyalty, that they need not be fearful, uncertain or helpless (as they contemplate who might be the next to go).
3. The need for fulfilment, satisfaction, and progression – that employees can trust the value that the organisation places on their current contributions and prior successes and relationships.[41]

A number of writers have referred to the so-called 'survivor syndrome' – the confusing mix of relief and guilt that characterises the feelings of those who have survived – so far – job-cuts in their place of work. Greenlaugh, Buch and others have put forward a 'threat-rigidity' thesis which suggests that the survivors, far from embracing the opportunity to innovate and take risks in the spaces provided in the 'lean and mean' organisation, often revert instead to the safest, narrowest, and most conservative modes of behaviour available to them.[42] This, they argue, is bound to be the outcome of fear. Fear, in turn, is the outcome of breaching the psychological contract.

The four main components of morale have been variously described as 'the satisfaction that is obtained from what you *do* (the job itself), enjoying the people you are working *with* (the work group), trusting the people you work *for* (management practices) and, finally, economic rewards'. Delayering and downsizing disturb these satisfactions. A recent Institute of Management survey of middle managers revealed that the two greatest dissatisfiers were 'perceived incompetence of senior management' and 'office politics'. In the 'lean and mean' organisation the pressure is on every job and job holder; inadequacies are ruthlessly exposed as spans of control widen. The survivors are not necessarily the most able people; in fact, the most capable and confident are highly likely to seize the generous severance packages generally on offer.[43] Downsizing, unless it is achieved with great care and skill, can lead to

> the creation of new demands for which retained staff have neither the skill
> nor experience to perform; oversubscription to voluntary severance schemes
> and the creation of a 'reluctant stayer' population; the replacement or

rehiring of previously severed posts; loss of older staff through early retirement with resulting structural blockages to promotion; and other unquantifiable 'hidden costs' such as the loss of organisational memory.[44]

Elliott Jaques, whose early research on levels of work theory is often cited to justify de-layering, has always argued that most employment hierarchies have traditionally been too long and steep.[45] However, he also warned that there is a natural and ineluctable increment of complexity and difficulty in hierarchy. If you strip out too many layers, you inevitably sever important connections between the levels of work, with catastrophic consequences – in fact exactly the consequences described in the IM survey. Even if you get the number of hierarchical levels right, it won't work unless the role incumbents at every level have the appropriate capability to deal with the complexity at that level. The psychological contract only works, Jaques argued, when the structure is exactly right and the capacities of all the people are almost exactly matched with the demands they face. Sudden and violent de-layering, unsupported by sound organisation theory, is bound to lead to distortion of work roles and a distorted and damaging image of the work itself.

There is another angle to the old psychological contract between employer and employee. In previous decades and centuries, few people took much notice of the costs of economic exploitation. There have been exceptions, such as slavery and child labour, but until the evidence about environmental pollution began to mount employee loyalty depended mostly on the reciprocal obligation to provide long-term employment and a 'career'. Prior to that, the word 'career' retained its original meaning – as in 'careering about', ie in an unpredictable and disorderly way.

In recent years, however, there has been a change in popular awareness about the purposes and outcomes of corporate activity. For example, 20 years ago it would have been unthinkable that employees who smoke cigarettes should be banished to the street to indulge their habit. A social change of this sort has the effect of exposing the impact that the major tobacco companies have on the well-being of their consumers. The reality has not changed but the quality of working life for all employees of such firms has altered irrevocably. Similar considerations apply in the case of firms known to pollute the environment, and even in the case of financial institutions known to oversell or mis-sell their products. The major armaments firms, of course, have faced particular problems in this respect. All of these social transgressions are being exposed publicly as never before.

Corporate recruiters report that potential employers' primary tasks (ie what the organisation exists to do) are increasingly prominent in the career choices of the best young graduates. If your purposes are perceived to be useful or valuable, you may well have a wider choice of the pick of the crop. Evidence from Australia suggests that this issue is particularly acute amongst young, outstanding women.[46] In the primitive hunting group, sympathy towards the hunted prey would be inimical to success – during the hunt; afterwards the cave artists clearly experienced some empathy, at least. In the home group, however, sympathy and bonds of female reciprocity would be crucial for social adhesion and resilience.

Not much has changed. In the modern corporation women, it seems, find it more difficult to insulate themselves from the embarrassing aspects of corporate primary tasks or effects ('the hunt'). Not only are high-rising women put off by the locker-room behaviour of male colleagues, they are much more likely to be pained by corporate wickedness in one form or another.

The likelihood is therefore that some of the most significant work roles of all – those within the core director groups at the top of major firms – will continue to be dominated by relatively amoral men. Only the Japanese, according to Hampden-Turner and Trompenaars, have a long-term strategy for getting out of 'dirty' technologies and into the 'virtuous' areas of work which must emerge. Chief amongst these is the pollution control and clean-up field. The awareness of the split between useful (virtuous) and pernicious or frivolous work is an emergent theme, not yet significant; but it would be foolish to ignore its implications for work satisfaction in the longer term.[47]

Conclusion

In the meantime employer practices have evolved in various UK firms, largely without restraint from government or from an emasculated union movement, that have had the effect of heightening the uncertainty of the lives of the least well-off in society and the additional effect of helping to create an anxious middle class. Very few big employers seem to have thought through the implications of this for their internal operations or for their immediate and longer-term environments. An important 1995 study by Future Perfect suggests that a minority of big UK firms has recognised the long-term risks of simply relinquishing the employer side of the psychological contract. These firms have worked hard to make the mutual expectations of employer and employee more transparent, to share information of plans, opportunities, scenarios; and they have stated a commitment to support the individual in a process of long-term career development. One of the firms studied put in 26,500 person-days in explaining its position to a workforce of 36,000 people. Future Perfect comments:

> We have little doubt that the very substantial investment that such companies are making will convert into competitive advantage for them, for we observe very high levels of management and staff commitment to, and belief in, the future of the organisation.[48]

But, as we have seen, the numbers remaining in these big organisations continue to dwindle. For the others, Ray Pahl suggests that we still have a great deal to learn from, and about, those people or couples who have succeeded in structuring a freelance or semi-freelance life. Ronco and Peattie make it clear that

> people have to learn to make both internal and external boundaries for themselves . . . they have to create for themselves categories of different kinds of tasks and segments of the work. They must learn to devise personal priorities and organise preferences. The external boundaries are also necessary to separate work from non-work activities. Doing all this will not be easy . . . Sadly, Government schemes focused on training and enterprise have a too narrow view of the problem. Recognising the real dilemma of people in their households with conflicting pressures from partners, children, parents, maybe even grandparents and the added complexity of previous partners and stepchildren would involve a massive broadening out of the narrow perspective of the Department of Employment or the Department of Trade and Industry.[49]

The third sector

It is becoming clearer that the efforts of firms to educate their employees for a more autonomous 'career' and the slow learning curve of the newly 'liberated' will not mop up the enormous problems surrounding work and work roles with which we began this chapter. It looks very much as though we are entering a period when governments are going to have to intervene more than they have done in recent decades, and employers are going to have to think hard about their 'freedoms' to operate as they please. This means that professional bodies such as the IPD and its sister organisations in other countries are going to be drawn into an unfamiliar, and perhaps uncomfortable, political posture.

The important Demos paper *The Time Squeeze* sets out the argument about the so-called 'third sector' with admirable clarity:

> The Third Sector becomes our last best hope for absorbing the millions of displaced workers cast off by corporate and government re-engineering . . .

In the United States there are currently more than 1,400,000 non-profit organizations, with total combined assets of more than $500 billion . . . The non-profit sector already contributes more than 6 per cent of the GNP and is responsible for 10.5 per cent of the total national employment . . . Britain's experience is closest to that of the United States: it has thousands of non-profit organizations, and in recent years has engaged in a similar political debate over the role of the Third Sector. There are currently more than 350,000 non-profit organizations in the United Kingdom, with a total income in excess of £17 billion, or 4 per cent of the gross national product.

The industrialized nations ought to consider making a direct investment in expanded job creation in the non-profit sector, as an alternative to welfare for the increasing number of jobless who find themselves locked out of the new high-tech global marketplace . . . An income voucher would allow millions of unemployed people, working through thousands of neighbourhood organizations, the opportunity to help themselves. Providing a social wage in return for community-service work would also benefit both business and government.

Paying for a social income and for re-education and training programs to prepare men and women for a career of community service would require significant government funds. Some of the money could come from savings brought about by gradually replacing many of the current welfare programs with direct income payments to persons performing community-service work. Government funds could also be freed up by discontinuing costly subsidies to corporations that have outgrown their domestic commitments and now operate in countries around the world.

Powerful vested interests are likely to resist the idea of providing a social wage in return for community service. Yet, the alternative of leaving the problem of long-term technological employment unattended could lead to widespread social unrest, increased violence, and the further disintegration of society.[50]

This is powerful stuff. If the IPD, for example, were to adopt a long-term 'human resource management' strategy even distantly similar to this, the potential for splits between the profession and mainstream corporate interests might be considerable. For a long time now, one of the main concerns of the personnel profession has been the status and influence of its senior managers in relation to line management. Membership of the board of directors, for example, has been looked on as a sign that personnel is taken seriously.

The Demos arguments about the Third Sector (expanded in a newer publication: *The Other Invisible Hand*[51]) reflect a wider international dissatisfaction with governments' ability to manage unemployment, and industry's perceived insularity and short-sightedness. The 'personnel' profession had some claim to professional detachment and values. The 'human resource' field seems to have been a willing ally, or accomplice, in cost-saving by the simplest route of all – 'downsizing', with little sense of the wider or longer-term questions addressed here. If the personnel profession really did have a breadth of vision, it might well be that the line executives, whose public repute has fallen steadily throughout the 1980s and 1990s, would seek to establish their status and influence with the personnel director.

End-notes

1   *Hansard*, 14 February 1995, p837; debate on poverty and unemployment.

2   Editorial, *People Management*, 18 May 1995, p57; Report on presentation of the IPD position paper, *People Make the Difference*.

3   PAHL, R, E, (ED.), *On Work – Historical, comparative and theoretical approaches*, Oxford, Basil Blackwell, 1989.

4   PAHL, (ED.), *op. cit.*

5   PAHL, R, E, *After Success – Fin de siècle anxiety and identity*, London, Polity Press, 1995.

6   REICH, R, in A. SAMPSON, 'Stuck in the nervous nineties', *The Observer*, 4 June 1995.

7   SCASE, R, AND GOFFEE, R, *The Reluctant Managers*, London, Unwin Hyman, 1989.

8   THOMPSON, E, P, *The Making of the English Working Class*, London, Penguin Books, 1979.

9   MALCOLMSON, R, W, *Life and Labour in England 1700–1800*, London, Century Hutchinson, 1981, cited in Pahl, (ed.), *op. cit.*, p12.

10   ATKINSON, D, *The Common Sense of Community*, London, Demos, 1994.

11   PAHL, (ED.), *op. cit.*, p19.

12   PAHL, (ED.), *op. cit.*, p2.

13   DUBIN, R, *The World of Work*, Englewood Cliffs NJ, Prentice Hall, 1958, cited in Pahl, (ed.), *op. cit.*, p14.

14   PRAHALAD, C, K, Keynote address to IPD National Conference, Harrogate, 28 October 1994.

15   MASLOW, A, *Common Knowledge: Motivation and personality*, New York, Harper, 1954.

16   PAHL, (ED.), *op. cit.*, pp12–13.

17   JAQUES, E, *Work, Creativity and Social Justice*, London, Heinemann, 1970, pp12–13, 64–65.

18   HANDY, C, *The Age of Unreason*, London, Basic Books, 1989.

19   HAMPDEN-TURNER, C, *Corporate Culture*, London, Piatkus, 1994, p80.

20   CHILD, J, 'Managerial strategies, new technology and the labour process', in D. Knight *et al* (eds), *Job Redesign*, 1985.

21   MARRIS, P, 'The management of uncertainty', address to the Tavistock Clinic Seminar: 'The Politics of Attachment', 31 March 1995.

22   BROWN, W, AND JAQUES, E, *Glacier Project Papers*, London, Heinemann, 1965.

23   HUTTON, W, *The State We're in*, London, Jonathan Cape, 1995.

24   HASKINS, C, in A. Sampson, *Company Man: The rise and fall of corporate life*, London, HarperCollins, 1995.

25   HAMPDEN-TURNER, *op. cit.*, p83.

26   SAMPSON, A, *Company Man: The rise and fall of corporate life*, London, HarperCollins, 1995.

27   KIECHEL, W, 'How we will work in the year 2000', *Fortune Magazine*, 17 May 1993, p45.

28   MURRAY, L, 'Personal and social influences on parenting and adult life', address to the Tavistock Clinic Seminar: 'The Politics of Attachment', 31 March 1995.

29   HAKIM, C, 'Homeworking in Britain', in Pahl (ed.), *op. cit.*, pp603–4.

30   COYLE, A, 'Dirty Business', West Midlands Low Pay Unit, 1986, in Pahl, (ed.), *op. cit.*, p606.

31   BARAN, B, 'Office automation and women's work: the technological transformation of the insurance industry, in Pahl, (ed.), *op. cit.* pp684–708.

32   SINCLAIR, A, *Trials at the Top*, Melbourne, Melbourne University Press, 1995.

33   HAMPDEN-TURNER, C, 'The structure of entrapment', quoted in *The Deeper News*, (Global Business Network), Vol. 5, No. 1, January 1994.

34   HERZBERG, F, *Work and the Nature of Man*, New York, Thomas Y Crowell, 1966.

35   RONCO, W, AND PEATTIE, L, 'Making work: a perspective from social science', in Pahl, (ed.), *op. cit.*, pp709–721.

36   SINCLAIR, *op. cit.*, pp7–8.

37   HAMPDEN-TURNER, C, 'The structure of entrapment', quoted in *The Deeper News* (Global Business Network), Vol. 5, No. 1, January 1994.

38   HAMPDEN-TURNER, C, AND TROMPENAARS, A, *The Seven Cultures of Capitalism*, New York, Currency Doubleday, 1993.

39   HAMPDEN-TURNER AND TROMPENAARS, *ibid*.

40   SCHEIN, E, *Organisation Psychology*, 3rd edn, Englewood Cliffs NJ, Prentice Hall, 1988.

41   HERRIOT, P, *The Career Management Challenge: Balancing individual and organisational needs*, London, Sage, 1992.

42 GREENLAUGH, L, 'Managing the job insecurity crisis', *Human Resources Management*, 22, pp431–44; AND BUCH, K. *et al*, 'OD under conditions of decline', *Organisational Development Journal*, 1990, p32–7, quoted in P. Kettley, *Employee Morale During Downsizing*, Institute for Employment Studies, Employment Brief 39, 1995.

43 KETTLEY, P, *ibid*.

44 KETTLEY, P, *ibid*.

45 JAQUES, E, *A General Theory of Bureaucracy*, London, Heinemann, 1976.

46 SINCLAIR, *op. cit.*

47 HAMPDEN-TURNER, C, AND TROMPENAARS, A, *op. cit.*

48 FUTURE PERFECT, *The Human Resource Implications for Organisations in Transition*, London, Future Perfect, 1995.

49 RONCO, W, AND PEATTIE, L, *Making Work: Self-created jobs in participating organisations*, London, Plenum Press, 1983, quoted in *The Time Squeeze*, London, Demos Paper 15/16, 1995.

50 DEMOS PAPER, *ibid*.

51 MULGAN, G, AND LANDRY, C, *The Other Invisible Hand*, London, Demos, 1995.

CHAPTER THREE
Organisational Structure

Keith Sisson

The ways in which tasks are divided, activities co-ordinated, and decisions taken within organisations are the basic building blocks for human resource management (HRM). Organisational structure, to use the short-hand to describe what is involved, is often ignored, however, in discussions about HRM – or even if not actually ignored, it tends to take second place to questions of 'culture'. In McKinsey's famous '7S framework', for example, structure is deemed to be only one of seven factors that make for effective management. It is also seen as part of the 'cold triangle', along with strategy and systems, rather than the 'warm square' of style, skills, staff, and subordinate goals.

Apart from its intrinsic importance, the particular reason for the focus in this collection is that major changes are taking place in the structure of organisations which have the most profound implications for HRM in general and the strategic prospects for HRM in particular. Superficially, these changes and implications are the same across the industrialised world and, according to some commentators, herald the dawn of a new era: the greater individual responsibility or 'empowerment' that changes in organisational structure are supposedly bringing about makes it seem possible to square the circle – to meet the demands for greater economic efficiency and at the same time make a significant contribution to improving the quality of working life. Organisational structure is deeply embedded in a particular context of institutions and legal frameworks, however, and so the implications of such changes can differ significantly from one country to another. Such is the context in the UK that the changes taking place, far from facilitating the strategic approach that many commentators say is essential to competitive success, call into question whether such an approach is a serious prospect.

This chapter develops the latter argument in more detail. It begins by briefly reviewing developments in the 'external' face of organisations in the UK; it goes on to look in more detail at what has been happening to their internal structure and at the rationale for the changes taking place; it then considers the implications for the strategic prospects for HRM both in general terms and in the specific UK context before concluding with a brief look forward to the millennium.

The changing face of British organisations

The 1980s and 1990s have been a period of intense change in what might be termed the 'external face' of organisations in the UK, with profound implications for organisational structure. Four developments have been especially important, namely, the changing portfolio of many companies, internationalisation, privatisation, and externalisation. In each case, therefore, there will be a review of the nature and extent of these changes based on the survey evidence and illustrated by specific cases.

Changing portfolios – merger and acquisition, investment and divestment

Ever since Chandler's (1962) pioneering work, the precise significance of an organisation's business strategy for its organisational structure has been the subject of intense debate and, in particular, whether the structure follows the strategy or vice versa. It is a truism, however, to suggest that business strategy is the key influence on the 'external' face of organisations which is the immediate concern. Especially important has been the nature and extent of diversification. Such diversification can take the form of expansion into related or unrelated activities (see, for example, Channon 1973). In the 1970s many British companies – Cadbury was just one example – embarked on substantial programmes of diversification in order to spread the risk of their investment. In the 1980s the fashion changed, largely as a result of the realisation that it was not necessarily easy to transfer particular management skills from one set of activities to another, and many drew back as substantially as they had expanded to concentrate on their 'core' activities or businesses – 'sticking to their knitting', as Peters and Waterman (1982) recommended. Movement around this axis has been more or less continuous ever since as companies have expanded and contracted activities, and bought and sold businesses, in the attempt to maximise their competitive advantage in an increasingly competitive environment.

Table 3.1 gives some impression of the sheer magnitude of the change taking place in the composition of the portfolio of UK companies. It comes from the second Company Level Industrial Relations Survey

(CLIRS) of 176 companies with more than 1,000 employees in the UK carried out in 1992 by the Industrial Relations Research Unit. Over the previous five years, more than two-thirds reported cases of merger and acquisition and a similar number reported investment in new locations. Almost the same number, however, reported the closure of existing sites, nearly half reported divestment, and 40 per cent the rundown of existing sites. Many of these changes were also associated with one another. Thus, the authors found that nearly three-quarters of the companies in the survey reported both growth and closure or run-down, with 20 per cent citing growth only and 8 per cent neither (Marginson *et al* 1995:20). A graphic illustration of the extent of change in this area is what happened to the composition of the portfolio of Unilever, one of the UK's biggest companies. Between 1983 and 1989 alone Unilever sold 124 companies valued at £2.4 billion and bought 163 worth £6.4 billion (Pollert 1993).

Table 3.1
EXTENT AND SOURCES OF ORGANISATIONAL CHANGE

Per cent mentioning	UK Dom.	UK Int.	O/seas	All
No change	6	8	3	7
Extent of changes in UK enterprise over 5-year period				
Merger and acquisition	65	78	67	70
Investment in new locations	72	66	64	65
Expansion at existing sites	58	72	69	66
Divestment	33	66	51	48
Closure of existing sites	63	62	62	62
Rundown of existing sites	31	43	51	40
Formation of joint ventures	24	52	33	36
Establishment of long-term contracts with suppliers or customers	28	46	36	37
Sources of change in internal structure				
Internal growth of business	54	58	44	53
Major new acquisition	44	38	36	40
Major new diversification	14	15	21	16
Shift from production to market logic	25	22	31	25
Increased accountability to business unit	43	57	67	53
Simplification/de-layering	28	43	41	37
Decentralisation	22	32	21	26

Base: All companies.
Respondents: Finance.
Source: Marginson *et al* (1995:21).

Internationalisation

The UK is distinctive not only because of the significance of large companies, but also because of their multinational character. Much attention has focused on the implications of the presence within the UK of foreign-owned multinational companies: in the 1950s and 1960s it was a question of US companies such as Ford, General Motors (Vauxhall), and IBM whereas more recently it has been a question of Japanese car manufacturers (Nissan, Toyota, and Honda) and, more recently still, of companies from other European Union member countries, such as BMW with its take-over of Rover. It is right to focus on this matter, because more than 15 per cent of the UK workforce in manufacturing is accounted for by foreign-owned multinationals (Business Monitor 1993). Even more significant, however, is the extent to which large UK-owned companies themselves have become multinational. In the 1980s the stocks and flows of international investment outwards from, as well as inwards to, the UK were proportionally higher than for the USA, Japan, Germany, or France (Dunning 1993). Or, to take another perspective, in the preparatory work for CLIRS in 1992, 975 companies were identified as having more than 1,000 employees in the UK . Of these companies 759 were UK-owned and 216 overseas-owned. Of the UK-owned companies almost half (360) were themselves multinational, including about one-third of the companies discussed below that had been privatised since 1979 (Marginson *et al* 1995:4, 20). Overall, then, almost seven out of 10 large companies in the UK were multinational.

Privatisation

One of the most obvious changes in the 'external' face of UK organisations has been as a result of the programme of privatisation undertaken by Conservative governments in the 1980s and early 1990s with the aim of achieving greater enterprise and efficiency. The sell-off of shares in British Petroleum and Cable and Wireless in the early 1980s was followed by the flotation of British Telecom (1984), British Gas (1986), British Airways and the British Airports Authority (1987), British Steel (1988), the regional water authorities in England and Wales (1989), the regional electricity distribution companies in England and Wales (1990), the electricity generator (1991), the Scottish electricity industry (1992), and what was left of the coal industry (1994). In addition many subsidiaries of former nationalised industries, such as *Travellers' Fare* in the case of British Rail, were sold. Of the major trading enterprises originally in the public sector, only the railways and postal services had not been privatised by the middle of 1995. British Rail was due to be privatised in the near future; the position of the Post Office was uncertain. Overall, the CLIRS team (Marginson *et al* 1995:20) found that some 10 per cent of the large companies in their sample had been privatised since 1979.

For present purposes, the significance of privatisation is especially important in employment terms. By the end of 1991 the total nationalised industry workforce had fallen from the 1979 figure of 1,849,000 to 501,000. Redundancy played its part, especially in coal, but the privatisation of the four public utilities alone removed some 560,000 employees from the public sector (Colling and Ferner 1995:492–3).

Externalisation

The fourth feature, the subcontracting of activities previously performed inside the organisation, is closely associated in many people's minds with privatisation, and understandably so. In an attempt to maximise the exposure of managerial decision-making in the public services to competition, the Conservative governments of the 1980s and early 1990s introduced compulsory competitive tendering (CCT) and 'market testing' for a wide range of activities. Managers, first in the civil service and National Health Service (NHS) and later in local authorities, were obliged to allow private sector organisations to bid for contracts to do work previously done by the organisation's direct employees. Initially, so-called ancillary services such as cleaning, catering, laundry, refuse, and ground maintenance were targeted. More recently the net has been widened to include professional services such as the work of architects, lawyers and solicitors, finance and personnel specialists in local authorities, and the collection of statistics and the management of information technology in central government.

The trend to put out to contract these and other activities has not been confined to the public sector. Many organisations in the private sector have done the same. The reasoning that led them to do so typically followed from a review of their 'core' activities, in some cases in the wake of relatively disastrous overdiversification in the 1970s and early 1980s, and from a determination to 'get back to basics' and to concentrate on 'core competencies' (Peters and Waterman 1982). The organisation had little or no expertise, it was argued, in carrying out many of the ancillary or professional services described above. Not only that: it had little idea of the market rate for such activities. In practice, it had tended to relate what it paid its employees doing these activities to the arrangements for the 'core' staff. At the very least, continued the argument, the organisation should put the activities out to tender to establish their true 'market' cost. Other things being equal, the organisation should subcontract these activities to the 'specialists' (who would be responsible for any research and development in their area) and concentrate its own energies and resources on the 'core' products or services.

This thinking has close affinity with that of the so-called *flexible firm* model associated with Atkinson (1984) and his colleagues (Atkinson and Meager 1986) at the (then) Institute of Manpower Studies. The status of the model, in particular its descriptive accuracy, has been the subject of considerable controversy (see for example Pollert 1987; Hunter and MacInnes 1991). At its heart is an organisational structure that many British firms are supposedly trying to introduce, and which is offered as a model for others to follow. This structure involves 'the break-up of the labour force into increasingly peripheral, and therefore numerically flexible groups of workers, clustered about a numerically stable core group which will conduct the firm's key, firm-specific activities' (Atkinson 1984:29). In the case of the core, which is assumed to be made up of managers and groups whose skills cannot readily be bought in, terms and conditions are designed to promote task or functional flexibility. They are likely to include, for example, single-status conditions, employment security, and performance assessment. In the case of the periphery, the emphasis is on numerical flexibility and the relationship is essentially market-based. Here several groups are involved: those that are full-time but have a job rather than a career; part-time and temporary workers; and those involved in subcontracting activities.

Much more substantial theoretical underpinning for externalisation, rarely mentioned in prescriptive texts recommending it, is to be found in the developing branch of economics known as transaction costs analysis. Briefly, this approach sees two ways to getting something done: one through the market and the other through hierarchy, ie the organisation (for further details see Williamson 1975, 1985; for a brief overview see Francis 1994:72–5). All things being equal, goes the argument, the market is the most efficient instrument. In a number of cases, for example, where specific skills are involved, the market does not work so effectively and therefore hierarchy may be more appropriate. In practice, as outlined in Table 3.2, it is possible to envisage a number of possible types of relationship. These range from the 'pure' market relationship, which can involve long-term relationships (such as Marks & Spencer or Japanese car manufacturers have sought to establish with their suppliers) as well as single so-called 'spot market' transactions associated with CCT, through to partnership and joint ventures, to different forms of hierarchy (intra-firm

Table 3.2
TYPES OF RELATIONSHIPS

Type of relationship	Basis of relationship
market/competitive	single transaction period contracts
partnership	supplier-dominant/buyer-dependent equal balance of power buyer-dominant/supplier-dependent
joint venture	joint ownership
hierarchy	intra-firm trading direct internal control

Based on Saunders et al (1994).

trading and direct internal control), which will be the subject of a later section.

Like the model of the *flexible firm*, the nature and extent of subcontracting has been the subject of considerable controversy (see for example

Table 3.3
INCIDENCE OF BUDGETARY TARGETS AND
REPORTING AT BUSINESS UNIT LEVEL

	Indicator targeted	Indicator reported	Of which reported:		
			weekly or daily	monthly	less often
	%	%	%	%	%
Sales	72	66	22	40	3
Return on Investment	40	37	1	30	7
Unit Labour Costs	47	40	10	24	6
Operating Profit to Sales Ratio	66	60	5	48	6
Sales to Capital Invested Ratio	18	14	–	13	1
Production Costs to Sales Ratio	31	27	3	22	2
Marketing Expenses to Sales Ratio	38	32	1	27	3
Admin. Expenses to Sales Ratio	41	35	3	29	4
Direct Labour Costs to Sales Ratio	40	35	5	27	3
None	6	15	–	–	–

Base: All Companies (N=176).
Source: Marginson et al (1995:7).

Pollert 1991). The best source of recent data, although it is primarily concerned with ancillary services, is the 1990 Workplace Industrial Relations
Survey (WIRS) carried out by Millward and his colleagues (Millward *et al*
1992). Table 3.3 gives details of the extent of 'complete' and 'partial' subcontracting for a range of specified services. Taking the two categories
together, it emerges that building maintenance was the activity most often
subcontracted, followed by cleaning, transport, and payroll. By sector, 85
per cent of manufacturing industries and 69 per cent of service industries
reported some 'complete' contracting. In central government, reflecting
the policies discussed earlier, the complete subcontracting of some activity was near universal (Millward *et al* 1992:340, 346).

An interim conclusion

These changes in the 'external' face of organisations have far-reaching
implications for organisations and their structures. It is not simply that
competitive pressures (in the usually accepted sense of the phrase) have
grown, leading to reductions in the size of many organisations – the UK
remains a country of large companies but their size, and that of their individual workplaces, has declined significantly in recent years. It is also that
many more workplaces in the UK find themselves competing for investment within multinational companies' internal market. The ability of
headquarters to use international comparisons of performance is a powerful weapon in driving costs down at the same time as improving quality
and reliability through the networking of best-practice solutions to problems. Also important is the increasing acceptance of the implications of
transaction costs thinking, namely that in many circumstances the market
is a more efficient way of managing activities than hierarchy. This means
that direct employment increasingly faces competition from subcontracting, joint ventures and other forms of market relationships.

Last, but by no means least in the case of the UK, there is perhaps the
most significant implication of privatisation, which very rarely receives the
attention it deserves. Traditionally, the public sector has been expected to
fulfil the role of the 'good' or 'model' employer whose management should
set standards for others to follow in the management of human resources.
With privatisation and CCT, this role has effectively been abandoned in
favour of a much more contingent approach.

On the inside

Changes in the internal structure of organisations have been wide-ranging as
well as fundamental. They go far beyond the 'right-sizing' euphemistically

associated with closures and redundancies. Five groups of such changes may be identified.

One group of changes reflects a move away from hierarchy with the reduction or de-layering of a number of tiers of management. A second group, which is to be found in services as well as manufacturing, involves the organisation of work. Specialisation (in which tasks, jobs, and functions are broken down and defined as narrowly as possible) is giving way to work organised into cells, groups, and teams. The third and fourth groups reflect similar processes at higher levels of the organisation. In the case of national companies and organisations, these involve the regrouping of activities on the basis of products or services rather than functions and include 'businesses within a business' as well as the 'strategic business units' (SBUs), 'divisions', 'sectors' and 'streams' associated with the fifth group (described below). In the case of international companies, the changes involve the regrouping of activities on the basis of products or services at the territorial level, such as Europe, North America, or the Far East, rather than on the basis of individual national company subsidiaries.

The fifth, and perhaps important, group involves the break-up of the large-scale hierarchical organisation into a number of semi-autonomous or 'quasi' businesses responsible for most, if not all, activities within their jurisdiction. In the case of many companies, and public-sector organisations such as British Rail and the Post Office, it has involved the creation of a number of 'businesses' or 'divisions'. In the civil service and NHS, it has involved the creation of 'executive agencies' and 'trusts', with 'opted-out' schools being the equivalent in education. In the case of companies such as Courtaulds and ICI there has been a true break-up: in effect, a demerger of what, in each case, was a single entity into two separate and independent companies. More generally, the talk is of 'federal' organisations (Handy 1984), 'network' organisations (Powell 1990; Miles and Snow 1992), and 'horizontal' organisations (Byrne 1993). (For fuller details see Wally et al 1995).

Three common developments underpin what might appear to be apparently unrelated changes. One is divisionalisation, the second budgetary devolution, and the third 'internal markets'. Each of these is considered here with the aim of getting behind the labels and the rhetoric to discuss what is actually involved.

Divisionalisation

Divisionalisation can take many forms and the different labels (for example, SBUs, 'sectors', 'streams', not to mention 'executive agencies' and 'trusts') can be very confusing. In practice, however, divisionalisation involves a number of major organisation changes which are more or less common. One is the disaggregation of the organisation into quasi-independent units, which will be referred to here as 'divisions'. Such divisions may embrace the activities of individuals, units, groups of units, or even of groups of companies. The principle of their organisation can be business activity or territory, or some combination of business activity and territory. In the case of Lucas, for example, many of the teams working under cellular manufacturing are quasi-businesses such as the diesel systems division and the automotive sector, both of which are organised on a worldwide basis. Examples of divisionalisation based on business activity would be the executive agencies in the civil service. Examples of divisionalisation based on territory would be the multiple retailers such as Marks & Spencer and Sainsbury or the main clearing banks, where individual retail stores and branches service specific geographical localities. An example of divisionalisation based on business activity and territory would be NHS trusts. Typically, NHS trusts organise the provision of health care by broad activity (such as acute services, ambulance, or mental health) within a geographical area roughly equivalent to the former district or regional health authorities of which they were once a part. In the case of many multinational companies, such as Nestlé or Unilever, divisionalisation operates at the international as well as the domestic level. Historically, such companies were organised around functions and national companies. Increasingly, however, the key decision-making unit is the international division, which has responsibility for individual products or related products either on a European or worldwide basis.

The second and third changes involved in divisionalisation are closely related. They are the separation of strategic from operating management and the decentralisation of responsibility for operating management to individual divisions. That is to say, strategic management (certainly in the sense of deciding the composition of the portfolio of the business) remains at the centre as does, in most cases, responsibility for the selection, development and reward of senior managers in the individual divisions. Day-to-day operations (and, in some cases, responsibility for strategic management in the sense of medium and long-term planning) is devolved to the divisions. In a phrase, the divisionalised organisation is 'decentralised operationally, but centralised strategically' (Whittington and Mayer 1994:6).

Whereas divisionalisation is a relatively recent departure in the civil service and the NHS, most large companies in the UK have long been run on some form of divisionalised lines (see for example Hill and Pickering 1986). The CLIRS results not only confirm the widespread coverage of divisionalisation but also offer further details on its nature. Just over half of the 176 companies in the survey reported that business activity was the basis of division, with the remainder split between territory and a mixture of business activity and territory as the basis. To illustrate the complexity of what can be involved, about 60 per cent also reported that they had intermediate divisions between the headquarters and the individual divisions. Most (70 per cent) individual divisions were 'mainly single-site' rather than 'mainly multi-site' (13 per cent), with the balance reporting a mixture.

CLIRS also confirms the importance of the developments associated with divisionalisation in accounting for the changes taking place in many large UK companies. Table 3.1 suggests that over the five years leading up to 1992 more than half of the companies had given increased accountability to the individual division (business unit), just over one-third had introduced some form of de-layering, and about one-quarter had moved in the direction of further decentralisation. Significantly, two-thirds of the 176 companies said that they had introduced at least one of the three developments associated with divisionalisation.

Budgetary devolution

Budgetary devolution involves the allocation of responsibility for managing activities within financial resources or targets (see for example, Henley *et al* 1992). Like divisionalisation, with which it nearly always goes hand in hand, budgetary devolution can operate at a number of levels. It can relate to the SBU within a company, or a trust within the NHS, or an executive agency within the civil service. It can also relate to the internal units within such divisions, and even to bundles of activities. Individual cells or teams in manufacturing, for example, may have budgets devolved to them, as may the different clinical directorates in a NHS trust or a social services department within a local authority.

Budgetary devolution can also vary in its scope. It can cover some or all items of income and expenditure. Whereas managers of individual departments in the local authority case described below had, for example, responsibility for keeping within staff budgets, they did not themselves set these budgets.

Evidently, too, the make-up of budgets can vary from situation to situation. Some idea of this variety can be gauged from Table 3.4, which gives details of the indicators in large private-sector companies reported in

Table 3.4

THE INCIDENCE OF COMPLETE AND PARTIAL SUBCONTRACTING OF SPECIFIED SERVICES, 1990

	Complete subcontracting %			Partial subcontracting %	Complete or partial %
	All establishments	Single independent	Part of multi-establishment organisation	Part of multi-establishment organisation	Part of multi-establishment organisation
Cleaning of buildings and premises	41	25	45	7	52
Security	21	17	22	6	28
Catering	17	9	19	8	27
Building maintenance	46	54	44	23	67
Printing and photocopying	18	30	15	13	28
Pay-roll	8	15	7	42	49
Transport of documents and goods	30	33	29	21	50
Base: all establishments Unweghted Weighted	2061 2000	253 418	1808 1582	1808 1582	1808 1582

Source: Millward et al (1992:341).

CLIRS (Marginson *et al* 1995:7). Significantly, too, one in five of the companies said they targeted seven or more of the specified indicators.

The operation of budgetary devolution also depends on whether the division is seen as a cost or a profit centre, for it is on either profits or costs that controls and targets have to bear. Individual divisions within an organisation, such as a cell or team or a department in a local authority, are typically cost centres, whereas a SBU within a company is usually a profit centre. It is not always as straightforward as this, however. In some companies, individual SBUs may be cost rather than profit centres. An example would be a motor manufacturer such as Ford which produces major components in several factories and assembles them in others: each of the factories, which may have thousands of employees, is essentially a cost rather than a profit centre. Arguably, even the individual outlets of some multiple retailers, such as Marks & Spencer and Sainsbury, which have highly centralised merchandising, are best seen as cost rather than profit centres: the local store manager has little control over many of the key elements that go into profit, such as type of goods and their price, let alone the decision about the location of the store, and is mainly accountable for running the store as efficiently as possible. In CLIRS most business units (85 per cent) were designated as profit centres (Marginson *et al* 1995:6).

To touch on a point that will be developed later, it is important to note that, paradoxical as it may seem, budgetary devolution is perhaps the most potent instrument of the centralisation of strategic control within organisations. Every one of the targets that appears in Table 3.4 above involves significant constraints as well as freedoms. Failure to keep within budgets or achieve targets can have drastic consequences. Respondents in 60 per cent of the CLIRS companies were able to recall at least one occasion when an individual division had been significantly off target. Asked what happened to the manager who was responsible,

> Forty-four per cent of the interviewees mentioned the removal, demotion, retirement or 'disappearance' of business unit managers, as against 24 per cent who referred to some form of support, such as revised objectives or new reporting requirements. Some or all the workforce lost their jobs in 53 per cent of the cases . . .
>
> Apart from the raw figures, the tone of many of the replies indicates that the headquarters of many of Britain's large companies have only limited tolerance of failure to meet targets. Perhaps the reply 'divisions failing to perform are sold', with its overtones of dispassionate routine, best exemplifies the attitude of our interviewees.
>
> Marginson *et al* (1993:23).

'Internal markets'

A third development is a variant of the externalisation discussed in the previous section. It involves a critical distinction between the purchasers and the providers of services within the organisation. This distinction is most obvious in the internal market of the NHS. The District Health Authorities, which were formerly responsible for total health care provision within a given area, have been split into two: the authorities or commissions, which are responsible for purchasing services from the most effective source available, and the trusts, which provide the services, in effect, to whichever authority will buy them.

An 'internal market' does not have to take such an extreme form, however. Many organisations practising an 'internal market' do not necessarily require the activities of 'providers' to be put out to subcontract or even market-testing. They do nonetheless expect services to be 'traded' and may give the purchasers the freedom to buy in services from outside agencies. In this way, so supporters argue, providers become more responsive to the needs of their 'internal customers' and have to ensure that the activity is cost-effective. Again, other things being equal, it enables the organisation to establish the cost of various activities.

A good example of the variety of forms that the 'internal market' can take is the delivery of specialist human resource activities. As well as the traditional department, one recent survey (Adams 1991; see also RDR 1991) of nearly 100 large UK organisations, identified no fewer than four main ways in which such activities were being delivered:

- the 'in-house' agency, in which the personnel department or some of its activities (for example, graduate recruitment), is seen as a cost centre and its activities are cross-charged to other departments or divisions
- the 'internal consultancy', in which the personnel department sells its services to the parent organisation or its units – the implication being that managers in the parent organisation will enjoy some freedom in deciding to go elsewhere if they are not happy with the service that is being provided
- the 'business within a business', in which some of the activities of the function are formed into a quasi-independent organisation which may trade not only with the parent organisation and its units but also externally
- the 'external consultancy', in which the organisation and its units go outside to completely independent business for help and advice on human resource and industrial relations matters.

As Adams (1991:44) points out, each of these four alternatives to the traditional department can be seen as representing a 'kind of scale of increasing degrees of "externalisation", understood as the application of market forces to the delivery of personnel activities'. Common to each of them, however, is some kind of service contract in which there is charging for the services delivered.

Kent County Council offers a good example of such arrangements in practice. It has drawn a distinction between centrally provided personnel activities that support the provision of direct services and those activities that serve corporate requirements. Under the process of budgetary devolution described earlier, individual service departments are given responsibility for all the resources that contribute to running their departments, and there is a process of negotiation and agreement with the 'provider' personnel department within the context of a medium-term planning cycle. Only the resources associated with those activities primarily concerned with the strategic functions of the council remain with the corporate personnel department (for further details see Griffiths 1989).

From management by task to management by performance

In focusing on the individual developments there is inevitably a danger of losing sight of their wider significance. Put simply, divisionalisation, devolved budgeting, and 'internal markets' add up to little short of a revolution in the ways organisations are being managed. Above all, they involve a fundamental shift from the management-by-task characteristic of traditional organisational structures to management by performance – in particular, financial performance.

The primacy of performance. Of course, divisionalisation, devolved budgeting, and 'internal markets' are not new concepts. Senior managers of such companies as General Motors and Du Pont (Chandler 1962) pioneered divisionalisation more than 70 years ago. The reasons why these ideas have been taken up so enthusiastically in recent years are twofold.

One reason is the pressure of competition. In the private sector this comes from increasing globalisation, and puts pressure simultaneously on costs, reliability and quality. In the public sector it is competition for scarce resources that is leading to the same outcome. In these circumstances, traditional organisational structures rooted in the hierarchy, bureaucracy, and task specialisation associated with so-called 'Fordist' or 'Taylorist' systems have proved to be not only costly and inefficient but also a major barrier to the flexibility increasingly required.

The second reason is the revolution in information processing facilities made possible by the coming of the microchip and associated developments in computer software. These facilities have produced instruments of management control and co-ordination that are far more effective and efficient than hierarchy and bureacracy. An organisation that can get data on sales and costs on a daily basis, for example, is in a position to do a number of things for which it previously needed substantial numbers of expensive managers – ranging from sending further supplies to making comparisons between divisions as a means of improving performance. No self-respecting senior manager in the mid-1990s has to issue an instruction to get his or her way as in the old days. Subordinates take heed of the implications of the performance information with which they are deluged – or else!

The significance of management by performance is very clear in a recent review by Owen and Harrison (1995) of the ICI demerger. There was much to be admired, the authors point out, in the 'old' ICI and yet 'a sense of the company as a protective shield, guarding employees from the harsh world outside' was seen increasingly as a barrier to further improvements in performance. A major objective therefore was to release energies deemed to have been submerged in the previous structure. To this end, strenuous efforts were being made in the two new companies to 'sharpen personal accountability at all levels'. The new' ICI, for example, has introduced what it calls the 'Triple A' project - accountability, achievement, and autonomy – which is 'designed to infuse the agility of a small company into the business while making the best use of its size and resources'.

As for the drawbacks of hierarchy, as regards in particular the relationship between headquarters and the divisions of the 'old' ICI, Owen and Harrison suggest that demerger was a response to a set of questions that every large multidivisional organisation needs to ask: 'What value does the head office add to our businesses?' and 'What are our distinctive advantages as a corporate parent – are they still relevant to our business?' The authors point out that as the divisions of the 'old' ICI had acquired greater responsibility, especially for their own profit-making, so the competence of headquarters to provide informed strategic direction had declined. This was especially true where the divisions had come to have very different interests. For example, in pharmaceuticals the emphasis had increasingly focused on new products, strengthening sales and marketing organisation, and improving the productivity of research and development. By contrast, the chemical businesses were cyclical, capital intensive, and less dependent on research. In these circumstances, the headquarters of the 'old' ICI concluded it was no longer capable of driving its world-class businesses hard enough. As Owen and Harrison (1995) state:

> Demerger has separated two distinct sets of management priorities and assigned them to corporate parents which are better equipped to deal with them than the old ICI. The narrower focus and greater homogeneity of the problems that the new head offices handle shorten and sharpen the lines of communication between headquarters and the operating businesses.

'Managed autonomy' rather than 'empowerment'? What about empowerment, ie the giving of greater responsibilities to individuals and teams, which so many pundits have proclaimed? There is, to be sure, very considerable devolution of responsibility in ICI and other organisations to managers and employees in individual divisions. It is a moot point, however, whether it is appropriate to dignify what is going on with the label of 'empowerment'. 'Managed autonomy' is a much better description of what is actually happening.

Crucially, the devolution of responsibility involved in divisionalisation, devolved budgeting, and 'internal markets' is by no means absolute. Indeed, as already suggested, in many respects the degree of co-ordination and control that senior managers at headquarters are able to exercise is much greater than in the most centralised of old-style hierarchical organisations. As well as the budgetary devolution that goes with divisionalisation and 'internal markets' there is a wealth of information that networking and benchmarking make available, for example, on 'best practice' developments inside and outside the organisation, to reward success and penalise failure.

Significantly, this also seems to be true of organisations such as ABB, which some commentators (for example Bartlett and Ghoshall 1993) have suggested has gone beyond the multidivisional model of organisation to develop new 'federal' or 'network' forms. In a review of the arguments, Whittington and Mayer (1994) point to the extreme decentralisation of a 'federation' of 1,300 companies, the leanness of the structure with only one intermediate level, the thinness of central staffs working as internal contractors, and the financial responsibility of front-line companies each with their own balance sheet, the capacity to retain one-third of their profits, and their own treasury management. They also point out, however, that the centre retains clear overall control over the portfolio of the company as a whole and that the rigorous reporting systems work effectively to increase the transparency of the internal capital market. Even the partial retention of profits, which is seen as a significant development of the original M-form, is provisional, and it has not prevented the closure and sale of many businesses.

A similar story emerges from a detailed study of the operation of budgetary devolution in one of the UK's largest local authorities (Keen 1995). The author emphasises the critically important distinction between devolution of budget management responsibility to middle managers and the devolution or delegation of decision-making authority, which may or may not form part of devolved budgetary process. In other words:

> managers may be held responsible for, and their performance measured against, financial and service delivery targets for, say, maintaining spending within their allocated budget totals. However, they may lack the authority to exercise control over key budget elements such as staffing, or to use overspends in one area to finance additional spend in another.
>
> Keen (1995:80–1).

So it emerged from Keen's interviews with 48 middle managers. The great majority welcomed the increased levels of control they had over resource management compared with pre-devolution days. In the words of one commercial services manager:

> Well, under the old system I had no budget. It was all done from above and we were all just a corporate cost, if you like. You were told you had eight people, you were the head and that was it – if things got a bit tight, you were tearing your hair out trying to work out how you were going to manage next. Now, I do have a budget – for telephones, for staff, for overtime, for temps, for all aspects of the business .
>
> Keen (1995:86).

The increased management autonomy over operational decision-making, which devolved budgeting is designed to encourage, was very qualified, however. In the words of one of the highways managers:

> In theory there is devolution down, but the reality is that devolution doesn't really exist at this level. It is really very cosmetic. There is very little equipment on my budget, my cost centre is effectively staff, and that is dictated . . . If I was, say, underspending on that budget, then in theory I have the ability to spend that money on additional staff or some bits and pieces. But the reality is that the group manager would want my underspend to balance someone else's overspend. Profits too – if my team was doing well and making an income, then the income wasn't mine to spend because that was wanted for the department generally.
>
> Keen (1995:92).

In the words of a social services manager:

You're told you're autonomous, that you've got responsibility but the reality is very different. I always feel a bit like Gulliver – you know – sort of pinned down. I don't feel that they've delivered what they promised . . . They don't actually trust us – it's an insult to our intelligence.

Keen (1995:92).

Keen's (1995:93–4) own conclusions are worth quoting in full:

Overall, budgetary devolution, in conjunction with the internal market system, appeared to have generated various tensions or 'pulls' between the various parts of the organisation competing to acquire greater power and influence . . . middle-management desires for greater autonomy, potentially available from devolution, conflicted with senior-management desires to increase levels of centralised control – especially over resource management and utilisation in a hostile environment of increasingly rigorous external funding and regulatory constraints. The purchase/provider split had generated a new set of 'horizontal' tensions between 'purchaser' managers' desires to maximise their control over service specification and design (to minimise cost), and 'providers'' desire to maximise their control over the service delivery process (and maximise the generation of surpluses).

The implications for strategic prospects

This example draws attention to two aspects of the changes in organisational structure that very rarely receive any attention. The first is that the changes are by no means straightforward in effect – they need very careful management – and bring some intrinsic problems of their own. The second is that the changes cannot be divorced from the specific context in which they are introduced. There are grounds for questioning whether the changes will necessarily improve the strategic prospects for HRM as some pundits seem to think.

Intrinsic problems

The case of budgetary devolution in local authorities suggests that whereas the new structures that are finding their way into many UK organisations may help to deal with some of the problems of traditional organisational structure, such as inflexibility between functions, they also bring their own problems. One is the relationship between 'purchaser' managers and 'provider' managers. The problem is the competitive element that the changes encourage. In the short run this may be important in achieving improvements in performance. The danger is, however, that the participants quickly adjust to the rules of the 'new' game. Individual managers become even more protective of their positions than under old-style hierarchy, with the result that individual departments and businesses may be performing well at the expense of the organisation as a whole.

The ICI case quoted earlier draws attention to another problem associated with the changes. The 'old' ICI had well-established arrangements for management development. ICI managers were regarded as a company rather than a divisional resource and could be rotated through jobs, which not only enhanced their own careers, but also improved the stock of talent available to the company as a whole. The demerger has reduced the scope for such development activities. Inevitably, the two fields are narrower. Owen and Harrison's (1995) conclusion – that it is not necessarily seen as a bad thing if the successor companies may have to look outside for talent – is poor compensation for what has been lost.

More fundamentally, the widespread adoption of divisionalisation, devolved budgeting, and 'internal markets' poses serious questions about the ability of organisations to develop and maintain a strategic response to HRM, for the human resource function is itself being crucially affected by the new developments. In particular, there is a considerable devolution of the specialist function from headquarters to divisions and the passing of responsibilities for HRM to line managers (see for example the review in *Employment Trends* 1994). On the face of it, both are to be welcomed, if they encourage greater local 'ownership' of the issues. There are inherent dangers, however. The run-down in the number of human resource specialists at headquarters potentially denies the organisation strategic capacity. In theory, specialists at local level can do what is required in close co-operation with line managers who have been convinced that HRM is the key to business success. Even with other things being equal, however, it is a moot point whether local managers will have the time or expertise to develop the kind of integrated approach to HRM that is needed. Moreover, combining strategic and operational responsibilities flies in the face of one of the original logics of divisionalisation. Bringing in consultants from outside is rarely the answer either. The 'best practice' solutions which they may promote may be important symbolically in suggesting that the organisation is doing what is expected of it, but are unlikely to make a lasting impact. More pragmatically, the dividing line between flexibility and inconsistency is extremely thin: too much inconsistency can be damaging to morale.

Critically, too, there is a need to have the strategic capacity to think through the HRM implications of the *extended* organisation which is being brought about by the substantial subcontracting and outsourcing of activities. There may be a shift of emphasis, from control through the employment relationship to control through the market. Externalising the problems associated with managing the employment relationship, however, does not mean that the problems disappear. Issues such as performance and quality, training and development, and health and safety, remain fundamentally important (see for example the discussion in Gilbert 1994). If the organisation itself does possess specialists with skills and expertise in these areas, it is very difficult to see how they will be able to help the subcontractors to develop them. Who, in this event, should take responsibility for training or health and safety is a worrying issue for all concerned.

The UK context for HRM

In any discussion of the implications of the changes in organisational structure it is important to consider the context in which they are introduced. As the author has argued in more detail elsewhere (Sisson 1994) several features of the UK context mean that it will be very difficult to ensure that HRM receives the attention it deserves, whatever the rhetoric. Especially important are the corporate governance arrangements, which make no serious provision for any stakeholder other than the shareholder and which encourage takeover as the most effective check on management performance. These place a premium on short-term profitability and payback criteria for investment, which is likely to be increased with the spread of divisionalisation, budgetary devolution, and 'internal markets'. There must be a danger that such developments will also reinforce 'numbers-driven' planning at the expense of 'issue-driven' planning and emphasise headcount reductions as the key to (short-term) financial success, which threatens employment security and employee motivation. They are also likely to reinforce the 'Cinderella' status of the human resource function – it remains the case, for example, that no more than 25 per cent of large UK-owned companies have a main-board personnel director, whereas twice that number of foreign-owned companies in the UK have one – especially if the role of headquarters human resource specialists is further weakened by the processes of devolution described above.

There are also few, if any, of the countervailing pressures found in many other countries to encourage management to give greater attention to HRM. The legal framework of employment rights in the UK is minimal, and there is no national training system comparable to that in countries such as France and Germany. The public sector, as already indicated, no longer has the role of setting standards for others to follow. Here and in the private sector the substantial decentralisation of collective bargaining, which the developments in organisational structure described in this chapter have massively encouraged, also means that the UK no longer possesses the institutional framework to set standards by sector, as is the case in other EU member states (for further details of these arguments, again, see Sisson 1994).

More generally, there are the implications of the sheer pace of change, especially as the result of merger and acquisition, that have to be considered. As Marginson *et al* (1995:26) suggest, the pace of change makes it difficult to develop coherent human resource policies and practices in *any* context, let alone the UK's. Inevitably, the time and energies of human resource specialists tend to be consumed in managing the operational implications of the changes. Inevitably, too, there is the danger that a significant measure of cynicism will creep in. Other things being equal, there seems little point planning for the future if things are so uncertain. This is especially so as the drive for improved performance means not only that short-term financial targets tend to replace market share and other longer-term performance targets as the overriding business objective, but also that they tend to take attention away from the less measurable aspects of competitive advantage such as the organisation's human resources.

It can also be argued that the complex of institutional arrangements that makes up the industrial relations or HRM 'regime' in the UK has seriously impaired the ability of British governments to deliver the stability of macro-economic policies that management in other countries such as Germany and Japan have enjoyed – a stability that has made it possible for organisations there to maintain a more strategic approach to HRM. In the words of one German manager (Bischof 1994), the transfer of responsibility for labour costs from company accounts to the government's, which the institutional 'regime' encourages in times of recession, 'turns a bad situation into a worse one'.

Towards the millennium

There are good reasons for believing that the pace of change will be as hectic in the second half of the 1990s as it has been in the first. Repositioning and restructuring are likely to continue to be extremely important as organisations seek to maximise their competitive advantage and their use of resources. At the heart of changes in organisational structure, whatever new labels are applied, will be the three issues discussed here: divisionalisation, budgetary devolution, and 'internal markets'. Organisations can be expected to fine-tune the arrangements as their experience and the external market changes. Significantly, too, restructuring is likely to remain the main instrument of change, whether or not the situation genuinely demands it, because of its symbolic importance.

If the analysis in this chapter is correct, it will be not only the changes themselves that are important, however. The context in which they will be introduced will be as, if not more, important. What happens in two areas in particular will be critical. One is the institutional context. Here the policy issue is whether an attempt should be made to shift the balance away from the 'market capitalism' which has been dominant in the UK to the 'relational capitalism' which many see as essential to the strategic prospects for HRM, and how this might be brought about. (See for example the deliberations of the RSA special inquiry on *Tomorrow's Company*, RSA Inquiry (1995); see also Hutton 1994.) The second, and related, area will be that of economic policy. Here the main issue is whether future British governments will be able to deliver greater stability so far as macro-economic policies are concerned, thereby encouraging UK organisations to think medium- and long-term, with all the advantages that this would bring for the strategic prospects for HRM.

References

ADAMS, A, (1991), 'Externalisation vs specialisation: what is happening to Personnel', *Human Resource Management Journal*, Vol. 1, No. 4, 40–54.

ATKINSON, J, (1984), 'Manpower strategies for flexible organisations', *Personnel Management*, August, 28–31.

ATKINSON, J, AND MEAGER, C, (1986), 'Is flexibility just a flash in the pan?', *Personnel Management*, September, 26–9.

BARTLETT, C, AND GHOSHALL, S, (1993), 'Beyond the M-form, toward a managerial theory of the firm', *Strategic Management Journal*, Vol. 14, Special Issue, 23–46.

ROBERT BISCHOF, (1994), 'Why German cycles give a better ride', *The Guardian*, 28 December.

BUSINESS MONITOR, (1993), *Report of the Census of Production 1991*, Summary Volume, PA1002, London, Business Statistics Office.

BYRNE, J, (1993), 'The horizontal corporation', *Business Week*, 20 December, 76–81.

CHANDLER, A, (1962), *Strategy and Structure*, Cambridge, Mass., MIT Press.

CHANNON, D, (1973), *The Strategy and Structure of British Business*, London, Macmillan.

COLLING, T, AND FERNER, A, (1995), 'Privatisation and marketisation', in P. K. Edwards (ed.), *Industrial Relations: Theory and practice in Britain*, Oxford, Blackwell.

DUNNING, J, (1993), *Multinational Enterprise and the Global Economy*, New York, Addison-Wesley.

EMPLOYMENT TRENDS, (1994), 'The centre cannot hold: devolving personnel duties', *Industrial Relations Review*, August, 6–12.

FRANCIS, A, (1994), 'The structure of organisations', in K. Sisson (ed.), *Personnel Management: A comprehensive guide to theory and practice in Britain*, Oxford, Blackwell.

GILBERT, R, (1994), 'An employer's view', *Employment Relations 2000*: Proceedings of a conference to launch the Centre for International Employment Relations Research, *Warwick Papers in Industrial Relations*, No. 50, Coventry, Industrial Relations Research Unit.

GRIFFITHS, W, (1989), 'Fees for house work: the personnel department as consultancy', *Personnel Management*, January, 39–9.

HANDY, C, (1984), *The Future of Work*, Oxford, Blackwell.

HENLEY, D, LIERMAN, A, PERRIN J, EVANS, M, LAPSLEY, I, AND WHITFOAK, J, (1992), *Public-sector Accounting and Financial Control*, London, Chapman & Hall.

HILL, C, AND PICKERING, J, (1986), 'Divisionalisation, decentralisation and performance of large United Kingdom companies', *Journal of Management Studies*, Vol. 23, No. 1, 26–50.

HUNTER, L, C, AND MACINNES, J, (1991), *Employer Use Strategies – Case Studies*. Employment Research Paper, No. 87, Sheffield, Employment Department.

HUTTON, W, (1995), *The State We're In*, London, Jonathan Cape.

KEEN, L, (1995), 'Organisational decentralisation and budgetary devolution in local government: A case of middle management autonomy?' *Human Resource Management Journal*, Vol. 5, No. 2, 79–98.

MARGINSON, P, EDWARDS, P, K, ARMSTRONG P, AND PURCELL, J, (1995), 'Strategy, structure and control in the changing corporation: a survey-based investigation', *Human Resource Management Journal*, Vol. 5, No. 2, 3–27.

MILES, R, E, AND SNOW, C, C, (1992) 'Causes of failure in network organisations', *California Management Review*, Summer, 53–72.

MILLWARD, N, STEVENS, M, SMART, D, AND HAWES, W, R, (1992),

Workplace Industrial Relations in Transition: the ED/ESRC/PSI/ACAS surveys, Aldershot, Gower.

OWEN, G, AND HARRISON, T, (1995), 'Parting of the corporate ways', *Financial Times*, 13 March, p11.

PETERS, T, J, AND WATERMAN, R, H, (1982), *In Pursuit of Excellence: Lessons from America's best companies*, New York, Harper and Row.

POLLERT, A, (1987), 'The flexible firm': A model in search of reality (or a policy in search of a practice)? *Warwick Papers in Industrial Relations*, No. 19, Coventry, Industrial Relations Research Unit.

POLLERT, A, (ED.), (1991), *Farewell to Flexibility*, Oxford, Blackwell.

POLLERT, A, (1993), 'The single European market, multinationals and concentration', *Journal of Public Policy*, Vol. 13, No. 3, 77–96.

POWELL, W, W, (1990), 'Neither market nor hierarchy: network forms of organisation', *Research in Organisational Behaviour*, Vol. 12, 295–336.

RECRUITMENT AND DEVELOPMENT REPORT, (1991), 'New ways of managing your human resources: a survey of top employers', *Industrial Relations Review*, March, 6–16.

RSA INQUIRY, (1995), *Tomorrow's Company: The role of business in a changing world*, London, RSA.

SAUNDERS, J, WONG, V, AND DOYLE, P, (1994), 'The congruence of successful international competitors', *Journal of Global Marketing*, Vol. 7, No. 3, 4–59.

SISSON, K, (1994), 'Paradigms, practice and prospects' in K. Sisson (ed.), *Personnel Management: A comprehensive guide to theory and practice in Britain*, Oxford, Blackwell.

WHITTINGTON, R, AND MAYER, M, (1994), 'Beyond or behind the M-form? Organisational structures in contemporary Europe', Paper presented at the Strategic Management Society Conference, Jouy-en-Josas, September.

WALLY, S, CARROLL JNR, S, J, AND FLOOD, P, C, (1995), 'Managing without traditional structures', in P. C. Flood, M. J. Gannon and J. Paauwe (eds), *Managing without Traditional Methods: International innovations in human resource management*, Wokingham, Addison-Wesley.

WILLIAMSON, O, (1975), *Markets and Hierarchies: Analysis and anti-trust implications*, New York, The Free Press.

WILLIAMSON, O, (1985), *The Economic Institutions of Capitalism*, New York, The Free Press.

CHAPTER FOUR

Employee Relations

Mick Marchington

Introduction

On the face of it, employee relations has gone through a significant period of change and adjustment over the last 20 years; observers could be forgiven for assuming that nothing remained of the collective institutions and practices that dominated the subject in the 1970s (Dunn 1990). Nowadays most presentations on employee relations by practitioners and academics focus on so-called 'new' employment practices such as team-working and empowerment, total quality management and business process re-engineering, non-union firms and performance-related pay. Even the terminology of employee relations is much more widespread than it was 20 years ago, and it is now commonly used for describing the regulation of the employment relationship (Marchington and Parker 1990:7–8; Blyton and Turnbull 1994:7).

At one level, the changes are very clear. Trade unions have lost substantial numbers of members from a peak of 13 million and a 55 per cent density of unionisation in 1979, and have experienced major difficulties maintaining a national voice during the 1980s and early 1990s. There has been a spate of trade union mergers over the last two decades, resulting in the creation of several new super-unions (such as UNISON), and the amalgamation of many others for financial and recruitment reasons. Indeed, the nine largest unions account for over 60 per cent of overall membership in Britain (Waddington and Whitston 1995:178). The extent of industrial action has declined dramatically, with days lost through strikes at a very low level. Whereas the number of working days lost through strike action during the 1970s and early 1980s averaged approximately 10 million per annum, during the 1990s it has been less than one-tenth of this figure. Similarly, the number of recorded stoppages continued to fall to a little over 200 per annum, compared with 2–3,000 for most of the post-war period (Edwards 1995:439). Accordingly, a whole generation of personnel managers has had little experience of dealing with disputes at work, and little understanding that the employment relationship is characterised both by conflict and co-operation. Collective bargaining now has lower levels of coverage and scope than at any time since the 1930s, whereas employee involvement has assumed a prominence that would have been unthinkable in the 1970s. This sort of data suggests that the last two decades can be characterised as a period of fundamental and deep-rooted change (Kessler and Bayliss 1995), an adjustment that has been reinforced by structural and occupational changes in the composition of the labour market.

Significant though these changes are, they need to be seen in perspective. Although trade union membership has declined substantially, it has not disappeared altogether: approximately one-third of employees remain union members. Trade unions are recognised by employers in about half of all workplaces employing 25 or more people, and about 10 million employees work in unionised establishments. Collective bargaining is less central to employee relations in the mid-1990s than it was a decade earlier, but it is still the mechanism by which pay is determined for nearly half the workforce. Strikes have not disappeared altogether, especially in the public sector and in certain parts of manufacturing, and discontent is also apparent through low levels of commitment to work and an increase in stress-related illnesses. Moreover, whereas the extensiveness of direct employee involvement has grown significantly during the last decade, this has not generally been as a substitute for representative participation, and indeed a number of large companies are now setting up works councils. Findings such as these support the notion that employee relations has been subject to continuity rather than change (Marginson *et al* 1988).

Whereas both interpretations (continuity *v* change) are valid at one level, they overlook the crucial point that *different* patterns of employee relations are found in *different* workplaces, sometimes in the same industry or sector. *Diversity* is more noticeable than similarity, *uneven* developments are more typical than common trends, and changes take place in different *directions* in different workplaces. The survey data allows us to identify differences between sectors and industries, which is invaluable in illustrating the uneven rates and directions of change, as well as patterns of continuity. In addition, the case-study data shows us how organisations in the same industry or sector adopt different policies and practices in response to the pressures and opportunities that affect specific employers. It also demonstrates that organisations with what appear to be the same practices (eg team briefing) have widely differing experiences and expectations from these, to a large extent depending upon why and how they have been implemented. It is important, therefore, to stress the range and diversity in patterns of employee relations in order to prevent readers from being seduced by the supposed attractiveness and apparent blanket coverage of 'new' developments (Blyton and Turnbull 1994:297).

The remainder of this chapter analyses the management of employee relations by focusing on a number of key issues: namely, union and non-union organisations, collective bargaining, direct employee involvement, and representative participation. This discussion is conducted against a backdrop of competing models of government regulation, intense and continuing competitive pressures, and the integration of employee relations management with wider business objectives. It concludes by arguing that employee relations is becoming increasingly bifurcated, not so much *between* union and non-union organisations but *within* each of these broad categories. Given the degree to which labour markets have been deregulated since the early 1980s employers now have greater flexibility in choosing appropriate styles and structures for managing employee relations, as well as a greater opportunity to integrate people-management strategies with those affecting the business as a whole. To do this effectively, however, requires employers to embrace a more strategic and externally focused approach to the management of employee relations; to be aware of the techniques adopted by other employers; and to disregard the latest fads and fashions if these are inappropriate for their own workplace. How many do this, of course, is another question.

Working with the unions

Despite the decline in union recognition and membership over the last 15 years many industries, and certain sectors, still boast a considerable union presence in the mid-1990s. According to WIRS3, a majority of workplaces in several industries (for example, metal products, post and telecommunications, water, central and local government, banking, finance and insurance) recognised unions for collective bargaining purposes. Within manufacturing, unions were recognised at approximately 80 per cent of workplaces employing more than 200 people, with only a slight decline over the latter half of the 1980s (Millward *et al* 1992:72). Moreover, single-union agreements were present in just one-third of all unionised workplaces, a figure that changed little between 1970 and 1990. In contrast, four or more unions were recognised at two-thirds of workplaces employing 1,000 or more people (Millward *et al* 1992:77–81). Indeed, it has been suggested that 'among workplaces with a strong union presence

. . . management support for trade-unionism remained high throughout the latter part of the 1980s' (Millward *et al* 1992:128).

There are a number of reasons why employers have chosen to work with, rather than against, unions at workplace level. First, management may regard trade-union representatives as an essential part of the communication process in larger workplaces. Rather than being forced to establish a system for dealing with all employees, or setting up a non-union representative forum, trade unions are seen as a çhannel that allows for the effective resolution of issues concerned with pay bargaining or grievance-handling (Marchington and Parker 1990:25). Secondly, gaining agreement with union representatives can bestow a legitimacy on decisions which would otherwise be lacking. It can also lead to 'better' decisions as well. Even if this method of decision-making appears more time-consuming than the simple imposition of change, less time is spent in trying to correct mistakes or persuade employees after the event of the efficacy of management ideas.

Thirdly, employers may desist from the use of aggressive strategies when the balance of power is firmly with them for fear that, should conditions change, shop stewards may seek to settle old scores. Compromise may be attractive because one of management's major employee relations objectives is to achieve order and stability in the workplace, especially in persuading employees of the sanctity of procedures for resolving industrial disputes. Indeed, it has been argued that 'responsible' workplace union organisation and 'responsive' management is mutually reinforcing (ACAS 1981; Roots 1986; Marchington and Parker 1990:25). Fourthly, some employers have taken the view that, given the nature of their workforce, the industry, and the region in which establishments are located, unionisation is inevitable. In this case, rather than engage in a fight with a number of prospective unions for recognition – and suffer both industrial relations and employee morale consequences in the process – it is far better to reach an agreement with a preferred union from the outset. This line was taken by Peter Wickens when at Continental Can and later at Nissan. He is quite explicit about this:

> the view was that if we sought to be non-union we could end up in a multi-union situation. Recognition claims would come from a variety of trade unions – skilled and unskilled, engineering, supervisory and administrative. There would then have rapidly developed a situation which would be difficult to control.
>
> Wickens (1987:129).

Fifthly, employers are typically more concerned with issues other than those relating to trade unions and, provided the latter do not present a major obstacle to the realisation of strategic goals, a union presence can be tolerated, or indeed promoted. This is even more relevant if trade unions are not engaged in a continual struggle with employers (Batstone 1984:310). Finally, even if employers are keen to reduce the role and significance of unions at the workplace, they may lack the power to carry through their intentions because of local constraints – for example, skill shortages of particular grades of labour may make wholesale dismissals unrealistic, as may fears that the tacit skills of workers will be lost, with the result of less effective and efficient organisations (Marchington 1992a:156–60).

The most coherent analysis of why and how employers might choose to deal with trade unions at the workplace has been articulated by Purcell (1979) in his 'strategy for management control in industrial relations', part commentary on and part prescription for the post-Donovan period. Of the eight core elements in his 'strategy', three refer specifically to the roles and activities of trade unions, whereas the others are concerned with matters such as dispute resolution, participation and involvement, and tactics to maintain control. The basis of his argument is that management will have greater success in achieving its objectives by working with trade unions, in particular by encouraging union membership and participation in union affairs, as well as by assisting unions to work together through support for joint shop-steward committees. He puts forward the idea of 'cumulation' (Purcell 1979:31), the notion that early experiences of industrial relations in an organisation influence subsequent behaviour, a process illustrated by developments at ICI.

After a period during the 1980s when such ideas seemed to have disappeared from the employee relations agenda, there has been a recent revival of interest in the idea of working with the unions, most recently promoted under the banners of 'mutuality' (Walton 1985), 'jointism' (Storey 1992), and 'partnership' (IPA 1993). The latter refers to the situation in which management is prepared to support the activities of the trade union(s) and, for their part, employees are more likely to regard union membership as an important aspect of their employment conditions. The approach to trade-union recognition and representation adopted by management in these organisations is broadly similar to the 'consultative' style of management outlined by Purcell and Sisson (1983). This could result in single or multi-unionism, and, in the case of the latter, joint shop-steward committees are likely to be well established and supported by management.

All the usual facilities are provided, as is data about the business, and there is an emphasis on information-sharing and joint problem-solving, with an integrative approach to the resolution of issues.

A good example of this is the IPA report (*Towards Industrial Partnership*), which is publicly endorsed by leading trade-union and management representatives, as well as by a number of well-known academics. Although not seeking to deny differences of opinions and goals, the report recognises the high degree of common interests shared by employers and unions, and stresses the need to accept the legitimacy of representative institutions. A number of case-studies have been published by the IPA (1995) which illustrate the partnership approach. For example, at Staveley Chemicals (part of Rhône-Poulenc), there has been a major shift from classic adversarialism to co-operation between the company and five separate unions. The process of building trust is shown to be a long and time-consuming process, with initial and understandable reluctance on the part of unions to accept the 'new' management style. But, over a six-year period, it was felt that each party had come to accept the legitimacy of the other, and had started working together through single-table bargaining to enhance the prosperity of the company as a whole.

Godfrey and Marchington (1994) show that shop stewards' reactions to partnership programmes depend fundamentally upon their trust in management. At some sites, shop stewards were highly supportive, referring to 'a new dawn', more open styles of management, and an increased influence over decisions. In other organisations, conversely, union representatives were highly sceptical about the meaning and extent of management's attempts to create partnerships, viewing them as nothing more than the latest fad and fashion, a device to weaken unions via incorporation.

Scott (1994:91) argues that management has much to gain from an approach that creates 'constructive' (that is, non-adversarial) employee relations. The question of whether unions gain more from partnership than they do from adversarial approaches, however, is highly dependent upon the situation and the viewpoint of the observer.

Edging out the unions

In contrast to those employers who have sought to strengthen their relationship with unions, others have opted for marginalisation or derecognition. In these situations employers have decided that their objectives are more likely to be achieved by reducing or removing the union presence, perhaps because of problems in the past. In some workplaces there may have been disputes that have slowed down or prevented changes in work-ing practices, or there may be concerns amongst managers about the degree to which they can work with trade unions. Others may simply have taken advantage of a superior power base to remove or restrict the activi-ties of unions, to reduce wage costs, and to enforce a stricter managerial regime, perhaps in line with some deep-seated antagonism amongst senior managers towards unions.

Some derecognitions have occurred as part of a drive towards single status, whereby groups of employees are placed on managerial or profes-sional contracts, and the removal of the union is undertaken in conjunc-tion with a shift to more direct methods of employee involvement. This is especially likely where management exerts considerable influence upon cultures that stress personalised customer service and performance-related pay schemes rather than collectively negotiated rates. In short, management is seeking to deny, rather than to legitimise, the role of one or more unions.

Even when trade unions are marginalised they nonetheless retain a pres-ence in the workplace and in many cases maintain the right to collective bargaining. In these situations, although the institutions of collective employee relations remain in place, they represent a much less important aspect of human resource policies and practices. A number of changes are typically associated with marginalisation: substantial reductions in the number of shop stewards at establishment level; a severe tightening-up on time-off for trade-union activities and facilities for undertaking union-related work; withdrawal of full-time shop-steward positions, often subse-quent to the dismissal (usually through redundancy or early retirement) of the existing role-holders; lack of support for check-off arrangements; a lower priority accorded to collective bargaining with unions and (in some cases) the upgrading of information-passing meetings for management to stewards; a greater emphasis on individualism and direct employee involvement/communications from line managers to all employees.

In recent years, as unions have become less able and willing to take industrial action, employers have certainly pruned the collective bargain-ing agenda and relied more heavily on written and verbal direct commu-nications to all staff, as opposed to union channels alone. Perhaps this stance is best summed up in the words of a manager from a food factory who said, 'It's pushing negotiations down to consultation, and consulta-tion down to communication' (Marchington and Parker 1990:144). In short, employers 'freeze out' shop stewards by allowing them less access to management whilst also making it more difficult for them to interact with their members.

Beyond marginalisation is derecognition, an idea that only really entered the vocabulary of British employee relations in the latter part of the 1980s (Claydon 1989), in contrast to the situation in the USA where traditionally there have been long and bitter battles over decertification at the end of a union contract (Beaumont 1987). In Britain the voluntarist and typically more pluralist traditions lost ground during the 1980s, so increasing the likelihood of derecognition. This has led some commentators to conceive of union derecognition as part of a wider conspiracy on the part of government and employers, 'a synergistic project to create a potent gradualist route to union exclusion' (Smith and Morton 1993:100).

Although there can be little doubt that derecognitions have increased, their impact on union organisation and membership in general has so far been slight. The complete withdrawal of collective bargaining rights and trade-union organisation for all employees at a workplace or throughout a complete employing organisation has been rare. The derecognition of specific groups or grades of employees has been rather more common, as has the removal of bargaining rights, but access to unions in the event of grievance or disciplinary cases has been retained. A number of surveys over the last decade have each indicated that only a small proportion of employers have undertaken derecognitions, the vast majority retaining arrangements in force at the beginning of the 1980s (Claydon 1989; Gregg and Yates 1991; Millward *et al* 1992; Marginson *et al* 1993; Gall and McKay 1994). Although the most recent survey by Gall and McKay points to an increasing rate of derecognitions during the early 1990s, they conclude that 'the scale of derecognitions to date is still fairly small. As yet, there is no stampede' (Gall and McKay 1994:434).

The types of employees most likely to lose their bargaining rights have been managers and other professional staff, although there have been well-publicised cases involving manual workers in firms such as Unipart, Esso and Tioxide in the late 1980s and early 1990s. In the Tioxide case, the TGWU was derecognised as part of a harmonisation package following a ballot of the workforce. A key aspect of this package was a new pensions deal, which attracted overwhelming support from a predominantly ageing workforce; it is however interesting to note that the company did not seek derecognition of the union at its Greatham plant, which had a much younger age profile.

Some derecognitions have also 'tidied up' union structures, as unions with few members lose bargaining rights at the same time as others continue to be recognised. Derecognitions also occur as union membership 'withers away', and the withdrawal of bargaining rights is not contested.

At North West Water, for example, two of the manual unions, with low membership levels, were derecognised as part of a move to single-table bargaining, whilst there was a complete derecognition of UNISON for professional, clerical, and technical staff as part of the company's move to a new central customer service and laboratory site (IRS 1992).

Managing without unions

Like derecognition, the issue of non-union firms received hardly any attention in the literature until recent times. It was well known that there were large numbers of small companies that did not recognise or deal with trade unions, but they were generally labelled 'traditionalist', unitarist, or 'sweatshop' employers, and castigated (often quite rightly) for their poor treatment of staff. It was only with the growing awareness of what Beaumont (1987:117) refers to as the 'household name' group – companies such as IBM, Marks and Spencer, and Hewlett Packard – that academic and practitioner interest started to blossom. These companies were praised for their forward-looking and progressive employee relations policies, which were designed to offer employees more than could be achieved by trade unions through negotiations.

It seems strange that it took so long to focus attention on non-unionism. After all, even at the peak of union membership in 1979, approximately 45 per cent of the workforce (over 10 million people) were not trade-union members. The density of non-unionism has grown steadily since then: by the mid-1990s about two-thirds of all employees did not belong to trade unions. Non-unionism is more extensive in certain parts of the country (such as the south-east of England) and in certain sectors of the economy (such as retailing, professional services, and hotels and catering) than in others. Younger and smaller establishments are also more likely to be non-union, and there has been some debate as to whether the high-technology sector is adding to the stock of non-unionism (Sproull and MacInnes 1989; McLoughlin and Gourlay 1992, 1994; Findlay 1993). In summing up the debate about the growth of non-unionism across the whole economy, Gregg and Yates (1991:365) point to the 'death' of establishments that recognised unions and their replacement (in statistical terms) by units that maintain a non-union stance.

But non-unionism can take many different forms, varying from the sophisticated and arguably more pleasant employment practices of the 'household name' group through to the sweatshops and 'bleak houses' of Dickensian employers (Sisson 1993). One of the problems with studies of non-union firms has been the lack of differentiation between these highly contrasting forms of employee relations, which have little in common beyond the basic refusal by employers to recognise trade unions for collective bargaining. For example, the idea that unions manage to achieve a pay and conditions 'mark-up' over non-union workers makes sense only if the latter are employed in 'bleak house' firms. Similarly, some of the 'household name' group have prided themselves on providing higher levels of training and better communications than their unionised counterparts. Guest and Hoque (1994) argue that the term 'non-unionism' is actually limiting in that firms are analysed only 'in relation to' unionised organisations. They suggest a fourfold categorisation of non-union firms: the good, the bad, the ugly, and the lucky.

First, and most celebrated by commentators, come employers who are probably leaders in their product market, those Guest and Hoque would classify as 'good'. They are organisations with a clear strategy for managing people and a wide range of human resource policies. Such employers have tended to operate a 'union substitution' policy (Beaumont 1987:136): they offer a complete employment package which can be seen by employees as an attractive alternative to trade-union membership. According to Foulkes (1980), Beaumont (1987), and McLoughlin and Gourlay (1994) this package includes some or all of the following:

1 a highly competitive pay, fringe benefits, and employee welfare package which is typically in excess of those offered by other firms recruiting from the same labour market

2 a comprehensive battery of recruitment techniques (including psychometric tests), designed to select individuals who match organisational norms

3 a high priority accorded to induction programmes which are geared up to socialising employees into the company ethos

4 a stress on training and development opportunities, both related to the employee's work and more broadly to their role in the company and society

5 a focus on employee communications and information-sharing within the enterprise, such as through team briefings

6 a system (such as speak-up) enabling employee concerns and anxieties to be dealt with by management

7 a commitment to providing secure and satisfying work whilst employed by the organisation, often involving regular moves to different types of job

8 single-status and harmonised employment policies between blue- and white-collar employees
9 an individualised pay and appraisal system differentiating between staff in terms of previous performance and future potential, designed to reward those who contribute most to organisational success
10 a focus on selecting and continuously developing managers who display interpersonal and leadership skills as well as high levels of technical expertise.

Of course, this is not to say that these organisations are above criticism. It could be argued that 'sophisticated' employment practices are merely an illusion designed to obscure the true nature of oppressive human resource management regimes in this type of company, or that workers are merely 'conned' by overt appeal into working harder not for their own rewards but for the company's ultimate benefit. Similarly it has been suggested that employers will continue to provide superior employment terms only under favourable economic and competitive conditions, and that product market problems will lead to their permanent or temporary withdrawal; in other words, the supposed employer commitment to employees as their 'most valuable resource' is both superficial and trite. The argument that these sophisticated non-union organisations offer good benefits only because of the previous and continuing efforts of trade unions in the economy at large also has a fair degree of credence.

The second type of non-union firm is the traditional sweatshop employer, often a small independent single-site company operating as a supplier to one of the sophisticated non-union organisations analysed above. Managements that deliberately deprive workers of their rights would be categorised as 'ugly' whereas those that offer poor terms and conditions without such a manipulative intent are referred to as 'bad'. The subordinate role that many of these small suppliers have with a larger company – dependent, dominated, and isolated – leaves them with little control over their own destiny and places a primacy on labour flexibility (Rainnie 1991:187). Such firms are under considerable pressure to control costs and enhance flexibility, goals which many of these employers believe to be achievable only without what they see as 'interference' by trade unions: thus, the high likelihood of these firms' remaining non-union by a strategy of 'union suppression' (Beaumont 1987:136). Their employment practices are almost the total opposite to those outlined above.

In these circumstances pay rates are likely to be low; formal fringe benefits and welfare arrangements would be virtually non-existent. Employees may get bonuses if the employer deems it appropriate, and requests for time-off/extra benefits are granted if a manager feels that the employee concerned deserves a break and is not a 'troublemaker' or a 'malingerer'. The regime in these small firms is highly personalised (Scott *et al* 1989:42). Recruitment practices are also likely to reflect the owner or manager's deep distrust of unions and other 'outsiders', in that much use is made of personal contacts. The lack of formal disciplinary procedures means that employee protection is haphazard and arbitrary at best, totally absent at worst. Scott *et al* (1989:56–60) provide many examples of employees receiving harsh treatment from an employer; they argue that the sanctions employed by the owner or manager typically depend less on the severity of the alleged misdemeanour than on the worker's status as 'friend', 'good worker', or 'troublemaker'.

The Third Workplace Industrial Relations Survey (Millward *et al* 1992:363–5) confirms this picture of a few procedures, highly personal relations, and harsh discipline; one-fifth of companies not recognising trade unions had no disciplinary procedure, a quarter had no mechanism for handling grievances, and a similar number had no health and safety machinery. Although managers in small non-union firms claimed that there was a substantial flow of information, formal meetings were rare and in about half the establishments there was no regular dissemination of financial information to employees. Moreover, dismissals in non-union firms as a whole occurred at twice the rate of their unionised counterparts. The picture that emerges is one of harsh informality, somewhat at odds with the claim that 'small is beautiful'. As Scott *et al* (1989:45–6) note, 'what often passes for good communication is usually the more negative situation in which no one has said anything' – the (probably false) assumption is that the employees must be happy because no one has complained!

Changing patterns of collective bargaining

Collective bargaining has long been a central aspect of British employee relations, certainly from the end of the First World War through to the 1980s when it was the principal method by which wages and conditions were determined for a majority of the workforce. In addition there is little doubt that collective bargaining outcomes (such as wage levels, hours worked, and holiday entitlements) also influenced the terms and conditions enjoyed by employees whose pay was determined by management alone. As we have seen, some employers explicitly offer terms superior to those negotiated by trade unions in order to remain union-free.

Over the last two decades collective bargaining has become less prominent, and it now covers less than half of all employees. The WIRS3 database (Millward *et al* 1992:91) shows that the proportion of employees in
establishments employing 25 or more people whose terms and conditions
are formally negotiated by collective bargaining fell from 71 per cent in
1980 to just 54 per cent a decade later. There are sizeable variations
between sectors, with the public sector showing the highest extent of coverage (78 per cent) and the private service sector the lowest (a third). In
total, over eight million workers had their terms and conditions determined by collective bargaining in 1990, of which over half were from the
public sector. Comparing results from the WIRS data-sets with that
extracted from the New Earnings Surveys leads Brown (1993:192) to conclude that only 47 per cent of *all* employees were covered by collective bargaining in 1990, an estimate confirmed by Milner (1995), who also notes
that coverage is now at a lower level than at any point since the 1930s. The
shape and character of collective bargaining also varies considerably
between workplaces, in particular in relation to the *level* at which bargaining takes place and the size or structure of the *unit* of employees covered
by any agreement.

There have been changes in the level at which bargaining takes place,
with a continuing shift away from the multi-employer negotiations considered the norm for much of the twentieth century. Several major multi-
employer deals were terminated during the 1980s, for example in
engineering, national newspapers, multiple food retailing, baking and
milling, and bus and coach operators (IRS 1993b). Jackson *et al* (1992)
note the existence of multi-employer bargaining in food retailing since the
1950s, even though a number of non-union firms such as Marks and
Spencer and J Sainsbury retained their own arrangements for pay determination. Problems arose when Tesco Stores decided to withdraw from
national negotiations to pursue their own in-house policies in 1988. The
company was experiencing major difficulties with staff retention in the
south-east of England; it wished to involve employee representatives; and
none of its major competitors was a party to the national agreements.
Bargaining at Tesco is now conducted directly with USDAW at company
level, and common rates of pay (apart from London allowances) and procedures apply across all stores. Multi-employer bargaining still exists, however, for many of the smaller, regional companies, once again illustrating the
diversity of management–employee relations.

Walsh (1993:429) shows that decentralisation took many diverse forms
in practice, as well as the fact that a number of companies had chosen to

maintain their existing bargaining structures. Indeed, it is important to place the decline in multi-employer bargaining firmly in perspective. According to Millward *et al* (1992:218), even though there was a sizeable reduction in the importance of multi-employer bargaining during the latter part of the 1980s it still formed the basis for the most recent pay increase in more workplaces than did single-employer bargaining. This aggregate prominence of multi-employer arrangements does however owe a considerable amount to its centrality in the public sector, where it was four or five times as important as single-employer bargaining. Of course, there are signs that multi-employer bargaining is now weakening, but it still retains a key influence over terms and conditions in this sector (Beaumont 1992:112–14). Within the private sector as a whole, the decline has been rather more pronounced; Brown (1993:195) estimates that single-employer bargaining is four times as likely here as its multi-employer equivalent. National agreements still operate in the footwear industry, construction, electrical contracting, and some parts of printing and publishing, where they continue to offer advantages both to employers and unions. Indeed, in the case of the construction industry, a survey of members in the early 1990s showed unanimous support for its continuation (Kessler and Bayliss 1992:179).

There are a number of factors that influence employer choices about the level at which negotiations are most appropriately conducted in multi-establishment organisations. Some of these factors relate to industrial and economic characteristics of firms whilst others reflect more deep-seated political and ideological pressures. Arguments in favour of centralisation include the ability to control costs, the provision of professional negotiating expertise, and large numbers of similar employment units. Conversely, those in favour of decentralisation make reference to local labour-market responsiveness, linking pay levels to establishment performance, and limiting union influence across plants (Thomason 1984; Kinnie 1987, 1993; Marchington and Parker 1990). It should be stressed, however, that choices about appropriate bargaining levels are not simple technical decisions, but depend upon judgements about the balance of power between employer and union, as well as the previous history of employee relations within the company itself. Equally, decisions about pay determination should not be made in isolation from other business policies; priorities in other parts of the business may take precedence over what appears 'appropriate' for employee relations. Indeed, there are dangers in compiling lists specifying the advantages and disadvantages of different levels of bargaining, because so much depends upon the industrial and organisational circumstances confronting any employer. In short, centralised or decentralised bargaining may prove highly attractive to one employer for reasons totally inappropriate for another.

There have also been changes over the last 15 years in the composition of bargaining units. This refers to the specific groups or categories of employees covered by a particular agreement, and this can range from narrow to wide, from a single category and sometimes small number of employees, through to a mass of jobs and grades dealt with in the same negotiations. Interest in recent years has focused on the increasing width of bargaining units, especially at workplace or company level, and the supposed attractions of single-table bargaining (STB). This needs to be seen in the context of multi-unionism, however, and the finding of Millward *et al* (1992:81) that, on average, 2.5 unions operated at establishments where there was recognition, and two or more unions were recognised at about two-thirds of all these workplaces. It is now rare for 10 or more unions to be recognised (although this does occur at some workplaces in the public sector and at a very few in manufacturing). By way of contrast, the simplest bargaining structures were found in foreign-owned and newer firms in the private sector.

The move to STB has accelerated since 1990, with an estimated doubling in its coverage in the early part of the decade (Gall 1993:13). Furthermore, the number of employees whose terms and conditions of employment are negotiated via STB increased over the same period from 30,000 to nearly a quarter of a million. Employers choosing this option include British Steel, Ilford, Southern Electric, Vauxhall, several of the water companies, and quite a number of NHS trusts. In the case of Ilford, for example, the single-table deal was implemented in 1992, replacing previous arrangements whereby the five recognised unions had operated under four separate bargaining units. For several years there had been discussions between management and the unions (through the joint shop stewards committee, which covered both the blue- and white-collar unions) about how to simplify pay-bargaining and overcome demarcations between different groups of employees.

Despite cases such as these, a recent survey (IRS 1995) suggests that STB might be 'an idea whose time has yet to come'. Whereas less than a quarter of the employers questioned already had STB deals, nearly half of the remainder were actively considering STB as an option. It is also interesting to note that several of the companies quoted in the Gall article made use of different arrangements (such as single-union deals and derecognition) at other sites, thus illustrating yet again the diversity of employee relations arrangements at plant level.

Both managements and unions can gain from STB. For the unions, the advent of STB can prevent 'divide-and-rule' tactics on the part of management and provide the opportunity for closer working relationships, which reduce the likelihood of interunion disputes. Rationalising the number of unions at establishment level, so that unions with lower levels of membership lose representative rights to larger unions, can also increase the effectiveness of union organisation. There is furthermore a feeling that STB deals have prevented employer-driven single-union arrangements, which has led to TUC support (Gall 1993:14).

For employers, STB has a number of advantages. It helps to encourage a common view across the site or company from all the unions represented, and make it unlikely that there will be 'leapfrogging' claims. It reduces the amount of time that has to be devoted to negotiating, an important consideration in some organisations where specialist industrial relations managers had traditionally three or more separate sets of negotiations with different unions at different times of the year. STB also allows employers to involve union representatives in questions of how to allocate overall pay and benefits packages *between* different grades of employee. Because harmonisation and single-status considerations have been a major impetus behind the drive for STB, persuading both blue- and white-collar union representatives to negotiate together has eased the process of change (IRS 1995). Indeed, STB has proved attractive more generally for the negotiation of flexibility provisions, such as those at Shell Carrington and Ind Coope's Burton Brewery (Marginson and Sisson 1990:47).

STB is not without its drawbacks, however. Issues of employee representation are of major importance to each of the unions, and agreements have to be achieved about how to allocate seats at the table, especially to unions with a minor presence. Problems can also arise if there are shifts in membership levels between unions. Although there may be advantages in meeting with all the unions at the same time, this also limits the potential to agree separate deals with different groupings of employees; in effect, it reduces the likelihood that one union can be played off against another. There are also doubts about the relevance of all single-table business to each participant. Any one of these concerns may lead an organisation to opt for a rationalisation of bargaining structures, but instead go for a compromise arrangement such as two-table bargaining, as at Seeboard.

Following the privatisation of the electricity industry and the termination of multi-employer bargaining, each of the companies involved formulated new arrangements for single-employer negotiations. Unlike those of its competitors which implemented STB, Seeboard opted for two-table bargaining, largely because management felt it was inappropriate for supervisors and professionals to have their terms and conditions indirectly determined by those they supervise. Accordingly, two new joint negotiating councils (JNCs) were set up, one for clerical and industrial staff, the other for professional and supervisory staff. The structures and procedures that govern the two JNCs are similar, and both allow for reviews of representation every two years in order to accommodate changes in staffing and union membership levels (IRS 1993a; Colling 1991).

The spread of employee involvement (EI)

In recent years there has been considerable academic and practitioner interest in whether methods of employee involvement (EI) are now taking the place of collective bargaining as the principal instrument by which organisations manage their employee relations (TUC 1994). It should be clear from previous sections that there is no simple, single answer to this question, and that in many workplaces collective bargaining and union organisation continue to form an essential component of workplace regulation. At the same time, there is little doubt that a large proportion of employers have extended EI arrangements over the last decade, in particular in the area of direct EI and communications.

This wave of interest commenced in the early 1980s, and is very different from most of those which have gone before it. The most recent manifestation of EI tends to be individualist and direct (as opposed to collective and conducted via representatives); it is championed by managements, often without any great pressure from employees or trade unions; and it is directed at securing greater employee commitment to and identification with the employing organisation. The terminology of EI is very apt, because it relates to managers giving employees more information or, in a few cases, more influence at workplace level. EI has grown without specific legislative support, although there have been repeated exhortations from government ministers to develop EI along voluntary lines. It is unlikely that the provisions in the 1982 Employment Act requiring large companies to report on action taken to introduce, maintain, or develop employee involvement has had any impact upon its growth throughout Britain (Marchington 1992b:35–8).

According to Millward et al (1992:175) there was a sizeable growth in direct EI and communications during the 1980s, a trend likely to have continued throughout the first half of the 1990s. The implementation of 'new' EI initiatives speeded up during the latter part of the 1980s, and the 'systematic use of the management chain' was described by respondents as the most frequently employed method of communication (Millward *et al* 1992:166). Regular meetings between managers and employees also grew, as did suggestions schemes and newsletters, but each was from a much lower base (Millward *et al* 1992:167). Again, there were variations between sectors, with the highest level of activity in the public sector and lowest in manufacturing, with a spurt in growth in private services. Research by Marchington *et al* (1992:14) shows that many organisations practised multiple forms of EI and, if anything, a wider range of techniques was employed in unionised firms than in their non-union counterparts. This study also demonstrates the variety and diversity of EI techniques in practice, and the way in which the 'mix' of these depends crucially upon managerial choice and organisational context. The influence of key groups within an organisation has a substantial impact upon the range and type of schemes introduced, as well as upon their ultimate success. 'Champions' played a key role in shaping this process (Marchington *et al* 1993).

Direct EI takes a number of quite distinct forms in practice. First, there is downward communications from managers to employees, the principal purpose of which is to inform and 'educate' staff so that they accept management plans. This includes techniques such as team-briefing and other regular structured techniques for information-passing; informal and non- routinised communications between managers and their staff; formal written media such as employee reports, house journals or company newspapers; and videos to convey standard messages to employees about the organisation's annual financial performance or to publicise some new managerial initiative.

These techniques provide employees with greater amounts of information from managers than most enjoyed previously, but whether or not this is of interest or relevance to them is open to question. In theory, employers gain because employees are 'educated' about the needs of the business and utilise their greater knowledge base to improve customer service or product quality, so helping to sustain competitive advantage. These gains are not always achieved in practice, owing to a lack of managerial commitment or skills and a lack of employee interest.

Most organisations that practise team-briefing hold meetings on a scheduled, monthly basis at most, and in many cases briefings are abandoned should more pressing business appear on the agenda or management lose interest in the technique. By contrast, daily team-briefings are practised in many Japanese-owned companies operating in Britain (such as

Nissan and Komatsu), and there are now signs that these ideas are spreading to other organisations (for example, Rover). These regular meetings at the start of each shift provide managers and employees with an opportunity not only to share information but also to develop team spirit as well. Team-briefings may not be appropriate in all types of organisation, however, and other methods for communicating information need to be established. For example, J Sainsbury has a long-established and well-polished house journal that communicates company-wide information to all staff and is supplemented by noticeboards and other forms of written information at each store.

The second form that direct EI has taken is upward problem-solving, designed to tap into employee knowledge and opinion either at an individual level or through small groups. The objective is to increase the stock of ideas within an organisation; to encourage co-operative relations at work; and to legitimise change. The best-known forms of this technique are quality circles, suggestions schemes, attitude surveys, and total quality management — at least in some of the forms the latter takes in practice (Wilkinson et al 1992). These offer employees the prospect of greater opportunities to contribute to discussions about work-related issues and employers the possibility of higher levels of productivity and quality. In a local authority examined as part of a wider project on TQM (Wilkinson et al 1996), quality service teams had been set up throughout the social services department. These teams are led by the manager responsible for the area and meet every six weeks to solve quality problems in order to improve the level of service to internal and external customers. This has resulted, amongst other things, in the establishment of a new annual audit of service standards and recognition in the shape of a quality award for one of the teams.

The third category of EI initiatives is task participation, in which employees are encouraged, or expected, to extend the range and type of tasks undertaken at work. As with the previous categories, these are also a form of direct EI of an individualist nature, some of which have their roots in earlier 'quality of working life' experiments in the 1960s and 1970s (Kelly 1982). Examples of task-based participation are horizontal job redesign, job enrichment, and teamworking. Each has figured in an increasing number of chemical and vehicle/components companies which operate their production systems on a teamwork and relatively autonomous basis. Task-based participation is probably the most innovative method of EI, given that it is focused on the *whole* job rather than comprising a relatively small part of an employee's time at work. Unlike team-briefing or quality circles, which can be viewed as supplementary to work itself, task-based participation is integral to work itself. This has led to assertions that 'workplaces have never been so democratic', but it is clear that these techniques do little to challenge existing patterns of power and authority in employment (Marchington 1995:55).

Finally, we can consider financial involvement, which encompasses schemes designed to link part (or occasionally all) of an individual's rewards to the success of the unit or to that of the enterprise as a whole. These schemes take various forms in practice, ranging from profit-sharing and employee share ownership schemes (Schuller 1989) through to ESOPs (Employee Share Ownership Plans), which are slowly beginning to emerge in Britain (Pendleton 1992; Wilkinson *et al* 1994). Financial involvement has similar objectives to those of the techniques already discussed, but it also operates under an assumption that employees with a financial stake in the overall success of the unit or enterprise are more likely to work harder for its ultimate success. Of course, much depends upon whether employees also identify such a link, and how much control they have over the performance of the unit concerned. In the case of employee share ownership arrangements, the most popular of these schemes, such control is negligible (Baddon *et al* 1989).

The re-emergence of representative participation

Joint Consultative Committees (JCCs) are the best-known example of representative participation in Britain, having had a long and somewhat chequered history comprising various periods of growth and decline; indeed, JCCs were effectively written off in the 1960s as unable to survive the development of strong shop-steward workplace organisation, only to re-emerge during the 1970s and decline slightly (especially in manufacturing) during the last decade (Millward *et al* 1992:153). JCCs are likely to be present in about one-quarter of all workplaces now, compared with approximately one-third in the mid-1980s. This decline owes more to the changing structural and sectoral composition of workplaces, in particular the falling number of larger establishments, than to any concerted attempt by employers to terminate existing arrangements or by unions to boycott committees (Millward *et al* 1992:154).

Unlike the methods of direct EI discussed in the previous section, JCCs are built upon the notion of indirect participation and worker representation in joint management–employee meetings. Joint consultation represents the most formal and potentially influential form of EI discussed so far in this chapter, and it is probably the closest that we get in Britain to models of representative participation practised throughout the rest of Europe. But JCCs can take a number of forms, often contrasting sharply with one another in terms of their objectives, structures, and processes (Marchington 1994:669-72). Consequently, in some organisations, JCCs can act as a safety valve (ie an alternative to industrial action) through which to address more deep-seated employee grievances, whereas in others they can be used as a device to hinder the recognition of trade unions or undermine their activities in highly unionised workplaces. In yet others, they may be irrelevant to management-employee relations, merely existing as a forum to debate various forms of trivia (Marchington 1992b:136–41). The relationship between collective bargaining and joint consultation in unionised workplaces can be a source of tension, particularly if management is trying to 'edge out' the unions.

The most important contemporary issue in this area is the European Works Council (EWC) Directive. The centralist philosophy that underpins this initiative is in sharp contrast with the voluntarist approach promulgated by successive Conservative governments since the early 1980s, whereby employers have been encouraged to adopt measures that suit their own circumstances and predilections, with an absolute minimum of statutory enforcement (Department of Employment 1989). Since the UK entered the EU in the early 1970s there have been a number of attempts to create a more coherent and uniform 'social' framework for the Community, and to harmonise certain standards of employment and company law across the member states. Commencing with the Fifth Directive back in 1972 (which proposed a two-tier board structure for all companies employing 500 or more people, with at least one-third of the suprevisory board drawn from employees), the idea of high-level representative participation has since re-emerged in various guises. More recently (in the latter part of the 1980s and early 1990s) further attempts have been made to harmonise policies in the areas of information, consultation, and participation.

Member states covered by the EWC Directive – that is, all states except the UK, which opted out of the Social Chapter at Maastricht in 1991 – are required to implement its provisions by September 1996. EWCs, or an equivalent information and consultation procedure, have to be set up in all community-scale multinational enterprises with at least 1,000 employees within the 16 states covered by the directive. There is scope for the negotiation of customised agreements, but in the event of a failure to agree a standard package will apply. In broad terms, this provides a template for the composition of the EWC and its remit, as well as a stipulation that an annual meeting should take place. At this meeting the EWC meets central management to be informed and consulted about the enterprise's progress and prospects in a number of areas, including the broad economic, financial and employment situation, as well as trends in employment and substantial changes in working methods. Obviously, a key point here is future employment projections, in particular closures, cutbacks, and redundancies. The Commission is to review the operation of the directive in 2001.

The directive does not have statutory force in relation to employees of multinational companies employed in Britain. In a similar vein, although the provisions do apply to British companies that employ people elsewhere in the EU, managements are not required to include in an EWC workers employed in Britain. Both of these facts create the potential for internal divisions, even more so because Hall *et al* (1995:12) estimate that just as many British companies will be affected by the provisions as are French or German organisations. As the authors note, this is something of a 'grey area' because data is not always available on employment patterns, but they reckon it will affect at least 140 British-owned companies; this can be compared with 150 German, 136 French, and 48 US organisations. The list includes employers such as Barclays, British Aerospace, Coats Viyella, Glaxo, Kingfisher, Lucas, Marks and Spencer, Rolls-Royce, United Biscuits, and Zeneca. It will be interesting to note how many of these companies choose to exclude their UK employees from an EWC.

More forward-looking British and overseas employers with employment units elsewhere in the EU can already decide of their own volition to set up EWCs so as to keep up with 'good' practice and be seen as model employers (Ramsay 1991; Hall 1992). By the middle of 1992, for example, approximately 20 EU-owned companies had already taken this opportunity (Gold and Hall 1992), a figure that had doubled by the end of 1994 (Hall *et al* 1995:15), nearly two years before this becomes a requirement. Amongst the companies with existing voluntary arrangements are Bayer, Nestlé, Volkswagen, and Thomson (whose first EWC was set up in 1985); by 1994 the first British-owned companies – BP Oil and United Biscuits – were signed up. Quite a number of these were not known as EWCs: the list of titles includes Employee Forum, European Group Committee, European Trades Union Committee, and European Information and Consultation Forum. Hall *et al* (1995) reprint the constitutions of a number of existing EWCs, and of those with employees in the UK some (for example, Bull and Thomson) do appear to invite representatives from these establishments to the committee.

The United Biscuits European Consultative Council (UBECC) is particularly interesting given that it is one of the first to be agreed in Britain. The Council comprises 20 representatives from around the company's operations in Europe, of which 13 are drawn from UK sites. Members are nominated by the unions or works councils, and up to four full-time union officials are eligible to attend in addition to the worker representatives; Hall *et al* (1995:17) note that the company has placed limitations on membership of UBECC, most importantly in being able to object to nominees if they are deemed 'inappropriate'. UBECC is chaired by the group human resources director, attended by the group chief executive and other divisional managers, and is scheduled to take place annually. The Council is to focus on the performance of the United Biscuits Group, on its overall strategic direction, on jobs and employment policy, and on the broad commercial factors that affect the operations of the company. It is anticipated that UBECC will consider how, if at all, the council might need to be adjusted once the directive comes into force in late 1996 (IRS 1994).

The UBECC is precluded from dealing with issues that are the preserve of national or local negotiating or consultative processes; instead it operates rather like the 'adjunct' consultative committees described in Marchington (1994.680-83). JCCs with a long history of co-operation as well as experience in dealing with strategic issues, albeit on an information-sharing basis, may be able to adapt their existing arrangements to fit in with the directive. It is therefore clear that despite the well-orchestrated and entirely negative response from many employers and from the Conservative government to these proposals organisations that already have workable structures for multilevel consultative committees may have little to fear from EWCs.

Future prospects: regulation and diversity

In summary, we can see that some major adjustments have occurred in the structure and operation of employee relations in Britain since the late 1970s. Many of these would have been difficult to predict when Labour was last in power, especially if post-war trends had been extrapolated through to the 1990s. For example, on that basis, one might have expected trade-union membership to rise further, or at least stabilise, whereas in fact it has dropped by over a third. Similarly, the significant shrinkage in the coverage of collective bargaining would not have been predicted, nor would the sizeable decline in strike activity. Moreover, 20 years ago most analysts would not have anticipated the growth of direct employee involvement or the individualism that now characterises so much of employee relations.

Perhaps the changing nature of employee relations, at least in aggregate terms, is best exemplified by the declining prominence of employers' organisations over the last 20 years. Then, the extensiveness of multi-employer bargaining arrangements and disputes procedures, as well as an increasing role in the provision of assistance for dealing with legal issues, meant that they were key players in the employee relations arena. Since that time their role has declined as a large number of private-sector employers have withdrawn from national wage-setting mechanisms and/or have decided to provide employee relations in-house. In addition the CBI was largely ignored by the Thatcher governments in favour of the Institute of Directors, which was more closely aligned with the Conservatives' free-market approach to the economy (Kessler and Bayliss 1995:195). In academic texts on the subject the amount of space devoted to employers' organisations has also reduced to the extent that they do not even gain a mention in the Index of Edwards' recent book (Edwards 1995).

In view of all the above, predicting future developments in employee relations is a hazardous exercise, not least because of the influence that government policies (both at a national and European level) have over the broad context within which organisations operate. Following the next election (due in 1997) we ought at least to have a clearer idea about the shape of government policy for the remainder of the century, especially in relation to EU social legislation. If elected, a Labour government would be committed to implementing the Social Chapter, which would be bound to have an influence over employers' policies regarding EWCs as well as their approach to other terms and conditions (for example, regarding part-time workers and the introduction of a minimum wage). This would have some effect on pay structures, especially in industries that have typically been towards the bottom of the wages ladder (such as the 'bleak house' forms of union-free firms), but the impact on the more progressive employers is harder to predict. It is also possible that there would be a rebolstering of the collective bargaining system and the introduction of new procedures governing union recognition (Trades Union Congress 1991; Beaumont and Towers 1992:129-30). More broadly, trade unions would probably be invited once again to play a role in the development of a social dialogue, both in the UK and in Europe. Conversely, a further Conservative government would be likely to continue with, and possibly extend yet further, its free-market philosophy, which sees little place for trade unions and no room for the Social Chapter. Furthermore, prospects for the low-paid and unorganised labour would then be likely to worsen, despite EU rulings to protect workers transferred from the public to the private sector (Rubery 1995:565).

Despite the influence of government over this organisational context it is however clear that space does exist for many, if not most, employers to develop policies suited to their own competitive and environmental conditions. Although it is appropriate and necessary to record broad trends in employee relations, the survey and case-study evidence demonstrates that not all organisations are moving at the same speed, let alone in the same direction. For example, WIRS3 shows an increase in the number of derecognitions and yet it also reports a number of new recognitions. Equally, whereas case-studies illustrate the emergence of 'new' forms of EI, they also record that 'old' forms are not disappearing. Similarly, if Labour forms the next government it is probable that rather more employers will set up EWCs than if the Conservatives remain in office; but, as we have already seen, quite a number of employers have established EWCs of their own volition during the first half of the 1990s. Moreover, just as unionised firms do not disappear under Conservative governments, neither will non-unionism be decimated under Labour. It is therefore crucial to remember that, despite the interest that broad trends and new developments attract, these are often less significant in aggregate terms than their 'old' counterparts.

It is clear, however, that employers do need to adopt a more strategic view about how employee relations can be integrated with wider business strategies and how they can be managed in a way that enables employee relations to contribute to the achievement of corporate goals. Many employers will never attempt this and so will continue to operate in an *ad hoc* and reactive manner to events, developing employee relations policies that are not designed in order to fit in with other aspects of personnel and development, let alone the remainder of the business. For those employers who aim to manage in a proactive manner, choices will have to be made about whether or not to continue relationships with trade unions, how to conduct collective bargaining, and which forms of EI are most appropriate. At the risk of simplification, it seems that the practice of employee relations is becoming increasingly bifurcated not so much *between* union and non-union organisations as *within* each of these categories.

In broad terms, employers who recognise unions can opt to work with or against them. Those who opt to develop closer partnerships with trade unions are likely also to find ways to enhance co-operation – through single-table agreements (possibly at local level), more effective consultative machinery, EWCs, and direct employee involvement designed to supplement and extend union channels. By contrast, employers who see little value in maintaining close relations with the unions are likely to seek ways to marginalise and remove them from any meaningful role in the organisation – through tightening up on union activity, failing to take collective bargaining seriously, and generally freezing out stewards. If EWCs become obligatory, then such management will do all it can to limit the role such a body can play eg by giving the minimum information necessary, and often under duress. At the same time, efforts are likely to be expended on weakening the link between unions and their members through direct EI and other individualistic techniques.

Trade unions are not merely passive agents in this process, and there has been debate about how to respond to recent employer initiatives, especially those paraded under the banner of HRM. The TUC has noted that HRM can be viewed in positive terms – in that 'good' employment practices are to be welcomed if they increase the quality of working life and training opportunities for members – instead of being seen solely from a more negative and conspiratorial perspective. But unions have to adopt a more radical stance if this is to be achieved: their decline is unlikely to be halted by a grudging acknowledgement of HRM (Guest 1995:138) and a cynical rejection of its practices.

Similarly, employers with non-union workplaces can also opt for policies and practices that aim to achieve closer co-operation between management and staff; alternatively they can seek to limit worker empowerment by reinforcing management prerogatives. In the case of the former (the 'good' employers), treating staff as assets and resourceful humans – by training and developing, appraising and rewarding, informing and consulting them – is seen as a philosophy that leads to competitive advantage. Conversely, in the case of the 'ugly' employers, the adoption of progressive employee relations policies is viewed as unnecessary and counter to the company's efforts to enhance profitability. Such employers see little point in recognising and rewarding effort or in involving staff in matters connected with their broader working environment.

Above all, however, employee relations in the UK is characterised by diversity; even a more regulated and centralised approach via EU initiatives is unlikely to bring about a 'standard' British system. The institutions and techniques used to manage employee relations show massive variation between workplaces, and even organisations with the same sets of procedures tend to operate these rather differently. Although an incoming Labour government is likely to implement EU initiatives in a variety of areas, the voluntarist emphasis and the absence of a centralised arbitration system will continue to allow for diverse patterns of employee relations in Britain.

References

ACAS (ADVISORY CONCILIATION AND ARBITRATION SERVICE) (1981), *Improving Industrial Relations: A Joint Responsibility*, London, HMSO.

BADDON, L, HUNTER L, HYMAN, J, LEOPOLD, J, AND RAMSAY, H, (1989), *People's Capitalism?* London, Routledge.

BATSTONE, E, (1984) *Working Order*, Oxford, Blackwell.

BEAUMONT, P, (1987), *The Decline of Trade Union Organisation*, London, Croom Helm.

BEAUMONT, P, (1992), *Public Sector Industrial Relations*, London, Routledge.

BEAUMONT, P, AND TOWERS, B, (1992), 'Approaches to trade union organisation', in B. Towers (ed.), *A Handbook of Industrial Relations Practice*, pp123–36, London, Kogan Page.

BLYTON, P, AND TURNBULL, P, (1994), *The Dynamics of Employee Relations*, Basingstoke, Macmillan.

BROWN, W, (1993), 'The contraction of collective bargaining in Britain', *British Journal of Industrial Relations*, Vol. 31(2), pp189–200.

CLAYDON, T, (1989), 'Union derecogniton in Britain in the 1980s', *British Journal of Industrial Relations*, Vol. 27(2), pp214–24.

COLLING, T, (1991), 'Privatisation and the management of industrial relations in electricity distribution', *Industrial Relations Journal*, Vol. 22(2), pp117–29.

DEPARTMENT OF EMPLOYMENT, (1989), *People and Companies: Employee Involvement in Britain*, London, HMSO.

DUNN, S, (1990), 'Root metaphor in the old and new industrial relations', *British Journal of Industrial Relations*, Vol. 28(1), pp1–31.

EDWARDS, P, (1995), 'Strikes and industrial conflict', in P. Edwards (ed.), *Industrial Relations: Theory and Practice in Britain*, Oxford, Blackwell, pp434–60.

FINDLAY, P, (1993), 'Union recognition and non-unionism: shifting fortunes in the electronics industry in Scotland', *Industrial Relations Journal*, Vol. 24(1), pp28–43.

FOULKES, F, (1980), *Personnel Policies in Large Non-union Companies*, New Jersey, Prentice Hall.

GALL, G, (1993), 'Harmony around a Single Table', *Labour Research*, June.

GALL, G, AND MCKAY, S, (1994), 'Trade union derecognition in Britain, 1988–1994', *British Journal of Industrial Relations*, Vol. 32(3), pp433–48.

GODFREY, G, AND MARCHINGTON, M, (1994), *Trade Unions: Partners in competitive success – the attitudes of shop stewards towards partnership programmes*, Paper presented to the IPD Annual Conference, Harrogate, October.

GOLD, M, AND HALL, M, (1992), *European-level Information and Consultation in Multinational Companies: An evaluation of practice*, Dublin, European Foundation.

GREGG, P, AND YATES, A, (1991), 'Changes in wage-setting arrangements and trade union presence in the 1980s', *British Journal of Industrial Relations*, Vol. 29(3), pp361–76.

GUEST, D, (1995), 'Human resource management, trade unions and industrial relations', in J. Storey (ed.), *Human Resource Management: A critical text.* pp110–41, London, Routledge.

GUEST, D, AND HOQUE, K, (1994), 'The good, the bad and the ugly: employment relations in new non-union workplaces', *Human Resource Management Journal*, Vol. 5(1), pp1–14.

HALL, M, (1992), 'Behind the European works councils directives: the European commission's legislative strategy', *British Journal of Industrial Relations*, Vol. 30(4), pp547–66.

HALL, M, CARLEY, M, GOLD, M, MARGINSON, P, AND SISSON, K, (1995), *European Works Councils: Planning for the directive.* London/Coventry, Eclipse Group/Industrial Relations Research Unit.

IPA (INVOLVEMENT AND PARTICIPATION ASSOCIATION) (1993), *Towards Industrial Partnership: A new approach to relationships at work*, London, IPA.

IPA (INVOLVEMENT AND PARTICIPATION ASSOCIATION) (1995), *Towards Industrial Partnership: Putting it into practice – Rhône-Poulenc Staveley Chemicals: a case-study in movement to single status*, London, IPA.

IRS (INDUSTRIAL RELATIONS SERVICES) (1992), 'Industrial relations developments in the water industry', IRS Employment Trends, No. 516, July, pp6–15.

IRS (INDUSTRIAL RELATIONS SERVICES) (1993a), 'Two-table bargaining and new pay structures at Seeboard', IRS Employment Trends, No. 543, September, p9–12.

IRS (INDUSTRIAL RELATIONS SERVICES) (1993b), 'Decline in multi-employer bargaining charter', IRS Employment Trends, No. 544, September, pp7–11.

IRS (INDUSTRIAL RELATIONS SERVICES) (1994), 'First British European works councils established', IRS Employment Trends, No. 574, December, pp4–7.

IRS (INDUSTRIAL RELATIONS SERVICES) (1995), 'Single table bargaining: an idea whose time is yet to come', IRS Employment Trends, No. 577, February, pp10–16.

JACKSON, M, LEOPOLD, J, AND TUCK, K, (1992), 'Decentralisation of collective bargaining: the case of the retail food industry', *Human Resource Management Journal*, Vol. 2(2), pp29–45.

KELLY, J, (1992), *Scientific Management, Job Redesign and Work Performance*, London, Academic Press.

KESSLER, S, AND BAYLISS, F, (1995), *Contemporary British Industrial Relations*, London, Macmillan.

KINNIE, N, (1987), 'Bargaining within the enterprise: centralised or decentralised?' *Journal of Management Studies*, Vol. 24(5), pp463–77.

KINNIE, N, (1993), 'Multi-plant industrial relations: fast foods', in D. Gowler, K. Legge, and C. Clegg (eds), *Case Studies in Organisational Behaviour and Human Resource Management*, pp106–13, London, Paul Chapman Publishing.

MARCHINGTON, M, (1992a), 'Managing labour relations in a competitive environment', in A. Sturdy, D. Knights, and H. Willmott (eds), *Skill and Consent: Contemporary studies in the labour process*, pp149–84, London, Routledge.

MARCHINGTON, M, (1992b), *Managing The Team: A guide to employee involvement in practice*, Oxford, Blackwell.

MARCHINGTON, M, (1994), 'The dynamics of joint consultation', in K. Sisson (ed.), *Personnel Management in Britain*, pp662–93, Oxford, Blackwell.

MARCHINGTON, M, (1995), 'Fairy tales and magic wands: new employment practices in perspective', *Employee Relations*, Vol. 17(1), pp51–66.

MARCHINGTON, M, AND PARKER, P, (1990), *Changing Patterns of Employee Relations*, Hemel Hempstead, Harvester Wheatsheaf.

MARCHINGTON, M, GOODMAN, J, WILKINSON, A, AND ACKERS, P, (1992), *Recent Developments in Employee Involvement*, Employment Department Research Series No. 2, London, HMSO.

MARCHINGTON, M, WILKINSON, A, ACKERS, P, AND GOODMAN, J, (1993), 'The influence of managerial relations on waves of employee involvement', *British Journal of Industrial Relations*, Vol. 31(4), pp553–76.

MARGINSON, P, EDWARDS, P, MARTIN, R, PURCELL, J AND SISSON, K, (1988), *Beyond the Workplace: Managing industrial relations in the multi-plant enterprise*, Oxford, Blackwell.

MARGINSON, P, AND SISSON, K, (1990), 'Single table talk', *Personnel Management*, May.

MARGINSON, P, BUITENDAM, A, DEUTSCHMANN, C, AND PERULLI, P, (1993), 'The emergence of the Euro-company: towards a European industrial relations', *Industrial Relations Journal*, Vol. 24(3), pp182–90.

McLOUGHLIN, I AND GOURLAY, S, (1992), 'Enterprise without unions: the management of employee relations in non-union firms', *Journal of Management Studies*, Vol. 29(5), pp669–91.

McLOUGHLIN, I, AND GOURLAY, S, (1994), *Enterprise Without Unions: Industrial relations in the non-union firm*, Buckingham, Open University Press.

MILLWARD, N, STEVENS, M, SMART, D, AND HAWES, W, (1992), *Workplace Industrial Relations in Transition*, Aldershot, Dartmouth Publishing.

MILNER, S, (1995), 'The coverage of collective pay-setting institutions in Britain, 1895–1990', *British Journal of Industrial Relations*, Vol. 33(1), pp69–92.

PENDLETON, A, (1992), 'Employee share ownership schemes in the United Kingdom', *Human Resource Management Journal*, Vol. 2(2), pp83–8.

PURCELL, J, (1979), 'A strategy for management control in Industrial Relations', in J. Purcell and R. Smith (eds), *The Control of Work*, pp27–58, London, Macmillan.

PURCELL, J, AND SISSON, K, (1983), 'Strategies and practice in the management of industrial relations', in G. Bain (ed.), *Industrial Relations in Britain*, pp95–120, Oxford, Blackwell.

RAINNIE, A, (1991), *Industrial Relations in Small Firms: Small isn't beautiful*, London, Routledge.

RAMSAY, H, (1991), 'The community, the multinational, its workers and their charter: a modern tale of industrial democracy', *Work Employment and Society*, Vol. 5(3), pp541–66.

ROOTS, P, (1986), *Collective Bargaining: Opportunities for a new approach*, Warwick Papers in Industrial Relations, No. 5, April.

RUBERY, J, (1995), 'The low-paid and the unorganised', in P. Edwards (ed.), *op. cit.*, pp543–68.

SCHULLER, T, (1989), 'Financial participation', in J. Storey (ed.), *New Perspectives on HRM*, London, Routledge, pp126–36.

Scott, A, (1994), *Willing Slaves? – British workers under human resource management*, Cambridge, Cambridge University Press.

Scott, M, Roberts, I, Holroyd, G, and Sawbridge, D, (1989), *Management and Industrial Relations in Small Firms*, Department of Employment Research Paper, No. 70, London, HMSO.

Sisson, K, (1993) 'In search of human resource management', *British Journal of Industrial Relations*, Vol. 31(2), pp201–10.

Smith, P, and Morton, G, (1993), 'Union exclusion and the decollectivisation of industrial relations in contemporary Britain', *British Journal of Industrial Relations*, Vol. 31(1), pp97–114.

Sproull, A, and MacInnes, J, (1989), 'Union recognition, single union agreements and employment change in Scottish Electronics', *Industrial Relations Journal*, Vol. 20(1), pp33–46.

Storey, J, (1992), *Developments in the Management of Human Resources*, Oxford, Blackwell.

Thomason, G, (1984), *A Textbook of Industrial Relations Management*, London, Institute of Personnel Management.

Trades Union Congress (1991), *Trade Union Recognition: A consultative document*. London, TUC.

TUC (Trades Union Congress) (1994), *Human Resource Management: A trade union response*, London, TUC.

Waddington, J, and Whitston, C, (1995), 'Trade unions: growth, structure and policy', in P. Edwards (ed.), *op. cit.*, pp151–202.

Walsh, J, (1993), 'Internalisation versus decentralisation: an analysis of recent developments in pay bargaining', *British Journal of Industrial Relations*, Vol. 31(3), pp409–32.

Walton, R, (1985), 'From control to commitment in the workplace', *Harvard Business Review*, Vol. 63(2), pp77–85.

Wickens, P, (1987), *The Road to Nissan: Flexibility, quality, teamwork*. London, Macmillan.

Wilkinson, A, Marchington, M, Ackers, P, and Goodman, J, (1992), 'Total quality management and employee involvement', *Human Resource Journal*, Vol. 3(2), pp1–20.

Wilkinson, A, Marchington, M, Ackers, P, and Goodman, J, (1994), 'ESOPs fables – a tale of a machine tool company', *International Journal of Human Resource Management*, Vol. 5(1), pp121–43.

Wilkinson, A, Marchington, M, Redman, T, and Snape, E, (1996), *Quality, Human Resource Management and Organisational Change*, Basingstoke, Macmillan, forthcoming.

CHAPTER FIVE
Organisational Behaviour

Cary Cooper and Barbara White

One of the key challenges for the future will be to clarify the role that organisational behaviour (OB) might play in human resource management (HRM). To meet this challenge it is vital to have a clear vision of what constitutes HRM. The relationship between the two disciplines has been made more complex by the observation that the term HRM has been used in two different ways. Some use it as a catch-all to encompass the whole field of 'people management'. In this sense HRM would include interpersonal skills training, organisational behaviour, and personnel management. HRM described as such is a broad umbrella, with no particular approach to management perceived to be preferable. In the second usage HRM is seen to be a new and unique approach which has been defined by Storey as:

> a distinctive approach to employment management which seeks to achieve competitive advantage through the strategic deployment of a highly committed and capable workforce, using an array of cultural, structural and personnel techniques.[1]

This second approach has been at the centre of the furore surrounding HRM, because it promises to provide solutions to the problems associated with managing people in a changing context. The question that must be addressed is whether OB can play a part only in the more diffuse approach to people management or whether it can make a valid contribution to the new and more business-oriented HRM.

In a critical review of the reality and rhetoric surrounding HRM, Legge expands the distinction between so-called hard and soft models.[2] The hard model focuses on the crucial importance of the close integration of human resource policies, systems, and activities with business strategy. The emphasis is on the quantitative, calculative, and business-strategic aspects of managing the headcount resource in as 'rational' a way as for any other economic factor.[3]

In contrast, the soft 'developmental humanism' model, while still emphasising the importance of integrating human resource policies with business objectives, treats employees as valued assets and as a source of competitive advantage.[4] Employees are considered to be proactive rather than passive inputs into productive processes. The emphasis is therefore on generating commitment, motivation, and human development, and it is towards this soft model of HRM that OB can make a contribution. In fact, the different emphases in the two models are not necessarily incompatible. Most statements of what constitutes HRM include both hard and soft aspects.[5]

To achieve an effective integration of HRM with OB it seems important that organisational behaviourists should acknowledge the implications of the major elements in the above definition. First, activity should be aimed primarily at managers and core-workers rather than at the non-managerial workforce. Secondly, priority has to be placed on competitive advantage through people and bottom-line results. Finally, attention must be given to the management of the organisation's culture. In defining the critical issues for the future of organisational behaviour in an HRM context it is essential that all of these elements are taken into consideration.

What is organisational behaviour (OB)?

As organisational behaviourists we do not find ourselves in the position of redefining the essence of our activity, as is the case for human resource specialists.[6] OB continues to be concerned with the human side of management. It draws from many theoretical frameworks including psychology, social psychology, political science, sociology, and anthropology in so far as they aid our understanding of individual and group behaviour in organisations. Luthans has defined OB as being concerned with the 'understanding, prediction and control of human behaviour in organisations'.[7]

Holloway also defines the goal of OB in terms of regulation of the workforce.[8] In a comprehensive documentation of 80 years of both work psychology and OB, Holloway suggests that what we see is a history of some of the tools produced to help regulate the workforce. She points to the lack of theoretical coherence between these strategies, which is attributed to the fact that they are not primarily the products of theorising but of changing regulation problems. The target of this regulation has been the individual at work. Over time we can see a story of several approaches to work regulation, each with a different model of the individual, for example scientific management, human factors, vocational selection, interpersonal skills training, work design, and leadership. Holloway predicts that, in the future, individuals will continue to be the object of OB strategies of regulation. The target has simply shifted from managing the workforce to managing the managers. This trend is likely to continue given the central role of line managers in HRM, a phenomenon reflected in the disproportionate amount of training activity and resources that are consumed by management development.

OB and HRM: a forced split?

Luthans has presented a meta-theoretical space to illustrate the relationship between different approaches to organisational management (see Figure 5.1). He distinguishes macro-level analysis (concerned with organisational design and structure) from micro-level analysis (concerned with individual and group behaviour). A distinction is also drawn between theoretical and applied endeavour.

There has been some convergence of the macro- and micro-levels of analysis in theory. The principles of scientific management espoused by Taylor are now recognised as being overly simplistic for today's complex challenges.[9] Human behaviour at work is much more complicated and diverse than the economic, security, working-conditions approach would suggest. It should be emphasised that although this may be recognised in theory, much of the practice of HRM still concentrates on individuals without sufficient consideration of the environment in which they operate.

The lines in Figure 5.1 are becoming increasingly blurred, because

Figure 5.1

THE RELATIONSHIP OF OB TO OTHER CLOSELY RELATED DISCIPLINES

	OT (Organisation theory)	OB (Organisational behaviour)
THEORETICAL		
APPLIED	OD (Organisation development)	P/HR (Personnel/ human resources)
	MACRO	MICRO

there is no universal agreement amongst academics or practitioners on what belongs to what. Luthans believes, however, that most would agree with his representation of the relationship of OB to other closely related disciplines. Personnel or human resource managers are found practising in organisations whereas organisational behaviourists are not. Confusingly, those managers who apply and draw on the field of OB are called 'human resource managers' because they are concerned with the management of people.

The field of OB serves as a basis for modern human resource managers. All too often organisations have sophisticated systems of evaluating everything except their management of people. OB seeks to counter this careless or simplistic tendency by carefully studying how people can best be assessed, motivated, led, trained, and developed at work. Without good theory, practice is blind. Organisational behaviourists have the potential to facilitate the prediction and control of human resources. This role will be critical to the goals of new approaches to management that will help to solve the problems and meet the challenges of the next millennium.

The critical challenges for the next millennium

Given the major objectives of HRM, our aim is to explore the ways in which OB can improve competitive advantage, facilitate the role of the line manager and help in the generation of effective organisational cultures. As Tyson and Jackson have pointed out, the behavioral sciences are still in early stages of development and do not offer universal laws or rules.[10] However, through the use of scientific enquiry and the search for practical solutions to management problems, it is thought that OB may make a unique contribution to some of the HRM challenges that organisations will face in the future. The objectivity of organisational behaviour should act to balance some of the unsubstantiated prescriptions emanating from the popular management literature.

OB consultants in uncharted territory

Shimmin and Wallis have described a trend in the way that work psychologists and organisational behaviourists have been making their contribution in recent years:

> The most conspicuous and profound change in the practice of occupational psychology in Britain in recent decades is the unprecedented growth of private psychological consultancies . . . In the last ten years the boom in

management consultancy of all kinds has provided opportunities for occupational psychologists. Client demand for these consultancies is almost entirely from management and not from trade unions, nor from individuals for whom the provision of special services is less than formerly.[11]

Many organisational behaviourists and work psychologists see themselves as technical experts able to advise on the detail of specific procedures such as psychometric testing, assertiveness training etc. If organisational behaviourists are to influence organisational functioning they need to move away from a technical specialist role towards that of a general business consultant. They must understand the organisational impact of their techniques, be able to work on macro-issues such as organisational change and human resource planning, and be able to demonstrate the likely financial impact of their recommendations.

Johns analysed why techniques advocated by organisational behaviourists are not adopted in organisations even if they seem to be based on good research and have the potential to save money.[12] He argues that the political and social contexts of organisations are often neglected. These issues loom larger in the minds of managers than the finer points of the organisational behaviourists' arguments concerning the technical merit of a given technique. Johns points out that managers will respond to how rival companies do things; what legislation requires; and what their bosses will readily find acceptable.

It seems vital, therefore, that the organisational behaviourists should have a grasp of the nature of the political context in which they are operating. As yet, organisational politics could be described as uncharted territory or an inadequately explored reality.[13] One of the key issues for the future will therefore be the development of a clear understanding of the nature and processes of organisational politics (OP). Our aim is to review definitions of OP, and to consider techniques used in the diagnosis of the political context of organisations.

Putting the humanity back into human resources

Another major concern for the future is that through the hard-headed approach HRM may have lost some of its humanity. Kanter suggests that the entrepreneurial spirit that has emerged in business throughout the last decade has affected people in many positive ways. It has provided them with new ways to contribute, to be rewarded for their contribution, and to increase the value of their skills. Yet she also points out that restructuring to create leaner and more productive organisations has had negative effects in terms of dislocated careers, diminished personal expectations, disrupted family lives, and work-related stress.[14]

Luthans goes one step further to suggest that the 'lean and mean' organisations which have produced short-term benefits of lowered cost and increased productivity will not meet the challenges of the future. The drive for productivity regardless of human cost has been at the centre of criticism surrounding HRM. The vision of personnel management as a 'caring' profession has been displaced by talk about sustaining and enhancing market competitiveness. Luthans predicts that if the current strategy is continued, the outcome will mean that organisations will not be

- keen enough to deliver higher service or to achieve leaps in productivity beyond easy gains achieved by screwing down on costs
- smart enough or sensitive enough to manage a diverse workforce or to satisfy the best employees.[15]

It will be demonstrated that OB can help to solve these problems by enabling a return to worker protection, reinvesting HRM with the humanity neglected in the hard model. As such, the management of diversity and health at work are thought to be central issues for the future. The British Psychological Society (BPS) also suggest that core topics such as motivation, training, and leadership will continue to be critical growth areas.[16] Other areas such as health at work, human computer interaction, women and ethnic minorities, cognitive approaches, and organisation change are also expected to take on more importance in the future. The BPS is not telling us anything really new, but it does reinforce the importance of these issues for future debate.

In our discussion of those topics which we believe will have particular relevance for the future we have chosen to focus narrowly on stress and health at work, equal opportunities and managing diversity, and organisational politics. Each topic is described in terms of the current state of knowledge and why it is an issue that will concern us as we move towards the next millennium. The current activities within OB as they impinge on HRM at both functional and strategic levels will be described. Attention will also be drawn to the ways in which organisational culture might be managed to achieve greater humanity in dealing with the workforce of the future.

Stress and health at work

It is currently estimated that nearly 10 per cent of United Kingdom GNP is lost each year owing to job-generated stress. We look at the nature of stress, what its sources in the work place are, and what we can do about it. Particular attention is given to the employee assistance programmes and the ways in which organisations might be redesigned to build healthy cultures.

What is stress?

Stress is generally recognised to be a result of the interaction between the individual and the environment. Lazarus proposed the transactional model of stress which takes account of evidence that *subjective perception* of a stimulus as a stressor by the individual is more predictive of physiological responses to it than *objective measures* of stress potential. As such, both the environmental stimulus and the reacting individual are vital elements in predicting stress. Lazarus would claim that

> Stress refers to a very broad class of problems that are differentiated from other problem areas because it deals with any demands which tax the system . . . and the response of that system.[17]

This definition redirects the focus of attention from the objective features of the work environment to the individual's subjective appraisal of environmental demands. This model could be criticised on the grounds that, although it may influence the way in which we conceptualise stress, it does not offer specific guidance as to what features of the work environment are most stressful.

More recent research has identified five chief categories of work stress.[18] These factors are thought to be common to all jobs but vary in the degree to which they are found to be causally linked to stress in each job. Much of the research on stress has been occupation-specific, the approach being to ask job incumbents to describe those aspects of the job which make them feel stressed. Unique attributes have been discovered, but there is a strong resemblance in the nature of the stressors from one job to the next. The individual appears as a mediating variable between the sources of stress and stress outcomes (see Figure 5.2).

In part the similarity in sources of pressure between occupations may be explained by the propensity of stress researchers to use similar questionnaires to tap the same set of theoretical constructs. However, even in studies that use more inductive qualitative methodology the sources of stress discovered are highly predictable. The consensus in the findings may be due to underlying mechanisms that are universally involved in the stress process. Alternatively we may be observing the effects of a widely held implicit theory about stress acquired from years of exposure to the popular press.

Figure 5.2
THE DYNAMICS OF WORK STRESS

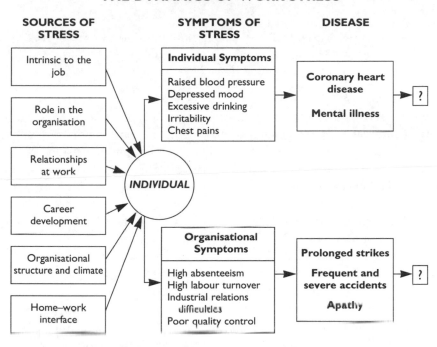

Stress as a problem for the future

The perception of employees as an organisational asset has generated a need to demonstrate that each employee is contributing and that his or her job adds value. Kanter reported a review of more than 800 studies of several thousand workplaces with productivity improvement projects that showed the most common workplace changes were towards flat, lean structures, multiskilled employees, and team configurations. These features lead to higher work absorption and overload. Although there may be fewer duplications, owing to effective business process re-engineering, there is simultaneously less slack in the new, leaner system, which means there are fewer people to do more tasks. Kanter has predicted that there will be a backlash in the form of resistance, cynicism, and fatigue at taking on so much change.[19] The conclusion that we may draw from Kanter's work is that the leaner organisations of the future will not be able to neglect the issue of stress if they wish to sustain productivity.

The belief that work stress is a causal agent in physical and mental disorders as well as organisational outcomes such as absenteeism and reduced productivity has gained widespread acceptance. Stress has been seen as a costly problem in many organisations for the last decade. McKenna states that

> companies have a major stake in promoting a healthier life style for employees, because of the potential benefits in reduced insurance costs, decreased absenteeism, improved productivity and better morale.[20]

It is impossible to arrive at an accurate determination of the costs of occupational stress because of the complexity of the problem. However, the literature does provide some estimates. Absenteeism is one of the most obvious costs of stress to employers. General indications are that absenteeism is an accelerating problem in many occupations. In 1978 the Confederation of British Industry (CBI) reported that absenteeism had 'risen alarmingly in recent years in spite of improvements in working conditions, income levels and family health'. By 1994 the CBI and Percom survey reported that 171 million working days were lost in the UK through sickness, compared with half a million lost through industrial disputes. We estimate that between 30 and 40 per cent of all sickness absence is stress-related.

High rates of employee turnover can also become expensive to a company. They raise training costs, reduce overall efficiency, and disrupt other workers. Although it is hard to estimate the actual costs of labour turnover, it is thought that they are often equal to about five times an employee's monthly salary.[21] US employers have been paying directly for stress-related illnesses through workers' compensation claims for several years, as Lubin describes:

> In general, claims for psychological disorders suffered as the result of job experiences have multiplied over the decade of the 70's . . . in 1979, the State of California alone received more than 3,000–4,000 'psychiatric' injury claims, half of which resulted in monetary awards.[22]

Many employers are being held responsible for employee stress, owing to the belief that they are doing too little to cut down the stressful aspects of many jobs. This may help to explain the growth of corporate stress and health management courses in the USA. The risk of potential litigation is now becoming a reality in the UK. In November 1994 the case *Walker v Northumberland County Council* made senior social worker John Walker the first person in the UK to win an action for negligence over stress. This success is likely to set a precedent which will spark many future claims.

The Health and Safety Executive published guidelines for employers at the end of May 1995. The production of the document had involved the consultation of organisational behaviourists who specialise in stress at work. The emphasis is on explaining symptoms of stress and the importance of removing the stigma attached to stress. Today it is commonplace to hear a working person talk about being 'stressed out': it is not seen as an admission of inadequacy. There is a growing acceptance that stress is normal, and that the availability of psychological advice, assistance, and counselling should be a facility in responsible organisations. Such provision in organisations is increasingly being seen not only as progressive and intelligent but also as cost-effective.

Stress management: the employee assistance programme

Employee Assistance Programmes (EAPs) are increasingly becoming part of the vocabulary of human resource managers. A workable, generic definition of the EAP is

> a programmable intervention at the work place usually at the level of the individual employee, using behavioral science knowledge and methods for recognition and control of certain work and non-work related problems (notably alcoholism, drug abuse and mental health) which adversely affect job performance, with the objective of enabling the individual to return to making her or his full work contribution and to attaining full functioning in personal life.[23]

They are supported not only by those who espouse the soft model or developmental humanistic philosophies of HRM, but also by hard-headed managers. EAPs are seen by managers as capable of playing a growing role in keeping organisations operating at a high level of efficiency. Such programmes are also seen to be cost-effective in individual and corporate terms as a new way of handling stress at work.

The EAP is distinctive in that it is embedded in the organisational processes of the firm. It should reflect and nourish the organisational culture and become part of organisational learning, problem-solving and adaptation mechanisms. These factors differentiate the EAP from external counselling or traditional welfare provision, which are designed to offset the damaging effects of work.

The effective EAP creates a reciprocity between employer and employee. The employer must acknowledge that sources of stress are potentially related to work, if not actually caused by work. He or she should also accept shared responsibility with the employee for the resolution of problems. On the part of the employee, by accepting participation in the EAP he or she implicitly agrees that a problem exists that may manifest itself in work. He or she must show personal commitment to tackling problems, obtaining and using help, and taking personal responsibility for the outcomes.

Another characteristic of an EAP which distinguishes it from former welfare services is the broad range of problems that come into its scope. This may be attributed in part to the greater expertise of the counsellors delivering the EAPs, but also to the more holistic philosophy underpinning the EAP. The range of issues dealt with by an EAP is shown in Table 5.1. Although this list is not exhaustive, and is expected to diversify, it illustrates that the EAP is designed to tackle the issues of stress in organisations in their *widest* sense rather than the restricted sense of job-related stress.

Table 5.1
COUNSELLING ISSUES FOR AN *EAP*

AIDS	Grievances	Relocation
Alcohol abuse	Indebtedness	Retirement
Bereavement	Induction	Sexual harassment
Career development	Job training	Smoking
Chronic illness	Lay-off	Stress (work-related)
Demotion	Legal matters	Stress (work-extrinsic)
Disability	Literacy and education	Substance abuse
Discipline	Marital problems	Suicide
Dismissal	Mental health	Verbal abuse
Divorce	Performance evaluation	Violence
Family problems	Physical fitness	Vocational guidance
Financial advice	Promotion	Weight control
Gambling	Racial harassment	Women's career breaks
Goal-setting	Redundancy	Young workers' problems

The 'core technologies' of EAPs

Berridge and Cooper acknowledge that although the standardised EAP does not exist, there are a set of core technologies and subsequent functions proposed by Roman & Blum that provide an analytical exposition of the key elements of EAPs (see Table 5.2).[24]

EAPs and HRM

The decision to adopt an EAP for an organisation is often the responsibility

Table 5.2
CORE TECHNOLOGIES OF EAPs

1 *Impaired job performance* (significant, documented) is the main basis of identification of the problem employee.

2 *Consultative assistance* is provided by the EAP to managers in ensuring the goal-directed operation of the organisation.

3 *Constructive confrontation* of the problem employee is central to motivating him or her to be involved in the EAP.

4 *Individual micro-linkages* (systematic, planned) are created between the problem employee and the EAP resources.

5 *Organisational macro-linkages* (longer term, systematic) are created between the EAP resources and the employer.

6 *Corporate culture integrates EAP* as a valid method of coping with the changing internal and external problems faced by the organisation.

7 *Improved job performance* (sustained, documented) is the main criterion of individual and collective success of the EAP.

The outcomes of these 'core technologies' are seen as 'functions' of the EAP:

- employee retention improved, with savings in training costs, expertise protection etc

- reduced managerial workload resulting from problem employees – shared with EAP

- disciplinary issues (even dismissal) treated more precisely, humanely, constructively

- improved financial control (of labour costs, insurance health-care cost management)

- enhanced employee morale.

of the human resource manager. At the functional level the benefits derive from the fact that EAPs relate to the employee as an individual. EAPs aim to tackle issues as close as possible to the problems as they are perceived by the troubled employee. This is consistent with industrial relations theory which suggests that conflict resolution should be as close as possible to the point of friction. EAPs are said to create a culture that emphasises problem recognition and resolution for work-related and other problems, leading to a positive and adaptive mode of behaviour. The aim is to raise the employees' awareness of a range of responses to organisational stressors, which should enhance their flexibility and trainability.

EAPs also represent a constructive way out of discipline problems, favouring positive reinforcement leading to behaviour modification. The business case for EAPs is that they are demonstrably cost-effective and they reduce the load for personnel managers and industrial relations officers. On a more negative note, line managers may feel that control over the workforce has been taken out of their hands and given to the counsellor. EAP participation may be a lengthy process when the line manager is looking for a quick fix to a current problem.

The responsibility for individual employee well-being in its fullest sense (not just in terms of performance) is increasingly thought to be part of the line manager's role. But managers vary in the time and attention they are willing to give to this holistic approach. They also vary in terms of their ability to handle the task. Therefore, although the EAP does not offer fast solutions, the majority of line managers will appreciate the EAP's double function as a safe haven for personal aspects of employee performance deficit and a source of guidance to themselves in handling difficult situations.

At the strategic level the major benefit of the EAP is that it represents a new facet to the culture of an organisation that recognises stress as a normal part of organisational life. It avoids placing blame and seeks to provide a remedy. EAPs can help to attain and retain high performance levels by providing stress-coping strategies and support during times of pressure. An EAP represents an affirmation of the firm's social responsibility in the face of the current lack of government action and the high costs of individual counselling services. The decision to introduce an EAP may therefore be viewed as a long-term strategic statement of philosophy on the part of the HRM function.

Redesigning for a healthy organisation

OB has offered employees stress-control techniques that operate at the psychological and physiological level. Psychological interventions have been popular, not least because they leave the structural conditions unchanged. But can stress-control techniques at the level of the individual improve the problem sufficiently to be effective? If causes are ignored psychology can probably effect only minor improvements. Organisational-level strategies are relatively rare, which means that OB tends to treat the symptoms of pressure and not eliminate the source.[25] Identifying and recognising the source itself, and taking steps to tackle it, might arguably arrest the whole stress process.

Elkin and Rosch have outlined a range of possible organisational-directed strategies which might be employed to reduce stress:

- redesign the task
- redesign the work environment
- establish flexible work schedules
- encourage participative management
- include the employee in career development
- analyse work roles and establish goals
- provide social support and feedback
- build cohesive teams
- establish fair employment policies
- share the rewards.[26]

The majority of these strategies increase employee participation and autonomy. It is recognised that social support and autonomy play an important part in moderating the stress response.[27] Many strategies that focus on changing the style of work in an organisation are often indirectly a vehicle for organisational change that moves the organisation towards a more open and 'employee empowered' culture.

Cartwright and Cooper have identified the characteristics of what can be described as a healthy organisation:

- stress levels are low
- organisational commitment and job satisfaction are high
- sickness absenteeism and turnover are below the national average
- industrial relations are good
- safety and accident records are good
- fear of litigation is absent.[28]

A healthy organisation is one that has been successful in creating a relatively stress-free environment in which the need for interventions such as EAPs will be minimal. Unfortunately, organisations have been slow to recognise the benefits provided by regular stress audits to ascertain their general 'state of health'. Organisational behaviourists have a role to play in conducting reliable and valid stress audits. Instruments such as the Occupational Stress Indicator measure sources of pressure and stress outcomes; they also incorporate measures of personality such as Type A, locus of control, and coping styles.[29] The identification of different stressors is likely to suggest different solutions. Therefore the diagnostic stress audit can be advantageous in terms of directing the organisation to areas when they can engage in anticipatory action to arrest the stress process before its negative effects have an impact on employee health. The organisation that is successful in eliminating or modifying environmental stressors will have less need for interventions that target the individual.

Equal opportunities and managing diversity

In recent years a controversy has arisen in both the popular press and within organisations about whether inequalities continue to exist between groups within the workplace. In a discussion of US corporate giants, Kanter has suggested that the barriers to an individual's ambitions are being challenged and eliminated as women and ethnic minorities begin to feel that no position is beyond their grasp. Within organisations people can aspire to greater achievements because of a weakening of the hierarchy and a broadening of participation in problem-solving. Kanter's optimism is reflected in the statement that

> business is gradually shedding the shackles of an artificial status order that told people what their place was – and to stay in it. [30]

This optimism cannot unfortunately be translated to the UK context. Both women and ethnic minorities continue to be located in what has been called the secondary labour market, in which they fill lower-level clerical and service-sector jobs.[31,32] Metcalf and Leighton have also provided an indication of the underutilisation of women in the workforce.[33] Their report gives information on occupational segregation that shows a lower proportion of women are professionals, employers, or managers.

We must be aware of what Blum and Smith have called the 'politics of optimism', which stems from images of upward mobility among women and ethnic groups.[34] This optimism serves to exaggerate the extent of integration and the opportunities available in the workplace. The danger associated with the politics of optimism is that the need for reform may be obscured, ultimately slowing down or even preventing progress.

The impact of such politics was evident in a survey carried out by Aitkenhead and Liff of 20 companies selected from the top 1,000 index (1987).[35] The aim of the study was to show how equal opportunities are understood. The respondents were those individuals in organisations who were responsible for equal opportunities. The results were as follows:

- It was generally believed that equal opportunities were already prevailing.
- Equal opportunities requirements were not conceived in terms of organisational structures requiring adaptation to individual needs.

■ Distributional changes were regarded as necessary and the criteria for evaluating equal opportunities were vague if they existed at all.

Although this represents a small-scale study, it paints a bleak picture for the future of equal opportunities, because most respondents felt that little needed to be done within their organisation to improve equality of opportunity. Equality audits demonstrate that it is common for male managers to believe that gender bias exists only in blue-collar or traditionally male trades and that discrimination and job segregation are remnants of a bygone age.[36] Although the audit may demonstrate that the problem of underrepresentation exists, there is often a temptation to explain it away in terms of women or minority workers not applying for posts, not having the required experience or qualification, or simply having different career expectations. It is not surprising, given the apparent blindness to inequality, that little is being done to tackle the problem.

Organisational behaviourists are also guilty of inaction on inequality at work. Holloway has pointed out that over the past decade the area has been dominated by the legal perspective.[37] The lack of success of the legal side, which requires employers to comply with equal opportunities regulation, has led to complacency. Organisations do not perceive the need for aid from organisational behaviourists to give advice about equal opportunities legislation and how to comply with it.

Equal opportunities as a problem for the future

One major reason why so little progress has been made in equal opportunities is that the white male predominates in positions of power in British organisations. Those who are best placed to promote change have no personal experience of discrimination. In addition, equal opportunities policies may have been perceived to conflict, and are frequently subordinate to, other organisational goals. However, we are beginning to see a shift in thinking as a business case emerges for equal opportunities.

There are demographic imperatives which suggest that organisations will have to acknowledge the increasing diversity of the workforce. Projections of the demographic make-up of new workforce entrants over the next 20 years indicate that white males, the traditional managerial and professional pool, will constitute only 15 per cent of this group. The remainder (non-traditional professionals and managers) will be made up of women and members of various ethnic and racial groups.[38] Davidson and Burke point out that this demographic situation will be exacerbated by increasing pressures for greater productivity, effectiveness, and innovation. Organisations will be forced to utilise their most talented and able performers, many of whom will be women and/or from the ethnic minorities. The acknowledgement of the need to use the potential of the entire workforce has created a need to understand how best to manage diversity.

Companies throughout Europe are having to learn to adjust to the changing workforce. Amadeus Global Travel Distribution serves the travel industry primarily in Europe, but its staff of 650 comprises individuals from 32 countries. Amadeus has developed a series of workshops to teach upper management how to lead multicultural teams and how to interact better with others from a variety of countries. Other companies that are taking steps to manage diversity include Mars Incorporated, Digital Equipment Corp., Hewlett-Packard Spain, Fujitsu Ltd, and British Petroleum.[39] It is recognised that managers must learn to adapt to the changing demographics. Employees will also need to be more tolerant of the differences among their co-workers.

The effective management of diversity is recommended not only

Table 5.3
SIX WAYS THAT MANAGING DIVERSITY CAN CREATE COMPETITIVE ADVANTAGE*

ADVANTAGE	CONTRIBUTION
Cost	Trim the costs of integrating diverse workers.
Resource acquisition	Companies that have the best reputation for managing diverse employees will have the best chance of hiring the best available diverse personnel.
Marketing	Increased insight and cultural sensitivity will improve the development and marketing of products and services for diverse segments of the population.
Creativity	Diversity of perspectives will improve levels of creativity throughout the organisation.
Problem-solving	Problem-solving and decision-making will improve through groups with more diverse perspectives.
System flexibility	Tolerance and valuing of diverse perspectives throughout the organisation will make the organisation more fluid, more flexible, and more responsive to environmental changes.

* *Source:* Adapted from Taylor H. Cox and Stacy Blake, 'Managing cultural diversity: implications for organizational competitiveness', *Academy of Management Executive*, August 1991, p. 47.

because it is a socially responsible thing to do but also because it can lead to competitive advantage. Cox and Blake have identified six ways in which competitive advantage can be created (see Table 5.3). Decreased personnel costs and improvements in the quality of personnel are two obvious benefits. In addition, the inclusion of diverse perspectives in problem-solving, decision-making, creativity, and product development are essential to creating competitive advantage in what is becoming an increasingly global market-place.[40]

Restricted access to top positions for women and ethnic minorities

Much OB literature on equal opportunities has defined inequality as differential access to senior organisational positions for members of different groups. One particular avenue which has been used to explain the underrepresentation of women and ethnic minorities at more senior levels within organisations has been to scrutinise assessment processes. In a review of gender bias in selection, Alimo-Metcalfe recommends that particular attention be given to the criteria against which the assessment will be measured; the method or technique adopted for gathering data that will form the basis of a selection decision; and the assessor's judgement of the individual's performance. Each of these factors will be discussed briefly in turn.

'Think manager – think white, middle-class, male' The evidence remains unequivocal on the prerequisite characteristics of an effective manager. In research on managerial sex-typing spanning more than 20 years, Schein has demonstrated that both men and women see a greater similarity between the characteristics of men and managers than they do between women and managers.[41] The difference continues to be significant among the male population, although the gap in perceptions is narrowing for women. These findings have led Schein to conclude that male managers continue to 'think manager – think male'. If what constitutes managerial effectiveness is so completely male then it is inevitable the entire selection process will be permeated with this androcentrism, in that it determines which dimensions are to be assessed.

Selecting the predictor Work in OB has attempted to influence recruitment through the premiss that there *is* such a thing as objective judgement. It is argued that a system can be devised that neutrally identifies the candidate with the characteristics that best fit the requirements of the job. Holloway suggests that this is however a fiction.[42] She states that psychometrics measure the 'problem' individual (female or black person) against the 'norm' (the white male norm) which was originally built into the test. This results in a tendency to blame the 'problem' individual. At best a standard selection system works more fairly because it goes hand in hand with selectors who actively support equal opportunities principles.

Inequality in performance evaluation Judgements in appraisals can have immediate and far-reaching effects, influencing decisions about training opportunities and career development. Within the selection process, performance judgements will influence whether the candidate gets the job, the pay, or promotion prospects. Alimo-Metcalfe points out that bias in performance appraisal is of particular concern for women in the UK, given the current interest of organisations in performance-related pay[43] Alimo-Metcalfe recommends that one way to minimise bias in evaluative appraisals would be to ensure that those people evaluating or appraising be required to provide specific observations of behaviours to substantiate their judgements.

The conclusion drawn by Alimo-Metcalfe is that, by attempting to increase fairness and objectivity of assessment processes through the adoption of sophisticated forms of assessment, organisations may be increasing the effects of bias. As the techniques become more complex, the bias simultaneously becomes more obscure and difficult to detect.

Opportunity 2000

Opportunity 2000 is an intiative that has focused specifically on the underrepresentation of women in senior organisational positions. It adopts a target-setting approach, with the aim of increasing the quality and quantity of women's contribution to the workforce, and operates as a 'target team' which is part of Business in the Community. This is a charitable venture providing a meeting-ground for top-level people to work on projects that address social and economic issues affecting the well-being of the community.

It is recognised that a substantial shift in organisational culture will be necessary before there can be any lasting change for women. The target team commissioned research to review the processes for bringing about major organisational change and these were compared with the implementation of equal opportunities. A model was developed from an examination of change in 150 companies. This showed clusters of critical success factors classified around commitment, behaviour, ownership, and investment. Specific factors included:

- the long-term and unstinting support of top management
- a clear business case for action
- many and varied actions that touched all parts of the business
- a complex system of encouragement and sanctions to bring about and sustain a climate for change.

In comparison, the equal opportunities initiatives were far less comprehensive and commitment was partial. Even if there was a champion he or she was unlikely to be on the board, and was rarely perceived as having any real power. Attempts to change were mostly focused on helping women fit into the existing culture. There was seldom any effort to build ownership of equal opportunities initiatives. Communication explaining equal opportunities objectives tended to be procedural and often omitted those most affected. There was little evidence of their aims or benefits being explained or how they related to the business situation. Hammond concludes that there was insufficient investment in the change in terms of resources, time, or money. It was clear that until equal opportunities were viewed as a business issue, there was unlikely to be much change.

Opportunity 2000 recognises that legislation and procedural change are not enough to bring women fully into the mainstream of organisational life. In November 1993 there were 216 members of Opportunity 2000, constituting around 25 per cent of the UK workforce. Members are required to make three commitments:

- to set their own goals for increasing opportunities for women in their workforce by the year 2000
- to publish these goals
- to monitor and report on progress regularly.

Each year all Opportunity 2000 members are required to take part in a detailed review. Details of best practice are collected and disseminated.

After three years Opportunity 2000 has moved from being an apparently ephemeral campaign to being a mainstream policy issue. It has been adopted and sustained through difficult times of recession. It has demonstrated progress in both difficult *and* good times. Hammond suggests that only time will tell whether Opportunity 2000 will bring about sustainable change for women, but it is clear that the campaign has already succeeded in raising debate and action.[44]

A change from equal opportunities to managing diversity

Kandola has expressed concern about target-setting such as that encouraged by the Opportunity 2000 initiative. Embedded within this approach is a notion of equality based on equal distribution rather than merit, in which managers are encouraged to appoint the right type of person. This, he points out, is a quantitative approach when what might be needed is a qualitative approach such as that embodied in managing diversity.[45]

The term 'managing diversity' has now been coined, but organisational behaviourists may be chastised for not being on this particular bandwagon. This is a reflection of their failure to get on the previous one: that of equal opportunities. It is predicted that a critical challenge for the future will be to understand the nature of diversity and how to manage it effectively.

Kandola and Fullerton have produced a comprehensive and practical guide to the management of diversity in which they suggest that

> The basic concept of managing diversity accepts that the workforce consists of a diverse population of people. The diversity consists of visible and non-visible differences which will include factors such as sex, age, background, race, disability, personality and work style. It is founded on the premiss that harnessing these differences will create a productive environment in which everybody feels valued, where their talents are being fully utilised and in which organisational goals are met.[46]

From assimilation to valuing diversity

There is a distinction between managing diversity and the assimilation theories that saw organisations as a 'melting-pot', whereby minorities were required to adopt the norms and practices of the majority. If the minority group was seen not to have been assimilated, the problem was thought to lie within that group rather than within the dominant culture. A similar shift of position has emerged in feminist literature. Feminist writers are no longer trying to prove that women are entitled to the same opportunities as men because they have the same qualities as them. There is now an acknowledgement that women have something unique to contribute, which should of itself give them access to equal opportunities.[47]

Kandola and Fullerton emphasise that the management of diversity expands current equal opportunities thinking by aiming to realise the potential of 'all' employees at all levels of the organisation. The main differences between equal opportunities and managing diversity are shown in Table 5.4.

Table 5.4
DIFFERENCES BETWEEN MANAGING DIVERSITY AND EQUAL OPPORTUNITIES

MANAGING DIVERSITY:	EQUAL OPPORTUNITIES:
■ ensures all employees maximise their potential and their contribution to the organisation	■ concentrates on discrimination
■ embraces a broad range of people; no one is excluded	■ is perceived as an issue for women, ethnic minorities, and people with disabilities
■ concentrates on movement within an organisation, the culture of the organisation and the meeting of business objectives	■ concentrates on the numbers of groups employed
■ is the concern of all employees, especially managers	■ is seen as an issue to do with personnel and human resource practitioners
■ does not rely on positive action/affirmative action.	■ relies on positive action.

A *diversity-oriented organisation*

Kandola and Fullerton outline their vision of a diversity-oriented organisation, which is comprised of six major characteristics.[48] These characteristics have practical implications for HRM in their efforts to build a culture that fosters and manages diversity effectively.

Mission and values Diversity-oriented organisations must develop a strong mission statement that incorporates managing diversity as a necessary goal for the achievement of long-term business objectives; the rationale behind this statement is derived from theories of group processes.[49] It is proposed that setting a 'superordinate' goal in the form of a corporate mission statement will require close and equal co-operation among members of different groupings. All employees should feel reliant on one another for overall success. This has the effect of directing attention towards similarities rather than differences.

Objective and fair processes Equality audits can be designed to provide the organisation with a comprehensive picture of patterns of employment of women and ethnic minorities. The effects of organisational working arrangements upon the potential for career development, and the relationship between current recruitment, training, and promotion should all be monitored. The audit may survey the attitudes of employers and their supervisors towards the present position and future changes. As such, audits ought to include both in-depth interviews and quantitative statistical analysis of the views of both men and women at all levels.

Skilled and aware workforce Employees should understand what diversity is and how to make it a reality. This will require training in how to recognise and acknowledge biases that can influence decisions and action. Managing diversity depends to a large extent on the capability of managers: Thomas believes that it is lack of managerial competence, as opposed to sexism or racism, that is at the root of managers' inability to manage diverse groups.[50] Management development is therefore crucial for the diversity-oriented organisation.

Active flexibility Hall and Parker have suggested that flexibility in work arrangements should be broadened to include the needs of all employees, and not just those with families.[51] Flexibility should also be present in the way work is carried out. This will involve challenging the existing norms. The focus should be on output rather than the number of hours worked.

Individuals, not groups A group-focused approach carries with it the danger of exaggerating the differences between groups. This can lead to the strengthening of stereotypes and the belief that all members of a group will conform to those stereotypes. A diversity-oriented organisation should adopt an individual approach so that the needs of all employees can be realised. Kandola and Fullerton state that an objective and fair organisation is one in which differences can thrive. In their opinion this is the crux of managing diversity.

Culture that empowers A diversity-oriented organisation must ensure that the organisational culture is consistent and complementary to managing diversity. This may involve not only the elimination of old discriminatory cultures but also the creation of a new, empowering culture. Such a culture would be trusting and open, one in which there was an absence of discrimination. Resources should be allocated on merit alone. An empowering culture facilitates experimentation and creativity. People should be given greater autonomy and be involved in decision-making. They should also understand the core values of the organisation, which will involve open communication between all levels. Managing diversity has to be acknowledged as a business objective which can lead to competitive advantage.

Within a diversity-oriented organisation recognition should be given to the possibility that processes such as motivation, career development, and job satisfaction do not work in the same way for everyone. For instance, many writers have argued that women's careers do not simply lag behind those of men: they proceed in a fundamentally different manner.[52] The role of organisational behaviourists in the future will be to provide a greater insight into how various organisational processes may differ between people. A variety of questions must be addressed if we are to build the foundations on which to manage diversity. For instance, are there differences in management style between ethnic groups? What leads to job satisfaction for men and for women? Perhaps more importantly, organisational behaviourists may begin to consider whether the benefits attributed to managing diversity materialise in practice. Kandola suggests that the lack of involvement of psychologists and organisational behaviourists on these issues has created a conceptual vacuum. It is imperative that we get involved in order to avoid serious mistakes which could only be detrimental for the long-term cause of equal opportunities.[53]

Organisational politics

Since the late 1960s it has been acknowledged that politics is an important factor in the successful outcome of any organisation development intervention.[54] Kumar and Thibodeaux comment that although the importance of organisational politics (OP) has gained increasing acceptance, organisational behaviourists have been cautious in grappling with the political realities of organisational development.[55] This caution is likely to become a liability in the future. Johns has pointed out that one of the reasons why organisational behaviourists fail to have their interventions adopted is because they do not take sufficient account of the political context in which they are operating.[56] This is particularly significant given the observation that current organisation conditions conspire to make organisations more political than ever.

Following a review of the literature, Miles has summarised several conditions that lead to an organisation's being political, as opposed to being rational. The amount of politics in an organisation is directly related to how critical or scarce the resources are. Ambiguous decisions on which there is a lack of certainty generate more politics that routine decisions. The more complex and ambiguous the organisational goals become, the more political the organisation becomes. Politics increases in a complex or turbulent environment; reorganisation or planned organisational development will therefore encourage political manoeuvring.[57]

Most of today's organisations meet the requirements for being highly political environments. As ambiguity and uncertainty increase, so there will be an increase in the degree of organisational politics. Therefore it is imperative that organisational behaviourists who are acting as consultants should have the information-base to be able to diagnose the client system. In this section the nature of OP will be outlined and an approach to political diagnosis will be presented.

What is organisational politics?

Drory and Romm suggest that two common themes have emerged from the exploration of the meaning of organisational politics. First, an examination of the outcomes of politics and the means adopted suggests that they all stray from formal organisational goals and means, or even contradict them. Secondly, the various means and outcomes all have another common characteristic: they all imply the notion of potential conflict. This element of conflict is not just another situational characteristic which may or may not be associated with the OP process: it is a central element built into the OP situation. Drory and Romm state that the essence of organisational politics may generally by captured through the minimal combination of three elements:

1 *Influence:* there is a wide consensus in the literature that political behaviour is essentially influencing behaviour in the sense or trying to change or affect someone's behaviour or attitude.

2 *Informal means:* the use of informal means is another element implied in most of the definitions. This element represents divergence from the formal organisational model.

3 *Conflict:* the presence of conflict is a central element. It is described as a situation where one individual or group seeks to advance their own interests at the expense of another.[58]

The lighter side of politics

Schein has described the political aspect of organisational life as an inadequately explored reality. It is claimed that power struggles, alliance formation, and strategic manoeuvring are as endemic to organisational life as planning, directing, and controlling.[59] Kakabadse shares the view that politics is an integral part of organisational life, based on the premise that differences, rather than similarities, between people form the basis of life in organisations. Kakabadse states that 'politics in organisations are ever present. No matter who you are or what you do, it is impossible to escape the power/political interactions that take place between people at work'.[60]

Hayes comments that individuals in organisations who do not acknowledge the informal system will become politically incompetent.[61] He suggests that many managers are less effective than they might be because they assume that choices are made rationally with the aim of maximising shared goals. Hayes proposes that a more realistic view of organisations is to see them as political organisms, within which individuals and groups attempt to influence one another in pursuit of self-interest. Derr (in her book describing the 'new careerist') confirms this view of organisations. She points out that the gap between actual and perceived states may lead many people to resort to politics in order to reduce the tension between what they want and what the organisation will allow. Skilled political behaviour is said to involve understanding how the organisation works and mobilising resources to achieve organisational purposes without subordinating personal needs or exploiting others.[62]

Arroba and James emphasise that, although politics in organisations does have negative connotations of immorality and deviousness, this is not necessarily the case.[63] Jones claims that

> Organisational politics as the 'darker side' is indeed part of the story in some organisations. But acknowledging this does not then require us to hold a narrow view of politics which consigns notions of trust and sensitivity to others and negotiated collaboration to that nice-but-naive category.[64]

Kakabadse also believes that politics is not all bad. Politics, in his opinion, is nothing more than getting done what you want done, preferably with the full permission and approval of others around you.

There is some controversy surrounding the 'lighter' and 'darker' aspects of OP. Some authors make a pragmatic case for the benefits of understanding and using OP to bring about organisational change.[65] Others argue that the use of such tactics and behaviours might be considered ethically unacceptable. Kumar and Thibodeaux suggest that to neglect the politics of organisations would be to deny reality. Although they do not make an exclusive argument for ends justifying the means they state that organisational politics is an organisational reality, and ensuring success of a change program may occasionally require tactical confrontation with this reality.[66]

Political diagnosis of organisations

To be complete, political diagnosis should attend to all levels of analysis: micro, intermediate, and macro. At the micro and intermediate levels we are concerned with individuals and coalitions. These are the politically active players who might influence the consultation process. Concern centres on how much power these individuals have and how they might use it. In contrast, at the macro level it is the context in which the actors are operating that is of interest. Cobb has identified a list of techniques that might be used to diagnose the organisation at each of these levels.

It is beyond the scope of the current chapter to provide a detailed exposition of all of these techniques. However, a brief synopsis of some techniques that might be employed to understand the individual level of the political context is given in order to provide an insight to the practicalities of political diagnosis.

Micro-level analysis of OP

There are two major objectives at this level: first, to identify individuals of political interest and, secondly, to assess those individuals' power and political skills.

Identifying powerful individuals There are three techniques: positional, reputational and decision analysis. Positional analysis focuses on an individual's formal power position in an organisation. The assumptions behind this approach are that powerful people occupy positions of power, and that these individuals will be most concerned with issues that directly impinge on their operations. These two assumptions may be challenged but are generally supported in the literature.[67] Methodologically the formal organisational chart is the diagnostic tool. In addition, consultants should account for: external contacts; informal contacts which cluster around the lines of workflow; and any new positions that might be created by the intervention.

Reputational analysis is a technique used to identify powerful individuals by assessing political reputation. The approach is to question people who are shown to be associated by the positional analysis. This can reach beyond the formal organisational chart and may assess the relative power of the players. The major drawback is that the data will be subjective.

The final approach used to identify powerful individuals is decision analysis. This is based on the observation that political players seek access to organisational decision-making. Therefore the approach is to seek out those people who have influenced decisions in the past. This relies less heavily on subjective data than does reputational analysis.

Cobb recommends that these techniques should be used to complement one another, because each has its own strengths and weaknesses.

Assessment of an individual's power and political skills An individual's power base may comprise a wide range of resources. The best-known classification is that provided by French and Raven.[68] Power is often derived from control over resources. Organisational intervention may affect the strategic importance of resources. Some individuals will therefore have a vested interest in resisting change. Consultants need to consider the

- individual's discretion over resources
- centrality of resources to the resolution of the issue
- centrality of the resources to the operations of the organisation
- substitutability of the resources
- resource range ie how applicable the resources are to different situations.

Baddeley and James have provided a useful framework for understanding political behaviour (see Figure 5.3).[69] They postulate two dimensions that influence political behaviour:

1 awareness and understanding of the organisation ie the individual's ability to 'read' the organisational world
2 the individual's awareness of being predisposed to behave in certain ways ie understanding what he or she carries into a situation.

To understand the organisation, the individual needs a knowledge of how it works – its processes and systems. It is important to have an understanding of the power bases *and* informal systems. Inability to read between the lines of the formal organisational chart will leave the individual organisationally illiterate.

The second dimension is concerned with the orientation of behaviour. At one end of the dimension, personal needs are of prime importance: they shape action with little concern for other people's needs and, as such, behaviour is self-oriented. At the other end, individuals are aware of organisational and their own personal needs. The issue is how to achieve

Figure 5.3
READING POLITICAL SITUATIONS*

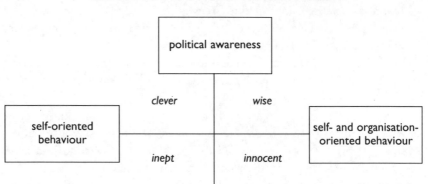

* *Source:* Baddeley S. and James K., 'Political management: developing the management portfolio', *Journal of Management Development*, Vol. 9(3), 1990, pp42–59.

organisational purposes without compromising personal needs. Each of the quadrants in Figure 5.3 presents behaviours – clever, inept, wise, or innocent, depending on the person's capacity to read the situation and their propensity either to play political games or to act with integrity. An understanding of such political styles will give the consultant greater insight into the motivations of political players. Tyson and Jackson also suggest that teaching people appropriate behaviours in business schools will in the future centre on helping them to understand and interpret organisational life and so become politically aware.[70] If we can encourage students to act with integrity, they will possibly act wisely.

The requirement for the future is to develop a map of the political territory of organisations that, to date, remains largely uncharted. The results of research in organisational behaviour will contribute to our understanding of the political landscape, which should facilitate effective intervention. Ensuring the success of OB interventions will require tactical confrontation with the reality of organisational politics.

Conclusions

Widely documented employment trends show that there are fewer full-time, permanently employed people at work, with companies dramatically downsizing, de-layering and, most significant of all, outsourcing. This will increasingly mean more contract workers, part-time employees, and individuals selling their services to organisations on a short-term basis. How this will be managed will be of critical importance over the next decade. Although contract working gives companies greater flexibility in the short term, it is unlikely to produce long-term benefits if contract workers are treated as resources to be brought in and displaced as the company requires them. This represents a backwards step towards the principles of scientific management, which equates motivation and commitment with financial reward. This short-term reliance on contract workers will not engender the adaptability, creativity, multiskilling, and willingness to take responsibility in employees that are prerequisites for success in an increasingly competitive market.

Our major concern has been to identify issues neglected since the introduction of the hard model of HRM. In the drive for competitive advantage companies have become 'lean and mean'. This meanness will not sustain the competitive advantage that will be needed for the future. To meet the commercial challenge of the future it is vital that companies build healthy and diverse workforces. OB has the potential to promote a better understanding of why people think and act as they do. This understanding may be used to help human resource managers to create empowered cultures which make full use of human resources. The notion that we must return some of the humanity to human resources is embodied in the words of John Ruskin, who wrote in 1851 that

> in order that people may be happy in their work, these three things are needed: they must be fit for it; they must not do too much of it; and they must have a sense of success in it.

End-notes

1   STOREY, J, *Human Resource Management: A critical text*, London, Routledge, 1995.

2   LEGGE, K, 'HRM: rhetoric, reality and hidden agendas', in J. Storey, *Human Resource Management: A critical text*, London, Routledge, 1995.

3   STOREY, J, 'Developments in the management of human resources: an interim report', *Warwick Papers in Industrial Relations*, No.17, IRRU, School of Industrial and Business Studies, November 1987.

4   GUEST, D, E, 'Human resource management and industrial relations', *Journal of Management Studies*, 24 (5), 1987, 503–21.

5   STOREY, J, (1994), *op. cit.*

6 MOLANDER, C, AND WINTERTON, J, *Managing Human Resources*, London, Routledge, 1994.

7 LUTHANS, F, *Organizational Behaviour*, 6th edn, Singapore, McGraw-Hill, 1992.

8 HOLLOWAY, W, *Work Psychology and Organizational Behaviour: Managing the individual at work*, London, Sage, 1991.

9 TAYLOR, F, W, *The Principles of Scientific Management*, New York, Norton, 1911.

10 TYSON, S, AND JACKSON, T, *The Essence of Organizational Behaviour*, Hemel Hempstead, Prentice Hall, 1992.

11 SHIMMIN, S, AND WALLIS, D, 'Change and survival in occupational psychology', Paper presented at the 4th West European Congress on the Psychology of Work and Organisation, Cambridge, 1989, 10–12 April.

12 JOHNS, G, 'Constraints on the adoption of psychology-based personnel practices: lessons from organizational innovation', *Personnel Psychology*, 46, 1993, 569–92.

13 SCHEIN, V, E, 'Individual power and political behaviour in organisations', *Academy of Management Review*, 2, 1977, 64–72.

14 KANTER, R, M, *When Giants Learn to Dance*, London, Simon & Schuster, 1989.

15 LUTHANS, F, 1992, *op. cit.*

16 BRITISH PSYCHOLOGICAL SOCIETY, *The Future of the Psychological Science: Horizons and opportunities for British psychology*, Leicester, BPS, 1989.

17 LAZARUS, R, S, *Psychological Stress and Coping Process*, New York, McGraw-Hill, 1966.

18 COOPER, C, L, COOPER, R, D, AND EAKER, L, H, *Living with Stress*, London, Penguin Books, 1988.

19 KANTER, R, M, 1989, *op. cit.*

20 MCKENNA, E, *Psychology in Business: Theory and applications*, London, Lawrence Erlbaum, 1987.

21 QUICK, J, C, AND QUICK, J, D, *Organizational Stress and Preventive Management*, New York, McGraw-Hill, 1979.

22 LUBIN, J, S, 'On-the-job stress leads many workers to file, and win, compensation awards', *Wall Street Journal*, 1980, 17 September.

23 BERRIDGE, J, R, AND COOPER, C, L, 'The employee assistance programme: its role in organizational coping and excellence, *Personnel Review*, 23 (7), 1994, 4–20.

24 ROMAN, P, M, AND BLUM, T, C, 'The core technologies of employee assistance', *The Alamacan*, 15 (3), 1985, 8–12.

25 MURPHY, L, R, 'Workplace interventions for stress reduction and prevention', in C. L. Cooper and R. Payne (eds), *Causes, Coping and Consequences of Stress at Work*, Chichester, John Wiley, 1988.

26 ELKIN, A, J, AND ROSCH, P, J, 'Promoting mental health at the work place: prevention on the side of stress management', *Occupational Medicine: State of the Art Review*, 5 (4), 1990, 739–54.

27 KARASEK, R, 'Control in the workplace and its health-related aspects', in L. Sauter, J. J. Hurrell and C. L. Cooper (eds), *Job Control & Worker Health*, Chichester, John Wiley, 1989.

28 CARTWRIGHT, S, AND COOPER, C, L, 'Coping in occupational settings', in M. Zeidner and N. Endler (eds), *Handbook of Coping*, 1994.

29 COOPER, C, L, SLOAN, S, AND WILLIAMS, S, *Occupational Stress Indicator: The manual*, Windsor, NFER Nelson, 1988.

30 KANTER, R, M, 1989, *op. cit.*

31 HANSARD SOCIETY, *Women at the Top*, London, L.A. Publishing Services, 1990.

32 BRUEGEL, I, 'Sex and race in the labour market', *Feminist Review*, 32, 1989, 49–68.

33 METCALF, H, AND LEIGHTON, P, *The underutilisation of women in the labour market*, IMS Report 172, University of Sussex, Institute of Manpower Studies, 1989.

34 BLUM, L, AND SMITH, V, 'Women's mobility in the corporation: a critique of the politics of optimism', *Journal of Women in Culture and Society*, 13 (31), 1988, 528–45.

35 AITKENHEAD, M, AND LIFF, S, 'The effectiveness of equal opportunities policy', in J. Firth Cozens and M. A. West (eds), *Women at Work*, Bristol, Open University Press, 1991.

36 CMPS AUDITS, *Commissioned research on barriers to women staff in public-sector organisations*, Stockport, Corporate Management and Policy Service, 1992–3.

37 HOLLOWAY, W, 1991, *op. cit.*

38 DAVIDSON, M, J, AND BURKE, R, J, *Women in Management: Current research issues*, London, Paul Chapman, 1994.

39 RUBIN, B, L, 'Europeans value diversity', *HR Magazine*, 78, 1991, 38–41.

40 COX, T, H, AND BLAKE, S, 'Managing cultural diversity: implications for organizational competitiveness', *Academy of Management Executive*, August, 1991, 47.

41 SCHEIN, V, E, 1977, *op. cit.*

42 HOLLOWAY, W, 1991, *op. cit.*

43 ALIMO-METCALFE, B, 'Gender bias in selection and assessment of women in management', in M. J. Davidson and R. J. Burke, 1994, *op. cit.*

44 HAMMOND, V, 'Opportunity 2000: good practice in UK organisations', in M. J. Davidson and R. J. Burke, 1994, *op. cit.*

45 KANDOLA, R, 'The challenge of managing cultural diversity', Address to the British Psychological Society, Occupational Conference, 1994, Jan 3–5.

46 KANDOLA, R, AND FULLERTON, J, *Managing the Mosaic: Diversity in action*, London, IPD, 1994.

47 MARSHALL, J, 'Feminist revisioning of careers', In D. T. Hall & Asssociates, *Handbook of Career Development*, Hove, Erlbaum, 1989.

48 KANDOLA, R, AND FULLERTON, J, 1994, *op. cit.*

49 TAJFEL, H, 'Experiments in intergroup discrimination', *Scientific American*, 223, 1970, 96–102.

50 THOMAS, D, A, 'From affirmative action to affirming diversity', *Harvard Business Review*, March–April, 1990, 107–17.

51 HALL, D, T, AND PARKER, V, A, 'The role of workplace flexibility in managing diversity', *Organisational Dynamics*, 22, (1), 1993, 4–18.

52 LARWOOD, L, AND GATTIKER, U, E, 'A comparison of the career paths used by successful women and men', in B. A. Gutek and L. Larwood (eds), *Women's Career Development*, Beverly Hills, CA, Sage, 1986.

53 KANDOLA, R, 1994, *op. cit.*

54 BENNIS, W, G, 'Unresolved problems facing organisational development', *Business Quarterly*, 34 (4), 1969, 80–84.

55 KUMAR, K, AND THIBODEAUX, M, S, 'Organizational politics and planned organizational change,' *Group and Organization Studies*, 15, (4), 1990, 357–65.

56 JOHNS, G, 1993, *op. cit.*

57 MILES, R, H, *Macro Organizational Behaviour*, Santa Monica, CA, Goodyear, 1980.

58 DRORY, A, AND ROMM, T, 'The definition of organizational politics: a

review', *Human Relations*, 43 (11), 1990, 1133–54.

59 SCHEIN, V, E, 1977, *op. cit.*

60 KAKABADSE, A, K, *The Politics of Management*, London, Gower, 1986.

61 HAYES, J, 'The politically competent manager', *Journal of General Management*, 10 (1), 1984, 24–33.

62 DERR, C, B, *Managing the New Careerist*, San Francisco, CA, Jossey-Bass, 1986.

63 ARROBA, T, AND JAMES, K, 'Are politics palatable to women managers? How can women make wise moves at work?' *Women in Management Review*, 10 (3), 1987, 123–30.

64 JONES, S. 'Organisational politics . . . only the darker side?' *Management Education and Development*, 18 (2), 1987, 116–28.

65 COBB, A, T, 'Political diagnosis: applications in organisational development', *Academy of Management Review*, 11 (3), 1986, 482–96.

66 KUMAR, K, AND THIBODEAUX, M, S, 1990, *op. cit.*

67 COBB, A, T, 1986, *op. cit.*

68 FRENCH, J, R, P, AND RAVEN, B, 'The bases of social power', in D. Cartwright (ed.), *Studies of Social Power*, Ann Arbor, MI, University of Michigan, 1959.

69 BADDELEY, S, AND JAMES, K, 'Political management: developing the management portfolio', *Journal of Management Development*, 9 (3), 1990, 42–59.

70 TYSON, S, AND JACKSON, T, 1992, *op. cit.*

CHAPTER SIX

Leadership in Times of Change

Andrew Kakabadse,
Lola Okazaki-Ward and Andrew Myers

In order to demonstrate the significant issues in leadership this chapter discusses a major research project that compares leadership amongst Japanese and European managers: a Cranfield Comparative Study of Top Japanese/European Managers. Unlike the other chapters in this book, the intention here is to discuss the results of one major study and use them to reveal what the key leadership issues are. 'Leadership' itself, it is argued, will continue to be seen as the critical dimension within management. This being so, questions concerning management development evolve into issues of performance based on relationships within management teams, styles of leadership, and how managers seek to affect performance. As organisations change, and as their operations become more international, the complexities of understanding management development in context increase considerably. This illustration of Japanese management development issues counterposed to those of European managers seeks to unravel the threads that constitute this complexity. (The survey was carried out with the co-operation of Masamichi Shimizu, chief researcher at the Japan Management Association in Tokyo.)

The background

In a lecture to the Royal Society of Arts in London Dr Kiichi Mochizuki, chairman of the Pacific Institute, drew a distinction between different forms of organisation. An obvious world influence is the Anglo-American organisation, stressing private stock ownership and based on concepts such as cost management maximising revenue streams and especially profit. It is oriented more towards short-term gains and characterised by top-down decision-making. As a contrast Mochizuki highlighted the Japanese organisation, which is more strongly influenced by social considerations. This type of organisation is driven by a management displaying a strong humanistic ethic. Its outlook is typically long-term, with an emphasis on employees, and is managed on a consensual philosophy. Shareholders have far less impact in the strategic direction of the organisation than do the management. The third type of organisation, considered by Mochizuki to fall somewhere in between, he loosely calls the European organisation.

Evidence from the Cranfield European Executive Competencies Study suggests however that these three forms of organisation do not fall into anything like such clear-cut regional distinctions. The socially concerned Japanese organisation is repeated across a number of European organisations, for example. The study highlights the fact that 50 per cent of Swedish, 48 per cent of Finnish, 26 per cent of Irish, 21 per cent of Spanish, 18 per cent of British, 11 per cent of Austrian, and 10 per cent of German companies are driven by considerations of community and a consensus approach to decision-making, as well as by business concepts such as revenue streams and profit. Equally, the strong leadership style characteristic of profit-driven Anglo-American corporations is found in 73 per cent of Spanish, 72 per cent of British, 62 per cent of Irish, 44 per cent of Finnish, 31 per cent of Swedish, 17 per cent of French, 9 per cent of Austrian, and 6 per cent of German companies.

What is just as evident from the survey is that the distinction between profit-motive-driven organisations and social-care-driven enterprises is being substantially eroded. The profit motive/share-ownership organisation is being considerably influenced by social and environmental rights movements. Pressure groups representing employees have been around for a long time. However, the last two decades have witnessed the emergence of powerful lobbyists representing environmental issues, civil rights concerns, ethical considerations, and even institutional shareholders have been pursuing their own 'political' agendas. A separate study at Cranfield highlights the fact that ethical considerations in decision-making have indeed reached such proportions in terms of influencing boardroom behaviour that detailed codes of ethics are commonplace in mid- to large-sized corporate organisations. US and non-US-based, shareholder-value-driven organisations face substantial problems and dilemmas in promoting and implementing codes of ethics at local country level, irrespective of whether the parent company is US or not.

Equally the 'employee first' policy of the consensual organisation has run into difficulty not only in Japan but also in the European countries mentioned above, notably Sweden. Specifically in Japan, corporations traditionally relied on bank borrowing for investment, and shareholders were mainly other companies content to make little demand in terms of return on their shares. Under conditions of continuous growth long-term investment was influenced by interest rate levels, with the banks heavily involved in the management of the corporation and in supporting its growth. Under such conditions policies of long-term employment were pursued, with the result that stability prevailed. However, with the bursting of the economic-growth bubble in the early 1990s, which left the banks with substantial bad debts and brought swift rises in interest rates, the number of Japanese firms raising cheaper capital from capital markets increased, expanding the body of private shareholders conscious of short-term profitability. Maintaining such a substantial fixed cost as people in a situation of overcapacity and continuous decline of profits has come severely into question. Also evident now is the long-standing concern over white-collar productivity, a problem that until recently has been pushed into the background.

Under similar conditions a rebellion against long-term employment has been growing in a number of European countries, especially Sweden. What has become crystal clear is that when the ethic of *work is social* dominates the fabric of the organisation then the corporation deteriorates into an inward-looking society concerned with the welfare of its members, most of whom are ready to sacrifice external gains for the preservation of a comfortable internal *status quo*. Has not tunnel vision and the rebuttal of unwelcome points of view been one of the causes of IBM's downfall? Diligence to task-related activity coupled with little shared dialogue about future prospects determined IBM's distinctive but inward-looking culture. For Japanese corporations the spate of law suits brought by shareholders under the recently reformed Commercial Code highlights an unwillingness to tolerate a system that at policy and strategic decision-making levels is driven by company insiders negatively disposed to the views (especially if controversial) of outsiders.

It is asserted that the twin forces of ethical consciousness and more short-term, shareholder-value-driven profitability are likely to change substantially both profit-conscious corporations and socially concerned organisations, with little likelihood of their returning to their familiar forms. In fact it is postulated that the organisation of the future will be concerned with promoting *stakeholder value*, of which employees and shareholders are just two of a number of stakeholder influences, all of whom can vary the impact they have on an organisation according to the agenda(s) driving the key players at the time. This idea is endorsed in the Keizai Doyukai's

(Japan Association of Corporate Executives) statement of January 1994 entitled *Japanese Management for the 21st Century — Establishment of Corporate Selfhood and Creative Management* as the future shape of organisations in Japan.

The dynamism of a stakeholder-driven organisation is likely to exceed either of the two previous forms because management will need to be responsive to external masters whose demands, for good reason, may not appear as coherent or consistent as before. Different stakeholders will have different needs and require different outcomes from the organisation, leaving management to reconcile seemingly irreconcilable demands. Whatever management may feel are the rights and wrongs of such a case, the likelihood of stakeholder-value-driven organisations emerging in force throughout the world is high. A well-informed public, a growing and educated élite, an ever-expanding professional and mobile female workforce, and shareholder demands for more concrete gains for their investment, will all require particular qualities of leadership. Such considerations provide the stimulus for this study.

Leadership

Born out of concern that changing economic conditions and the emergence of new institutional forms are set to challenge present practices of leadership, the Top Executives Competency Surveys were initiated at the Cranfield School of Management. In pursuing an examination of top management performance, particular attention was paid to working within a theoretical framework that would capture the reality of the demands made on managers.

Most studies of top managers have tended to fall into one of two categories: those that focus on examining the attributes of individuals in terms of behavioural, attitudinal, or deeper personality dimensions, and those that are driven by job, role, or organisational type criteria. The original and insightful work of Professor Elliot Jaques, who in the 1950s examined different cultures within the workplace, provides the conceptual bridge between individual behaviours and role requirements. Crucial to the work of Jaques is the concept of *discretion*. The discretionary element of role refers to the choices the incumbent needs to make in order to provide shape and identity to their role and to that part of the organisation for which the incumbent is accountable. The contrast to the discretionary element of role is the *prescriptive* side, namely the structured part, which is predetermined and which drives the individual's behaviour. In effect, the prescriptive part of a manager's job is that part over which the manager has little choice other than to undertake the duties required of him or her.

Professor Paul Evans of the International Business School of INSEAD (Paris) draws a similar distinction when he refers to the manager's job as a split between the leadership elements (discretionary) and the management elements (prescriptive). Such a distinction is particularly pertinent, because providing leadership for stakeholder value is likely to make considerable demands on the discretionary elements of a senior manager's role. The individual manager will need to make choices between unclear alternatives and also need to devote considerable attention to nurturing key interfaces with influential internal and external stakeholders in order to ascertain their commitment to a meaningful way forward.

What choices are made and how commitment is negotiated highlights the impact that the stakeholders have on the organisation, as well as the capabilities of senior managers to respond effectively to such challenges. There is no reason to assume that even if the capacity of top management in the organisation is considerable, each of the members of the senior executive would form similar conclusions as to the shape, size, direction, and desired qualities of the total organisation and thereby the shape and cost of each of the key functions/divisions/business units in it. Hence, senior managers, who share the same challenges to address may form different views as to the configuration of their organisation and how it should be led. Exploring each senior manager's beliefs concerning what to lead, how to lead, and when to lead, highlights a key question: to what extent do senior managers share their views and concerns with one another?

On this basis, high-quality dialogue amongst the members of the senior executive is fundamental to effective leadership of an organisation. The preliminary results of interviews and case-study analyses examining the behaviours and capacities of senior managers both in Japan and Europe indicate that where the quality of dialogue is high and the relationships amongst senior managers are positive the issues and concerns facing the organisation are likely to be more openly addressed. Where, however, relationships are tense and the quality of dialogue restricted, certain issues and problems tend not to be raised, because to do so would generate unacceptable levels of discomfort amongst certain or all of the members of the senior executive. In effect, such discomfort would be experienced as too unwelcome to face up to the problems confronting the organisation. Ironically, the case-studies reveal that unless the top team is working reasonably effectively then issues that need to be addressed are not: in other words senior management knowingly allows the organisation to deteriorate because they feel too uncomfortable to discuss and attend to the key issues and challenges facing them.

The Cranfield Comparative Study

The study concentrates on examining the relationship between individual attributes, role and organisational requirements, and the quality of dialogue amongst senior Japanese managers. Comparison is made between the Japanese respondents and the respondents in surveys conducted in eight European countries: Britain, France, Germany, Sweden, Spain, Ireland, Austria, and Finland. Preliminary interviews and case-study analyses conducted in Britain, Ireland, France, Sweden, Greece, Austria, Germany, and Spain, as well as in Japanese firms located in the UK, significantly influenced the design and content of the Cranfield Executive Competencies Questionnaire. The questionnaire attempts to capture elements of national and organisational culture, and key attitudes and behaviours displayed by managers in doing their job. The structure of the questionnaire allows comparisons to be made between different groups of respondents. Back translations and further screening were employed to assure consistency in interpretation. Hence, in examining the exercise of discretion, individual preferences, strategic intent, and cultural considerations are encompassed in the design of the study.

Through the support and co-operation given by our partner, the Japan Management Association (JMA), questionnaires were distributed and collected in Japan. The opinion of the researchers is that the quality of the results can be directly attributed to the fact that the senior managers who returned the completed instruments were able to do so in privacy and anonymously. A total of 701 top Japanese managers completed the questionnaire in the JMA survey over the spring and summer of 1994. Over 2,500 European respondents also returned completed questionnaires.

The survey data from the Japanese study has already been analysed, interpreted and published as an outline report in Japanese by the research partner, the JMA. We therefore keep mention of the Japanese-only data to a minimum, concentrating on the comparative analysis of the Japanese survey with that in Europe. Five key areas of exploration are reported:

- *issues of demography* ie age of incumbents, levels of educational background, areas of responsibility, number of years in present job and organisation, and seniority of role
- *quality of dialogue* amongst members of the senior executive ie the extent to which 'sensitivities' within the senior group inhibit discussion of key business concerns affecting the current and future performance of the organisation. Further examination concentrates on how that, in turn, is likely to affect the extent to which members of the senior executive

hold a shared view on both the future direction of the organisation and on the issues to address in order to promote its well-being. 'Sensitivities' refer to issues perceived by group members as difficult to discuss (bearing in mind the different views and positions adopted by individual members) and which affect their relationship and may in turn negatively influence the openness of their conversation.

■ *managerial behaviour and leadership styles* adopted by different levels of Japanese manager, exploring whether the demands of different roles influence the attitudes and behaviours of managers and whether this in turn affects the performance of the organisation both within Japan and on an expatriate basis

■ *organisational performance factors* that are likely to arise and their effect on the organisation eg if members of the senior executive exhibit poor-quality dialogue and lack a shared vision of the future and/or the manner in which the organisation is to be enhanced

■ *leadership implications for Japanese managers* arising from the results of the survey.

Comparisons are made throughout between the Japanese and European respondents. Cluster, regression, and correlation analyses were utilised to explore the relationship between certain of these characteristics. Finally, recommendations are given on the development needs of senior Japanese managers both as a way of illustrating how management development itself requires research, and as a way of showing what the organisations' systems will themselves require in the development process.

Issues of demography

Data concerning role seniority, age, areas of responsibility, educational background, years in present job, and years in present organisation, is provided.

As for role seniority, the respondents are classed into 10 levels; their positions are given in Table 6.1.

Positions 1 to 6 in Table 6.1 comprise members of the board and account for 90.9 per cent of the total. Within that, the chairman/president group account for 24.6 per cent, the vice-president/senior managing director group 14.1 per cent, and the executive director/director 52.2 per cent. Positions 1 to 4, in groups of 6 or fewer people, typically comprise the members of the *jômukai* (executive board), who meet once a week with the avowed purpose of keeping in close contact with one another and driving the strategic agenda. A recent survey by Tôyô Shinpôsha revealed that the average number of directors on the directors' board of the Japanese company listed

Table 6.1
POSITION OF RESPONDENTS

	Position	Number	%
1	Owner of the business, chairman, vice-chairman	27	3.6
2	CEO, president	160	21.0
3	Vice-president	30	3.9
4	Senior managing director	78	10.2
5	Executive director	168	22.1
6	Director of the board	229	30.1
7	Auditor	12	1.6
8	Senior advisor	4	0.5
9	Non-board director	5	0.7
10	General manager, divisional manager	33	4.3
	No response	15	1.8

on the first section of the Tokyo Stock Exchange in 1994 was 15.5 persons. It is also understood that the majority of the members of the directors' board in the large companies have come through the internal promotional route. Auditors are formally not on the board of directors, though they are legally appointed (mostly from among the retired company members) to ensure that the way the company is run is in complete accordance with the 1983 Commercial and Company Code of Japan. The recent reform of the Company Code imposed the appointment of an external auditor to ensure that the function of auditor is strengthened. The senior advisor is an ex-member of the board, often an ex-chairman. Non-board directors and general managers are the senior middle management, but the former do not usually have line management responsibility.

Of the total in Table 6.2 almost 88 per cent are aged 51 or above, and 24.7 per cent are aged 61 or over. Only 11.7 per cent are aged 50 or below.

The 41 per cent of the respondents in Table 6.3 accountable for the total

Table 6.2
AGE OF RESPONDENTS

Age	Number	%
Up to 40	7	0.9
41–45	29	3.8
46–50	53	7.0
51–55	187	24.6
56–60	294	38.6
61–65	149	19.8
65 and over	39	5.1
No response	3	0.4

company match almost exactly the proportion of the sample population in levels one to four. These are members of the executive committee, and are

Table 6.3
AREAS OF RESPONSIBILITY

Responsibility	Number	%
Total company	312	41.0
Number of divisions/departments	211	27.7
Single major division/department	175	23.0
Other combinations	50	6.6
No response	9	1.2

responsible for the total company business. Executive directors are usually responsible for two or more departments, whereas the responsibility for a major division/department usually falls on the director.

Of the total in Table 6.4 only 8.6 per cent hold secondary education qualifications. Those who have undertaken undergraduate and HND equivalent programmes account for 82.1 per cent of the total, and a further 9.1 per cent have postgraduate degrees. Also 10.1 per cent have recognised professional qualifications.

A comparison of educational attainment with managers in the European

Table 6.4
EDUCATIONAL BACKGROUND

Qualification	Number	%
O-level equivalent	4	0.5
A-level equivalent	62	8.1
HND	26	3.4
BA, B.Sc.	599	78.7
MA, M.Sc.	38	5.0
MBA	8	1.1
Ph.D.	23	3.0
Professional qualification	135	10.1
No public qualification	476	62.5

study has proved to be difficult because of the different systems in each of the countries: the only reliable way is to compare qualifications beyond A level or its equivalent. On this basis, the Japanese respondents with post-A level qualifications account for 91 per cent, whereas the figures for the UK, Germany, and France are 59 per cent, 64 per cent, and 86 per cent respectively. Yet at postgraduate level the figures reveal a different story:

9 per cent of Japanese, 22 per cent of UK, 26 per cent of German, and 42 per cent of French respondents have postgraduate qualifications. Two-thirds of the sample in Table 6.5 (68.9 per cent) have been in their current post for four years or less, with those who have been in the post for three to four years accounting for the largest number. Almost half of the respondents have been in the present job between one and four years. Just over 10 per cent have been in the current post for more than 10 years and, of

Table 6.5
NUMBER OF YEARS IN JOB

Period	Number	%
< 6 months	35	4.6
6–11 months	112	14.7
1–2 years	179	23.5
3–4 years	199	26.1
5–6 years	86	11.3
7–8	52	6.8
9–10	13	1.7
> 10 years	77	10.1
No response	8	1.1

these, chairmen and presidents predominate. Within Europe, most respondents for most countries have been in their job for either one to four years or for five to ten years.

It usually takes 28 years or more for one to become a board director in most large companies where 'lifetime' employment is the norm. The fact that in this survey nearly half of the respondents have been in their com-

Table 6.6
NUMBER OF YEARS IN THE COMPANY

Period	Number	%
< 6 months	3	0.4
7–11 months	22	2.9
1–2 years	35	4.6
3–4 years	72	9.5
5–6 years	53	7.0
7–8 years	36	4.7
9–10 years	26	3.4
11–15 years	43	5.7
16–20 years	45	5.9
21–25 years	67	8.8
26 years or more	365	46.8
No response	3	0.4

panies for more than 26 years is not surprising. However, it is striking to find that 24 per cent of the respondents had been with their company for six years or less, particularly given that 88 per cent of the sample are aged 51 and over. One explanation could be that many of these respondents had recently been transferred to their current company from the parent company, or appointed from outside, for example from the government ministry, the main bank, or other companies in the same *keiretsu* (group of companies).

The largest group for France and Austria were those who had been with the company for four years or less, accounting for 33 per cent and 28 per cent respectively. By contrast, in Britain, Ireland, Germany, and Finland the largest group were those who had been with the company for 11–15 years, comprising 28 per cent, 39 per cent, 31 per cent, and 38 per cent respectively. In the case of Japan, Sweden, and Spain the largest group were those who had been with the company for 21 or more years, accounting for 56 per cent, 29 per cent, and 27 per cent respectively. The proportion of Japanese respondents who had been with their company for 21 years or more (56 per cent) was exceptionally large, and can be attributed to the 'lifetime' employment system and seniority-related promotion.

Quality of dialogue

Comparisons were drawn between the Japanese respondents and 2,514 European respondents representing eight European countries. In the research there is an exploration of differences of view that may exist concerning the future direction of the organisation; those sensitive issues (if any) that the respondents consider merit, but do not receive, attention at top management levels; and differences of view that may exist between top managers and their general managers at lower levels concerning key aspects of managerial behaviour.

Future direction In terms of strategic intent, one key question is asked: 'Do the members of the senior executive (presidents, chief executive officers, managing directors, executive directors, general managers) hold different views as to the future direction of the company?' (See Table 6.7.)

Table 6.7 shows that 23 per cent of Japanese respondents indicate that differences of view exist at senior management levels concerning the shape of the organisation and the future pathways it should pursue. The Irish highlight greatest differences of view, with 48 per cent of respondents indicating diversity of perception at senior management levels concerning the strategies the organisation should pursue. The Swedish respondents

Table 6.7
FUNDAMENTALLY DIFFERENT VIEWS ON COMPANY DIRECTION (%)

	Japan	UK	France	Ireland	Germany	Sweden	Spain	Austria	Finland
Yes	23	30	39	48	32	20	40	31	25

highlight the least degree of differences of view on strategic direction at senior management levels (20 per cent).

Addressing sensitivities In terms of issues requiring resolution at senior management levels, one question was asked: 'Are there issues or "sensitivities" that merit, but do not receive, attention in the top team?' (See Table 6.8.)

The Japanese respondents reveal the greatest number of concerns, with 77 per cent of the sample stating that important but unattended issues predominate at senior management levels. The Irish sample rate the second highest score with 68 per cent, closely followed by the Austrians and Spanish. The British, Finnish, and French identify the least number of sensitive issues.

However, even with the French, for whom 36 per cent of respondents

Table 6.8
SENSITIVITIES THAT MERIT BUT DO NOT RECEIVE ATTENTION IN TOP TEAM (%)

	Japan	UK	France	Ireland	Germany	Sweden	Spain	Austria	Finland
Yes	77	47	36	68	61	50	63	67	49

identify outstanding issues remaining unaddressed at senior levels in the organisation, the results highlight the strain senior managers are likely to experience in responding positively to difficult challenges. Hence, the nature and quality of the behaviour that senior managers adopt in order to implement their intentions and decisions require examination.

Managerial behaviour

Six aspects of senior manager behaviour were explored: approachability, addressing sensitivities, being understanding, trust, commitment to decision implementation, and the long-term/short-term orientation of management.

A distinction was made between the responses of presidents, chairmen, chief executive officers, managing directors, executive directors and those holding general manager (GM) positions. The aim was to identify whether compatibility of view exists between top-level managers and the general managers below them concerning the behaviour and effectiveness of the top team. Overall, the Japanese respondents provided the greatest compatibility of view.

Similar responses across all of the country respondents emerged from the question, 'Are the members of the top team easy to talk to?' Only the Irish and German GMs considered their senior managers less approachable than those senior managers would consider themselves.

Substantial differences of response across all the country respondents emerged however from the question, 'Do the members of the top team openly discuss sensitive issues?' For example, 69 per cent of Japanese top managers considered they openly address sensitive issues, whereas 47 per cent of Japanese GMs considered that the top team tended to address safe issues. The Irish and Spanish responses veered more towards the negative: 52 per cent and 44 per cent respectively of top managers considered they addressed sensitivities openly whereas 60 per cent and 61 per cent respectively of their GMs considered that safe issues were discussed. In contrast, and on the more positive side, 68 per cent of top German senior managers considered they openly discussed sensitive issues, and 63 per cent of their GMs agreed that was so.

Regarding the issue of understanding, Japan was the only country where the views of both the top managers and GMs were positive and supportive. In contrast, the percentage of GMs in the UK, Ireland, Germany, and Spain who considered that their top managers do not understand one another was higher than that of top managers who considered they had a good understanding of one another. In France, Sweden, and Austria the percentage of top managers who considered that they understood one another was higher than that of their GMs who thought that their top managers lacked understanding of one another.

On the issue of trust, the Japanese responses reveal similar levels of compatibility to those of the Swedes. For both samples the top managers indicated that the levels of trust amongst the members of the top team was high, an opinion shared by their GMs. The greatest level of incompatibility of response arose from the Irish, UK, and German samples: 67 per cent, 68 per cent and 69 per cent respectively of their GMs considered that the behaviour of their bosses indicated low levels of trust amongst the members of the senior executive.

Equally, compatibility of scores from the Japanese respondents emerged in response to the question, 'Do the members of the top team implement decisions made jointly in the top team?' The result was that 89 per cent of the top management group indicated they did, and 76 per cent of their GMs agreed. A contrast of scores between the top management group and the GM sample is identified by the UK, Irish, and Austrian respondents. The Irish respondents provided the greatest contrast, with 91 per cent of top management indicating that decisions made jointly in the top team were implemented, whereas 50 per cent of their GMs considered that senior managers implemented only those decisions that personally suited the individual, irrespective of whatever had been agreed jointly.

In response to the question, 'Do the members of the top team address long- and short-term issues?', the Japanese respondents provided the most comparable, positively oriented responses: 75 per cent of the respondents in the top management category considered that they addressed both long- and short-term issues, and 62 per cent of the Japanese GM sample agreed. The Spanish respondents emphasised compatible but negatively oriented responses, whereby 61 per cent of top management and 60 per cent of GMs considered that the top team addressed short-term only issues. For the remaining respondents, differences of view were identified between senior managers and the GM group

Leadership styles

Through cluster analysis – using role seniority, length of time in present job, length of time in present organisation, and age of respondents – three distinctly different groups of respondents emerge from the Japanese sample. Subsequent factor analysis of attitudinal and behavioural questions was undertaken within each of the clusters, with distinctly different combinations of attitude and behavioural characteristics emerging between the three groupings. Interestingly, age of respondents is identified as having no significant impact on the clusterings. It is then concluded that the significant determinants of senior managers' attitudes towards jobs, people in the organisation, and the organisation itself are seniority of role, length of time in current job, and length of time in organisation.

In effect, three groups of leaders emerge from the analysis of Japanese organisations. First there are those managers who hold senior office, whose fundamental preoccupation is the discussion of and generation of policy (policy makers). The second group are those managers whose primary concern is the achievement of company objectives and the meeting of targets (business drivers). The third group are those managers whose primary concern is with the implementation of strategy (implementors). Table 6.9

identifies the key demographic characteristics of the three management groups in terms of role seniority, length of time in the organisation, and also in the job.

Table 6.9
DEMOGRAPHICS OF LEADERSHIP

Manager style	Role	Company years	Job years
Policy makers (n=204)	Chairmen, president/CEOs VPs/SMDs	>20 years	>10 years
Business drivers (n=213)	SMDs EDs Directors	<5 years	2–3 years
Implementors (n=285)	Directors GMs	>20 years	<2 years

Key: CEO = chief executive officer   VP   = vice-president
      ED   = executive director   SMD = senior managing director
      GM   = general manager

NB Total = 702. The remaining 59 respondents were not classified, owing to missing data.

Characteristics of policy makers Policy makers are more likely to be currently holding a senior role such as chairman or president, chief executive officer, vice-president, or senior managing director and will have been in the company and held their position for a substantial period of time. In terms of size of the company, policy makers are scattered – 46 per cent work in small- to medium-sized organisations (up to 500 employees), 28 per cent in medium- to large-sized organisations (500 to 2,499 employees), and the remaining 26 per cent work in large-sized organisations (2,500 or more employees). Policy makers are found mainly in manufacturing (57 per cent), the remainder being split into retail (14 per cent) and services (29 per cent).

Characteristics of business drivers Business drivers are people who are more likely to hold senior managing director, executive director, or director roles, and will have been in the same job for about three years on average, and are more likely to have been employed in the same company for a limited period (under five years). Some have been employed for up to 10 years but, in this sample, no longer than that.

In terms of company size business drivers are scattered, like policy makers, although more towards organisations with 2,500 or fewer employees –

48 per cent work in small- to medium-sized organisations (up to 500 employees), 36 per cent in medium-sized organisations (500 to 2,499 employees), and the remaining 16 per cent work in large-sized organisations (2,500 or more employees). This grouping differs from the other two groups in terms of industry sector, there being roughly an even split between manufacturing (44 per cent) and services (46 per cent). The services sector is considered volatile, which could explain why some business drivers have been in the company for a limited period of time. Furthermore, they may have been transferred to their current company from their parent company, and many of them may also be mid-career entrants. The remaining 10 per cent in this category are in the retail sector.

Characteristics of implementors Implementors may occupy a director or GM position, and are more likely to have been in their present job for under two years (certainly no longer than four years) but they will have been employed by the company for a substantial period of time. In effect, implementors are awarded different assignments, but within the same company. In terms of the organisation, 77 per cent work in medium- to large-sized companies (500 or more employees). They are found predominantly in manufacturing (60 per cent), 10 per cent are in retail, and 30 per cent in the services sector.

Style of policy makers Three characteristics emerge through factor analysis which portray the underlying attitudes and styles of management of the policy maker: being disciplined, being focused, and being communicative. Particularly prevalent is the need for being disciplined and focused. The policy maker, in order to promote a well-structured working environment, is identified as procedures-oriented, attentive to details, responsive to rules, and is disciplined. Clarity in terms of ways of working is uppermost in the policy maker's mind, because for him or her effectiveness of performance is enhanced if people are clear as to the accountabilities and responsibilities in their role. The policy maker creates clear job boundaries and promotes clear goals. The focus on structure and order is driven by the belief that success at a personal and organisational level is driven by being disciplined about tasks.

In order to action such values, policy makers exhibit considerable respect for command. The same degree of respect is shown towards the procedures and systems applied in the organisation, because these are considered the fundamentals that hold the organisation together. At a personal level, the policy maker is identified as flexible and positively responsive to people in the organisation.

Policy makers consider themselves satisfied with their work circumstances and stretched in terms of being challenged in the job. Equally, they display high commitment to the organisation. They seem able to combine focus and discipline with a positive inclination to interact effectively with others. One example of effective interpersonal skills is that policy makers are rated by others as listening-oriented. Furthermore, the individual is seen by colleagues as well informed, accepting of others, and approachable.

In terms of overall impact, policy makers are rated high by colleagues in terms of sharing and being co-operative and helpful. Their contribution to the organisation is appreciated, as is the manner with which they address the issues and challenges they face.

Style of business drivers Business drivers are identified as portraying a strong results-orientation to tasks and to the management of the organisation. Motivated by a need for challenge, they are self-directing, independently minded, and capable of taking the more unpleasant decisions. They are identified as robust in responding to strain and pressure. They tend to see issues in black-and-white terms, which is strongly epitomised by the fact that they consider that there is a right and a wrong way to address challenges. Their independence is especially displayed in their dislike of unwelcome intervention, which they would consider interference in the discharge of their responsibilities and a possible undermining of their role.

Self-reliance is coupled with being disciplined and systematic. Business drivers believe that effectiveness of performance can be truly achieved only by being structured and disciplined as a matter of daily practice. The same philosophy is used to promote effectiveness of communication. Business drivers insist on being regularly briefed concerning new and existing initiatives. They also demand ever greater attention to systematic follow-through on decisions made.

The discipline applied to communication is coupled with an attentiveness to the quality of managerial relationships. For business drivers, being effective at communication requires sensitivity to feedback. Making themselves available for comment is central to generating an environment in which staff and management feel comfortable about offering their views as to how improvements in the work environment could be achieved. The vehicle for achieving a more open environment is through teams. Business drivers consider themselves team-oriented, attempting to promote collegiate relationships so as to achieve a high-quality level of dialogue.

Encouraging group cohesion is viewed as a necessary aspect of work-directed behaviour.

Furthermore, for business drivers (as was the case for policy makers), personal satisfaction and openness of relationships are viewed as necessary to achievement. Hence commitment to making the organisation profitable involves the application of task-related skills, clarity of decision-making, and a structured and disciplined approach to undertaking tasks at work, in conjunction with more open, team-oriented relationships, recognising however that team relationships are secondary to results.

For the business driver, task achievement and organisational success are paramount. The flexibility of style portrayed is a 'lever' to achieve those ends.

Style of implementors The implementor is identified as disciplined, conscious of following through on decisions made, consensus-oriented, and committed to generating a stimulating working environment. A manager whose focus is on implementing strategy needs to be structured and disciplined in the way his or her daily workload is handled. Equally, it is important to follow established procedures to ensure consistency of application. Such practice can be effectively applied only if respect both for existing rules and for the traditions of the organisation is displayed. As a part of being disciplined, teamwork is considered important in order to promote understanding and co-operation. Implementors consider that constantly encouraging group cohesion is fundamental to engendering positive and stimulating relationships. Coupled with being satisfied with his or her job, the implementor considers that success is achieved by having a management that is well disciplined.

Implementor-oriented managers are equally conscious of follow-through on key decisions, emphasising the need for personal discipline and being systematic in application. In addition, openness of dialogue and creating an environment where work problems can be discussed is considered as important as being personally rigorous. As part of generating positive work relationships, being accessible as a senior manager is seen as a necessary condition.

Underlying the discipline and application is a strongly held belief that openness of communication is vital. Creating a climate where people feel they can effectively work together is considered fundamental. For the implementor, it is important for staff and management to feel that they can share their work problems. In order to achieve positive levels of communication, checking out plans with colleagues and subordinates in order to encourage greater understanding and sharing of work-related issues is pursued. Furthermore, the implementor feels it important to promote an image of a sensitive and responsive management, so that lower-level management hold top management and the command structure of the organisation in respect. As part of promoting an image of a more cohesive organisation, the implementor feels it important that they and their staff display respect for protocol in the way official engagements and formal relationships are managed.

A positive attitude to the job is also portrayed. The implementor feels that his or her work affords a stretching and challenging experience. Satisfaction with the organisation extends to being committed to it, evident in the positive attitude the implementor displays towards systems and controls in the organisation. The implementor identifies him- or herself as responsive to the opinions of others, and works towards establishing a culture of tolerance amongst senior managers.

Overall the implementor is concerned with promoting a positive working environment in the organisation, believing that, with greater encouragement, staff and management will become more self-confident. In this way, those within the organisation are more likely to be open about personal, task-related, and organisational issues that require attention. For the implementor, attaining high levels of consensus is an end in itself. For the policy maker, in contrast, effectiveness of communication is crucial to promoting clear direction, whereas for the business driver, openness is one lever for goal attainment.

Organisational performance factors

From the initial unstructured interviews particular aspects of organisational performance were identified. For example, the issues raised covered internal organisational performance concerns such as the motivation and performance of employees, management of costs, structuring of the organisation, effectiveness of interfacing, quality of products and services, current product/services portfolios, and viability of sales and marketing practice. Externally oriented matters were also discussed, such as competitive advantage and its sustenance, insights into the behaviour and intents of competitors, quality of service to clients, response to feedback from the market-place, and a number of other factors. Issues such as these were included in the Japanese Executive Competencies Questionnaire. Respondents were asked to identify those items that, in their opinion, were relevant to the current and future performance of their organisation. The single items identified were factor-analysed, with five key factors emerging.

Two organisational performance factors are identified by the Japanese respondents, namely, quality of dialogue in the top team and a sense of harmony amongst senior management colleagues; four factors were identified by the European respondents, namely, quality of dialogue in the top team, performance motivation, market responsiveness, and strategic orientation. The Japanese and European respondents share the same factor concerning quality of dialogue within the top team.

Quality of dialogue in the top team (Japan/Europe) Effective dialogue within the top team requires being:

- understanding of one another
- trusting of one another
- able to discuss sensitive issues
- easy to talk to
- able to implement decisions made jointly
- able to address long- and short-term issues.

Both European and Japanese senior managers considered that in order for senior management to perform effectively as a team the quality of dialogue amongst the members of the team needs to be open, so as to allow for full examination of the issues facing the organisation. The respondents considered it imperative for team members to have the confidence in one another to discuss sensitive issues of an individual, departmental, or organisational nature that affect the performance of the company. In order to create an environment where confidence and openness of dialogue is possible, the levels of trust amongst team members are considered as needing to be high. One element for enhancing levels of trust is for relevant senior managers to understand one another as people. Mutual understanding, through appreciating the strengths and weaknesses of one another's style(s) and through recognising the challenges and pressures each senior manager faces in his or her role, allows comments to be made more sensitively, according to the issues facing each colleague. Such a working environment allows for a level of comfort in senior management relationships which acts in turn as a springboard for a fuller exploration of the challenges facing the organisation.

Two key issues in particular are identified by both senior Japanese and European leaders as crucial elements to teamworking: the addressing of long- and short-term issues, and the confidence that decisions made in meetings will be implemented jointly. The Cranfield Comparative Study identified no particular distinction between working on longer- or shorter-term objectives. In essence, it is considered that both sets of objectives need to be addressed, and virtually at the same time. Discussing longer-term issues may be experienced as stimulating, because conversation may focus more on concepts, priorities and options. Discussing shorter-term issues may be experienced as more sensitive, because the performance of senior colleagues and/or their departments or functions may come under scrutiny. Evolving a mature relationship is important to be able to discuss both ends of the spectrum.

Quality of dialogue in the meeting influences the effectiveness of decision implementation. A poor top team is one where, on having discussed and decided ways forward, each senior manager implements only what personally suits him- or herself. Such behaviour signifies no meaningful commitment to 'cabinet responsibility' or to the decision-making processes amongst senior management. Growing a sense of shared responsibility within senior management so that decisions made are implemented jointly requires a positively oriented team environment.

Harmony (Japan) The Japanese respondents identify harmony as:

- enhancing employee morale
- stimulating greater trust
- improving employee performance
- enhancing internal organisational relationships.

Particularly relevant to the Japanese respondents is the concept of harmonious work relationships. Harmony is identified as creating an environment in which enhancing employee morale occurs naturally. As a result, people within the organisation are likely to be more trusting of one another and of their leadership. Within a culture of improved morale and greater trust it is considered that performance from employees will naturally improve as pride in the workplace increases. As motivation and relationships improve at the individual level, then greater attention and care is likely to be given to the quality of interfacing between departments and functions.

Performance motivation (Europe) The European respondents identify that motivating people to improve performance involves:

- enhancing employee morale
- stimulating greater trust

- having fewer people leaving
- having fewer inaccurate commitments made internally
- improving employee performance
- generating improved internal organisational relationships.

Positive working relationships are as important to the European as to the Japanese respondents, but greater emphasis is placed by the former on promoting a positive attitude to work-related performance than quality of relationships in their own right. As with the Japanese respondents, creating a stimulating environment whereby effective working relationships are considered important is a priority. Through improved working relationships greater levels of trust can be achieved between the levels of management and across the whole organisation. Being more stimulated in the workplace is seen to lead to improved performance by employees. Improvements in morale and the quality of working environment is identified by the Europeans as reducing employee turnover. Equally, as staff and management feel more positive about the organisation, it is likely that fewer inaccurate commitments are going to be made between functions or departments or between managers and their staff. The overall result is that improved internal organisational relationships are likely to emerge.

Market responsiveness (Europe) The European respondents identify that being responsive to the market-place involves:

- discussions concerning competitor impact
- being able to handle competitors
- focusing on key customer groups
- being committed to clients
- being responsive to new initiatives
- providing better relationships
- being able to deliver goods or services
- becoming profitable through effective sales and marketing.

For the European respondents a key measure of organisational performance is being market-responsive. Particularly pertinent is the quality of dialogue inside the organisation concerning developments in the market-place. The openness and honesty of discussion amongst managers within the organisation concerning competitor impact is viewed as vital in order to enhance understanding of opportunities within the market-place. Some conversations are likely to focus on the ability of staff and management to respond to competitors, which is one side of the equation; the other side is responsiveness to customers. A particular concern of the Europeans is the degree to which managers respond to the requirements of key customer groups. Appreciating the varying needs and demands of the organisation's customer base is necessary in order to fulfil existing and future commitments to clients. Equally, it is considered that being market-responsive requires attention to be given to the effectiveness of service delivery.

By attending to internal and external organisational requirements, the ability of staff and management to respond to new initiatives is likely to be more proficient. As a result, improved external relationships are likely to follow. Overall, sensitivity to interfaces internally and responsiveness to the markets externally provides the foundation for the effective application of sales and marketing. In effect, profitability through sales and marketing is the result of effective internal and external interface management.

Strategic orientation (Europe) The European respondents identify that being strategic requires examining:

- issues affecting the long term
- the future of the company
- the quality of products or services
- cost management
- the product or service portfolio.

The European respondents identify particular perspectives which for them are prime strategic considerations, and which they consider make an impact on the longer-term viability of the company. The degree to which management are aware of the issues affecting the longer-term prospects of the organisation and have formed a view as to how future developments are likely to affect the company is highlighted as an important element of strategy generation. Equally, issues pertaining to the quality of the current range of products or services and the effectiveness of cost management within the organisation are viewed as considerations of strategy.

Leadership implications for Japanese managers

Having identified the different characteristics of Japanese leaders, and the people- and organisation-related performance challenges that both the Japanese and European respondents consider important to address, cross-correlation analysis is undertaken to examine the relationship between leadership and performance. The following results highlight the likely impact Japanese managers will have both within Japanese organisations and in holding senior expatriate positions where they lead a European staff and management.

Impact of policy makers The orientation to effectiveness of communication is rated as having a positive impact by the majority of the country managers in the sample. Being attentive to good communication is rated by the Japanese respondents as enhancing team identity, team purpose, and cohesion amongst team members. The British, Irish, Germans, Swedes, Spanish, and Austrians reveal that Japanese leaders who are effective at communication are likely to affect positively team relationships, the motivation of staff and management to improve performance, the responsiveness of staff and management to be sensitive to market and customer requirements and the overall awareness of employees concerning strategic issues and the future development of the company.

The discipline element of the policy maker's style is identified by the British respondents as having a positive contribution to helping managers be more market-responsive. In contrast, the French respondents identify the application of discipline as counter-productive in terms of assisting French managers to focus on strategic issues. The Spanish and Austrians also find the disciplined Japanese manager unhelpful in addressing organisational performance issues. Specifically, the Spanish indicate that motivation to perform, being market-responsive, and being more strategically aware are hindered by the application of a disciplined approach to management. The Austrians indicate that team relationships and performance motivation are negatively affected by the application of discipline.

Japanese leaders who are focused are considered by the Japanese respondents as enhancing team relationships. The British, Spanish, and Austrians similarly consider that a Japanese leader with a focused approach provides a positive impact on organisational performance. In particular, the British consider that team relationships, motivation to perform, and the manager's awareness concerning strategic issues are improved by a focused style of management. Equally positive sentiments are expressed by both the Spanish and Austrians, who consider that team relations, motivation to perform, being market-responsive, and being more strategically aware are all enhanced by the application of a focused approach to managing. In addition, the Irish respondents consider that motivation to perform improves, for the Swedes and Finns, team relations improve by the application of a focused style.

Impact of business drivers The results-oriented style of the business driver is identified by the Japanese respondents as a positive influence in terms of promoting effective team relationships. However, in terms of promoting harmony within the organisation, the Japanese view being results-oriented as negative.

As far as the European respondents are concerned, being results-oriented is seen not to have any particularly significant impact other than on certain organisational performance measures in certain countries. The Irish respondents consider that Japanese leaders who are too results-oriented are likely to have a negative impact on staff and management's motivation to perform in their job. In contrast, the British respondents indicate that too results-oriented an approach undermines strategic awareness and limits the opportunity for strategic dialogue. The Spanish respondents indicate that those Japanese top managers who lead a Spanish management and workforce and who display a results-oriented style are likely to have a negative influence on team relationships, the motivation of people to perform, the market responsiveness of staff and management, and the strategic orientation and awareness of management. The Austrians reveal a negative impact on their employees in terms of worsening team relationships and a reduction in staff and management's motivation to perform.

Impact of implementors The orientation towards being ordered and systematic is identified as having a significant impact on the French, Spanish, and Austrian respondents. The French consider that being ordered and protocol-driven has overall a positive effect on team relationships amongst French managers.

In contrast, the Spanish consider that an ordered style has a counter-productive impact on team relationships, performance motivation, being market-responsive, and strategic awareness. The Austrians consider that Japanese leaders who apply an ordered work approach have a negative effect on team relationships and the motivation of staff and management to perform. However, generating a working environment where staff and management are satisfied with their organisation stimulates far more positive results. The Japanese respondents consider that an organisational environment which staff and management find satisfactory has a positive impact on team relationships. The British, Irish, Swedish, Spanish, and Austrian respondents consider that satisfaction with one's working environment enhances team relationships, increases people's motivation to perform, helps staff and management to be more market-responsive, and promotes a greater willingness to comprehend the strategic challenges facing the organisation. The French respondents highlight a positive impact on team relationships, staff and management performance motivation, and stimulating greater strategic awareness amongst management. The German respondents indicate that with improved levels of satisfaction within the organisation, team relationships and the performance motivation of staff and management are likely to improve. The Finnish respondents display a similarly positive inclination, highlighting improvements in team relationships and greater focus on market-related challenges.

Being disciplined at follow-through is identified by the Japanese respondents as having a positive influence on team relationships. The French consider that effectiveness at follow-through has a positive effect on the motivation to perform on staff and management. The Swedes, in keeping with the French, consider that those Japanese who apply follow-through are likely to improve the motivation of staff and management. In contrast, the Spanish consider that effectiveness of follow-through is likely to be counter-productive with staff and management in terms of being market-responsive or more strategically oriented. The Irish also consider that Japanese managers who apply a follow-through style are more likely to demotivate staff and management.

A consensus-building style of systematically working with others, sharing problems and promoting more open communication is considered by certain respondents as beneficial to team relationships. The British respondents think that Japanese managers who apply a consensus-oriented approach have a positive impact on team relationships, performance motivation, and strategic awareness. The French and Spaniards rate consensus-oriented management as having a positive influence on the performance motivation and the strategic awareness of their staff and management, whereas the Swedes highlight a positive correlation with performance motivation. The Finns indicate a positive correlation between a consensus style and the enhancing of team relationships.

Summary

- The Japanese respondents, in comparison with the European respondents (excepting the Swedish), identify the least degree of divergence of fundamentally different views concerning the future direction of their organisation.
- The Japanese respondents, in comparison with all the European respondents, identify the highest degree of divergence in terms of addressing known sensitive issues within their organisation.

- The Japanese respondents, in comparison with the European respondents, provide the least divergence of incompatible perceptions of behaviours between top management and general management below.

- Seniority of position, length of time in company, and length of time in job are identified as key determinants of the managerial styles and attitudes of Japanese business leaders.

- Three approaches to business leadership amongst the Japanese respondents are identified: amongst those managers who occupy a policy-making role; amongst those who are results-driven; and amongst those who are concerned with the implementation of strategy.

- The Japanese respondents identify two organisational performance indicators: effectiveness of team relationships; and harmony within the organisation.

- The Europeans identify four organisational performance indicators: effectiveness of team relationships; performance motivation; market responsiveness; and strategic orientation.

- Particular elements of each of the approaches are identified as having a positive impact on Japanese and European managers: being communicative; being focused; and attempting to create an environment in which staff and management are satisfied with their organisation.

- The consensus-oriented approach, although identified as having a positive impact on Japanese and European managers, is also identified as having less impact than effectiveness of communication, being focused, and nurturing an organisational environment with which staff and management can positively identify.

- The results-oriented approach is identified as having more of a negative impact on Japanese and European managers.

Leadership for stakeholder value

The implications

'Paradoxical' is a word that summarises the nature of the results of the Japanese top manager survey. On the one hand, the approaches of seeking consensus, attaining effectiveness of communication, and promoting a satisfactory work environment are identified as positive and enhancing work relationships within the organisation. On the other hand, the focused, disciplined, results-oriented style counter-balances the 'softer' approaches, and significantly correlates with promoting disruptive and inhibitingly tense work relationships.

The Japanese respondents also emerge as the most cohesive in identifying with the mission of their organisation and portraying higher levels of trust and consistency of behaviour when compared with the managers from European countries. In contrast, the Japanese highlight the greatest degree of difficulty in addressing known concerns compared with the Europeans.

In effect, the Japanese respondents indicate that although they can trust one another, can move forward jointly and share a greater sense of 'cabinet responsibility' than the Europeans do, they nonetheless find it considerably more difficult to address those issues that need attention in order to promote added-value service. What are the implications of such a paradox in leading the stakeholder-value organisation of the future?

In the foyer of the London office of the Fujitsû subsidiary, ICL, a notice clearly reads, 'Do 1000 Things 1% Better'. This interesting motto encapsulates the essence of the stakeholder-value organisation, namely, the organisation and its infrastructure are well constituted and focused, but sustained competitive advantage comes from constant attention to all those little things (details) that together make the difference. Making the difference is not something that can be prescribed: it is more a requirement of effective leadership.

Developing leaders

Paying attention to those concerns that require discussion, especially when discussion is difficult, is seen as crucial in today's world. The leadership that can knit together conflicting demands is the leadership required for the stakeholder-value organisation. In order to promote such effectiveness, four areas of leadership and management development are identified: acknowledging reality, content of dialogue, expatriate placement, and general management development.

Acknowledging reality What issues do the Japanese respondents find difficult to raise? Table 6.10 identifies the most quoted areas of sensitivity.

Whatever else is done, a first major step is to acknowledge that such challenges exist and that they affect the various levels of management ie inhibit people from raising these issues. Supporting the questionnaire results, the interviews with top Japanese managers highlight the ever-growing concern over white-collar productivity. The only significant and consistent theme over the question of white-collar productivity to emerge is the seeming lack of insight as to how to manage this problem. Other than that, the above remaining issues can be classified into two groupings: relationship-oriented, and being strategic. As can be seen in Table 6.10, the relationship-oriented issues are highlighted with greater frequency than the strategy issues. Top Japanese managers found people-related issues the most difficult to address. Particular attention may need to be given to leadership style, because that has emerged as the most dominant of the people-oriented issues.

In order to proceed, examination of the following questions may be of assistance:

- What key issues (if any) affecting the organisation have not been adequately examined?
- For how long have particular concerns been recognised as pertinent to address?
- If it is inhibiting to talk of such issues, why is that?
- What are the opportunity costs to the business if it does not enter into dialogue over these issues?

Content of dialogue Having identified key areas of sensitivity, respondents to the questionnaire were asked to list how much better things would have been if such concerns had been resolved earlier. The list in Table 6.11 outlines the most quoted issues. Other than the issue of increased profitability, the remaining issues that represent areas for improvement are people-oriented.

From experience it is postulated that attention to the 'softer' synergies provides the extra cutting-edge in terms of customer loyalty, customer retention, effectively determining longer-term relationships, and effective marketing. This is likely to be the case especially for Japanese business organisations, because the questionnaire highlighted the following interesting views. The following questions were asked:

Q. *How would you rate your competitors?*
A. Customer-oriented (61 per cent of responses).

The response to this question was higher by almost 15 per cent than that given to a question on cost-orientation, which came second out of eight possible answers.

Q. *What is involved in the marketing of your products/services?*
A. Establishing longer-term relationships with clients/customers (90 per cent of responses).

Table 6.10
SENSITIVE AREAS FOR JAPANESE MANAGERS

Area most quoted	N	%
Productivity of white-collar workers	265	35
Issues affecting the long term	205	27
Leadership style	184	24
Decline of young people	180	24
Different values held by young people	170	22
Cost management and control	168	22
Relationship between departments	164	22
Future of the company	162	21

N = Number of times quoted.
% = percentage of responses.

Table 6.11
AREAS NEEDING EARLY RESOLUTION

Area	N	%
Improved employee morale	323	42
Increased profitability	299	39
Improved clarity of strategic direction	268	35
Better employee performance	262	34
Improved response to new initiatives	257	34
Improved quality of decision-making	228	30
Greater trust	195	26
Greater commitment to decisions	190	25
Fewer inaccuracies to clients/customers	158	21
Better focus on customer groups	154	20

N = Number of times quoted.
% = percentage of responses.

The key business issues that top Japanese managers feel need to be addressed require positive internal dialogue and appropriate feedback so as to make continuous re-adjustment in order to perform effectively as an organisation. The evidence emerging from the Cranfield study suggests that the content of senior management dialogue should emphasise the 'softer' concerns of management.

In terms of enhancing quality of dialogue within Japanese companies, consideration of the following questions may assist:

- What is the nature of the sensitivity that inhibits appropriate dialogue from taking place?
- What forums do senior management attend in order to examine and

understand the workings of the organisation?

■ How and by whom is the agenda constituted at these forums?
■ How responsive are senior management to giving and receiving feedback?
■ To what extent do senior management seriously request feedback?
■ How remote are senior management from the reality of organisational life?

The response to these questions is likely to provide a view as to management's intent and capability to discuss the issues facing their organisation. As management in the future are likely to experience ever greater levels of ambiguity in responding to the conflicting demands of different stakeholders, the honest views emerging to the above questions are likely to highlight senior management's level of robustness to provide effective leadership.

Expatriate placement Business management literature is awash with books and articles on expatriate managers, the preparation of expatriates for placement, their compensation packages, approaches to monitoring their performance, and considerations for repatriation. However, the Cranfield study results captured on pages 151–172 highlight an additional interesting finding: the impact on local European management of the various styles of Japanese business leaders. Most positive results are gained through effective communication, providing clarity of direction and generating circumstances that help local management feel satisfied with the organisation. Although a consensus-oriented approach is viewed positively, it is thought to have less impact than the above three. The styles that induce more negative orientation are those concerned with a need to enhance results while paying less attention to relationship management. What are the consequences of these styles for Japanese expatriate managers?

Intensive case-study analysis conducted in Europe has identified the fact that adopting a leadership style viewed as inappropriate by the local country management can have a detrimental impact not only on relationships but also on sales and marketing. Crucial to adjusting to local conditions is the appreciation of differences within each locality in terms of sales and marketing. The Cranfield study highlights the fact that companies within the same industry sector pursuing similar customers with comparable products may display quite different approaches to sales and marketing. Why? Because regional variation is an important factor. What 'sales and marketing' means for a product range in Greece is likely to be different from what it will mean in France. Misunderstandings can easily arise as to the conditions and requirements of different markets in any region, or between regions. The time taken by the expatriate manager to appreciate the business circumstances they face depends on his or her ability to integrate locally.

Being able to integrate depends on the quality of the relationships that the expatriate manager evolves with local management. One obvious way to damage relationships is to adopt styles of leadership that the locals find unwelcome. Another way is to have targets set from the centre that are considered unattainable in the operating business owing to local market conditions. A newly appointed expatriate senior manager who too readily – and against the advice of local management – accepts targets set from above faces the prospect of losing credibility with the local team. Targeting that is out of step with local market circumstances leads to defensiveness on the part of local managers. For the expatriate manager this may mean renegotiating targets set by the centre. A common experience in multinationals is that, whatever targets are set, they are prone to renegotiation. Managing the process of negotiation effectively (especially on cost and revenue targets) between the corporate centre and the subsidiary takes time to learn.

Local managers can quickly recognise when the targets they have been given are out of keeping with the reality of their business circumstances. Within a short while local management can become demotivated. A demotivated local management will demotivate the staff, which in turn will have a negative effect on the performance of the organisation.

The learning point here is that it is necessary to understand the nature of the circumstances a company faces in different parts of Europe, or any other region of the world, and then build the necessary network of relationships in order to do business. The Cranfield study indicates that those Japanese leaders most prone to not growing the necessary positive relationships with local management are the more results-oriented 'business drivers'.

For Japanese organisations facing problems with their local country management consideration of the following questions may provide clues as to ways forward:

- Do constraints exist at local management level, in one or more country sites, within the multinational organisation?
- Do substantial problems of business and organisation result from such constraints' not being addressed?
- Have the constraints been identified and discussed with local management?

■ To what extent is there ownership at local management and expatriate/corporate centre management levels, to address such constraints?

■ To what extent has a partnership philosophy between local management and expatriate/corporate centre management been adopted to overcome the problems identified?

■ To what extent have all the key interfaces been consistently nurtured so as to improve the quality of dialogue and relationships?

■ To what extent is expatriate management really listening to local management and attempting to integrate with local circumstances?

■ If all else has been done, is it necessary to remove people?

Case-study analysis conducted by the Cranfield team in Britain shows that those Japanese companies that are more likely to face problems with local country management are those in non-greenfield site situations. Japanese management has here to manage and change an existing culture and does not have the luxury of starting with a clean sheet!

General management development In the above section, style of leadership emerged as a topic that the respondents find difficult to discuss. A number of reasons can explain this. First, hierarchical distance makes senior management appear too remote to be meaningfully involved in dialogue; secondly, the quality of conversation, even through consensus, is perceived as insufficient or not sufficiently penetrating.

Whatever the reasons, such a result indicates a deeply felt concern. In order to help both existing and younger, emerging managers to address issues of style better it is recommended that enhancing management style should be viewed in conjunction with meeting the challenge of effectively performing as a general manager. Therefore, areas of general management development are outlined: career planning; early leadership experience; general management training; and personal development.

■ *Career planning.* Numerous managers from the Cranfield European study outlined the advantages of having worked in more than one function in the same firm rather than working in more than one firm but staying in the same function. Greatest benefit from cross-functional experience was gained prior to the age of 35 years. The learning gained by crossing organisational boundaries provides the basis for being capable, once in a senior role, to communicate effectively with colleagues in other functions. This system of 'development by rotation' has been well instituted in large Japanese corporations and allows managers there to evolve effective networking, on which the successful functioning of many organisational processes depends. Furthermore, cross-functional experience promotes the development of a more realistic overview of the organisation, and this is all the more important because the Japanese regard highly the ability of senior managers to have a global view of their organisation. In fact, a considerable number of the respondents in the Cranfield/Japanese survey rated holding a realistic overview of their company as second only to leadership ability. However, the system of developmental rotation has too often been based on the expediency of company needs, with individual preferences given secondary consideration. Granted that the up-and-coming generation is likely to need more meaningful job experience in order to be well motivated, such considerations may need to become part of a career development programme in which the individual's preferences for their career development are regarded as an input of equal importance in the existing HRM practices of Japanese companies.

■ *Early leadership experience.* An additional area of practical development for prospective leaders is personal leadership. The implication is that individuals need to be given the responsibility for managing people. Unless a manager is exposed to learning how to allocate work, chair meetings, motivate team members, discuss understandable differences of opinion, and reach a resolution – and above all be held accountable for the decisions made – the individual may not move to high office with the confidence required for effective performance. Other Cranfield studies conducted in the USA and the UK indicate that most up-and-coming managers received their first leadership post before the age of 30 years. In the Japanese corporate context, where the practice of 'slow-burn' promotion is still the norm, early selection of future business leaders for training and leadership experience is probably difficult, particularly as the survey carried out by the JMA in 1994 shows that seniority consciousness is regarded as the greatest obstacle to such a change being introduced. Selection at too early a stage could adversely affect the morale of the remaining employees. At the personal level, selected individuals could experience intensive ill-will from their peers. The survey by the JMA indicates that few companies (3.3 per cent) currently have a policy of selection and training for employees under the age of 30. However, 28 per cent of top management think that such a process should begin around the age of 30. In addition, 81 per cent of senior managers feel that providing more specific career-path opportunities for younger, talented employees will be necessary in the future. Appointment to head office is cited as the most effective way of developing business leaders (83 per cent), with early appointment to a middle management post as a close second choice (66 per cent). Because 73 per cent of firms in the survey felt they lacked the quality of people to assume business leader positions, it is clear that existing practice requires urgent revision and improvement. An earlier leadership posting within a fast-track promotion system is one possible longer-term solution. Such a strategy, which amounts to merit-based promotion rather than the traditional seniority-based practice, clearly entails adjustments to many existing personnel arrangements, the least of which is to devise an effective way of selection, relying more on objective measures that are seen to be fair and reliable by employees. The question is whether Japanese companies can afford not to introduce such measures if they are to ensure their long-term survival.

■ *General management training.* General management programmes can be valuable in growing the potential of those who exhibit capacity for senior office. From experience, the following elements have been considered as valuable parts of general management programmes:

Issues-based teaching A strategic perspective should be taken in the presentation of the key subject areas of finance, marketing, information systems, manufacturing strategy, design, business strategy, and HRM. Most major US and European business schools are teaching, or are working towards teaching, integrated case-studies.

International and research-driven Insights concerning improvements in multinational corporations (MNCs) and different regions of the world should be standard on most general management programmes. A 'cutting-edge' programme is research-driven, highlighting the latest trends and practices across key markets, providing information on the latest techniques, and promoting new perspectives on issues such as managing change. Added value, in terms of management development for the future, will depend on research results of a cross-comparative nature.

Current issues and society In order to prepare managers to lead the stakeholder-value organisations of the future broader social, ethical, and legal perspectives need to be adopted to stimulate an understanding of the key relationships between society and business. Esoteric sociological and political science contributions will not do! Pragmatic teaching is required on those aspects of society likely to influence the criteria for decision-making at general management level. For managers who work in mid- to large-sized corporations, taking a broader societal perspective provides the tools for considering medium- to long-term strategic developments and, in effect, makes issues such as business ethics and corporate responsibility realistic concerns rather than ephemeral interests.

Network of contacts Making contacts with other programme participants during and after the programme is an important element of executive development programmes in business schools. The calibre of the programme participants and their experiences are important ingredients in promoting learning from one another and forming mentorship relationships that can make a lasting impact on each manager. It is appreciated that networking within Japanese organisations and between affiliated companies has been applied effectively to date. But the question is whether, with the emerging business challenges and increasing internationalisation of business, this will continue to the same degree of effectiveness. To have the opportunity to network with others from different business organisations, from different industry sectors, from public-sector organisations, and with managers from different countries widens the management horizons of each individual.

■ *Personal development* Personal development is the foundation of an executive development programme. A high-calibre programme should bring together quantitative learning inputs such as strategy, functional business skills, and economic and political trends along with more qualitative concerns such as the personality of the manager and how that affects his or her performance and decision-making capacity, the importance of management style, and how attitude can be a powerful enabler or inhibitor to individual and team performance. Personal counselling, the use of psychological and management-style tests, and even well-planned outdoor activities are fruitful mechanisms for helping managers understand what they are like as people, how they 'naturally' manage, and what further on-the-job development experiences they need to undergo in order to stimulate further development. Once learning becomes an emotional experience, especially if the manager is receiving feedback on his or her capacity to shape an identity for the function or organisation to which he or she is accountable, or on how differences of personality and style could severely inhibit discussion within the top team or dampen the enthusiasm of others, it is likely that an impact will be made on how that manager performs at work. Each participant internalises learning and gives serious consideration to what he or she will do after returning to work. Considerable time needs therefore to be built into the programme for group and individual counselling and feedback.

Conclusion

The ever greater demands being made on management are evident. In the *White Paper on the Enterprise* published in January 1994 by Keizai Doyukai (Japan Association of Corporate Executives) Japanese companies are portrayed as standing at the crossroads, where the future is not clear and where they are experiencing a massive structural change described as the biggest discontinuity since the end of World War II. Never has strong leadership been more earnestly sought from corporate top management. That 81 per cent of the Japanese respondents of the Cranfield Executive Competencies Survey cite *leadership* as the requirement for top management to carry out its responsibilities effectively, placing it as the number-one priority, is not surprising. Meeting the expectation of different stakeholders who affect a business organisation is a process fraught with strain. The normal response to this situation is likely to be, 'We can never get it right'. The quality of leadership to provide a pathway through such ambiguous circumstances is a crucial factor in determining the effective performance of the organisation.

In terms of qualities of leadership, the Cranfield study highlights three crucial questions which we propose Japanese managers should consider:

- What impact does the quality of dialogue (or lack of it) amongst the members of the top team have on the effectiveness of Japanese business organisations?
- What are the management development issues facing Japanese managers now and in the future, bearing in mind that values differences (for example between 'policy makers' and 'business drivers') in ways of working and managing relationships are likely to affect the styles adopted in Japanese business organisations?
- What is the impact of the emerging Japanese management styles on local managers in overseas operations? Does further consideration need to be given to expatriate placement and length of expatriate tenure?

If nothing else, bearing in mind that the younger generation are less and less likely to accept certain current values (such as seniority-based promotion), and will instead press for greater financial reward based on performance and merit, leadership for stakeholder value is likely to be a requirement for the future.

Responding to the above three questions is a must, not an option.

Acknowledgements

The research team at Cranfield acknowledges the help, support, and co-operation given by our partner at the JMA who carried out the main part of the questionnaire survey on our behalf in Japan, and produced the report on its part of the questionnaire survey in Japanese in co-operation with the team. The team would also like to thank Keizai Doyukai (Japan Association of Corporate Executives), who have not only been instrumental in providing the team access to its members for interviewing but have also provided, as have the JMA, opportunities for holding a discussion and presentation of our comparative Europe–Japan research results in Japan. Thanks also to British Airways and ICI Japan, whose sponsorship made it possible for us to travel to Japan and to undertake this interesting survey. We owe a number of individuals our very special thanks; they are Mr Y. Kume, chairman of Nissan Motor Co. Ltd, Mr Y. Kobayashi, chairman and CEO, Fuji Xerox Co. Ltd, Dr J. Miyai, OBE, president of the Japan Productivity Centre for Socio-Economic Development, and Professor S. Aida, visiting professor at Cranfield University, all of whose support and assistance have been invaluable. Finally, but not least, the team are grateful to the managers who completed the research questionnaire and especially to those who kindly gave their time to be interviewed.

CHAPTER SEVEN

The Management of Careers

Peter Herriot

Introduction

In the late 1970s the title of this chapter would not have been problematic. Most people assumed that they could look forward to a careeer in their organisation, though the idea of 'career' meant different things to different types of employee. To managers and professionals it signified a steady progression up through a sequence of managerial grades; to the general workforce it meant the prospect of retaining their job and the regular pay-rises that went with it. Either way, it was the responsibility of the organisation to manage careers. Individuals merely had to appear to work to the best of their ability and effort, and be compliant in order to benefit.

In the mid-1990s things could not be more different. It is possible to question whether either of the terms in the chapter title carries much meaning today. Can we even talk of organisational careers, when the essence of the careers of the 1970s – security and promotion prospects – have all but disappeared? Is it feasible to manage careers today when the organisational and business environments are so unpredictable as to make any sort of planning next to impossible? And how can organisations take time to manage careers when all their efforts are directed towards surviving in an ever more competitive world?

The revolution in the nature of careers has been profound. However, I will argue that it is only part-way through. Just as the stable socio-economic and business environment of the 1970s has given way to the cost-competitive and productivity-obsessed 1990s, so new conditions necessary for organisational survival and success will arise by the next millennium. And just as stable hierarchical structures and systems have today given way to what might rudely be termed chaos (but, politely, change) so new organisational forms will evolve tomorrow to address the new issues of the twenty-first century. As for how we think and feel about our careers, the sea-change in attitudes towards the employment relationship which we perceive today will by then have become a transformed perception of the nature of organisations and of our dealings with them.

The structure of this chapter reflects the course of this ongoing revolution. I will consider the 1970s, the 1990s, and the twenty-first century in turn. I will describe the context, the structures, the systems, and the perceptions of careers typical of each period. Inevitably the treatment will be schematic and oversimplified. There are, for example, some organisations already operating with the structures and systems of the twenty-first century; others are only just moving out of the 1970s. Likewise some individuals still delude themselves into feeling secure whilst others are already constructing boundaryless careers for their futures.[1] Nevertheless there is considerable agreement about what was and still is typical of the 1970s and the 1990s; we can even discover some slight consensus about where things are going.

The 1970s: the organisational womb

The growth factor

The context of the 1970s was one of steady and predictable economic growth. The occasional faint blips on the ever upward curve served only to highlight the overall trend. Markets were stable and regulated, and the cold war stabilised the political environment, albeit by means of a stalemate between two opposed power blocks.

In such a favourable and predictable context organisations could construct optimistic metaphors to describe their structures.[2] If they, too, were growing steadily, like the Western economy, then they thought of themselves as organisms, adapting in an evolutionary way to the changing environment. If they were in a steady state, they could adopt the machine metaphor, becoming ever more efficient and well-oiled at serving the same market.

Internal labour markets

The structures matched the metaphors. Most organisations approximated to a greater or lesser extent the idealised internal labour market.[3] That is, they:

- recruited and promoted from within
- maintained a structured promotion ladder
- experienced low labour turnover
- developed company-specific knowledge and skills.

The degree to which organisations conformed to this structure varied, depending upon:

- their business strategy[4]
- their main technology
- their national origin
- the stage of the economic cycle
- the department or division being investigated.

However, despite these variations the generally hierarchical and closed structures reflected, and were adapted to, the steady state of their external environments. From a career perspective, such structures offered the prospect of security of employment, with a steady progression through frequent promotions up many rungs of the ladder, with status and salary increasing with age. Because most organisations were structured according to functional divisions it was possible to remain within one's professional specialisation while being repeatedly promoted.

Managed careers

Organisations took responsibility for managing careers within the internal labour market. Managerial control of such a closed system was not considered too formidable a task. Personnel professionals planned individuals' careers and established accepted career paths which were recognised routes to the top. They set up assessment centres to identify individuals of high potential, and provided fast-track placements for these high-flyers. They distinguished two career tracks: professional/technical, and managerial.[5] They constructed elaborate succession plans, with two or three individuals earmarked as suitable to fill specific top management jobs.[6] Although the reality did not always conform to the prescriptions of these plans, such systems at least expressed the intent to manage careers, as well as the belief that they could be managed.

The relational contract

Perceptions of the employment relationship were all of a piece with these structures and systems. Many employees, especially managers and professionals, believed that they had a relational psychological contract with their organisation.[7] That is, they felt that the deal that they had went beyond a mere instrumental transaction (for example, pay in exchange for effort). Rather, each party would be willing to go the extra mile for the other when the need arose – to be a 'good citizen'.[8] Many believed that their psychological contract with the organisation ran something along the following lines: in return for security, promotion, and paternalistic care they provided loyalty, conformity, and good-citizenship behaviour.

Along with this perception of the overall employment relationship went other perceptions of the nature of careers in the organisation. Given an overwhelmingly male entry immediately after the completion of full-time education – and given a steady and predictable series of promotions – it was possible to look at a career as though it were a timetable.[9] If one had not reached a certain level by a certain age, then one had fallen behind. This might well be due to having failed at one round of the tournament (usually an early one).[10]

Along with perceptions of careers as a timetable and tournament went a variety of stereotypes of the players. Because in Anglo-Saxon culture we need to believe that people get the jobs they deserve, people's position in the corporate hierarchy was attributed to their own characteristics rather than to the inevitable consequences of hierarchical structure. Thus the middle levels were said to be peopled by 'high-fliers', 'solid citizens', or 'dead wood'.[11] In fact these attributional categories tended to refer to those (respectively) who had changed jobs frequently, had changed jobs relatively rarely, or had been in the same job for a very long time. It goes without saying that in any pyramidal hierarchical structure opportunities for movement across or up become fewer the higher up the hierarchy you rise and the older you get. People are 'plateaued' because the mountain gets narrower, not necessarily because they cannot climb. So much for the static 1970s.

The 1990s: the organisational survival stakes

Savage competition

Consider the high-tech, information-based corporate high-fliers of the 1970s: the Digitals, Hewlett-Packards and ICLs of this world. They were so confident in the brave new dawn of their industry that they all played an equal and generous part in the training and development of their young scientists and engineers. When an individual left for a competitor, this was considered inevitable and, indeed, a beneficial cross-fertilisation of industry-wide talent. All contributed to the common good. Not any more: high-tech organisations try today to ensure that they reap for themselves some benefit from the training costs they have sown. But at the same time they attempt to seduce already trained experts and so gain benefits from others' investment.

This particular scenario is indicative of the transformation in the social, political, economic, and business environment in which organisations operate today. Its main feature is the tremendous increase in the severity of competition. Markets have been deregulated, as have sectors. Any financial institution can now offer practically any (legal) financial service, for example. Moreover, business has become globalised. Transactions can be accomplished instantaneously between the world's financial centres. Global organisations can achieve economies of scale by locating particular functions in the most appropriate centres: research and development, for example, in countries with a well-developed scientific base, or production where there is plentiful, cheap, and reliable labour. Finally, although information technology (IT) offers competitive advantage for a brief period, it rapidly becomes a necessary – but not a sufficient – condition for survival. Which bank, for example, would now survive without EFTPOS (electronic fund transfer at point of sale)? Which supermarket chain would survive without the IT-based integration of sales, pricing, ordering, transporting, and warehousing? Add to these competitive pressures three further difficulties, two of them peculiarly British:

- the longest and most savage recession since World War II
- the ideologically driven determination to privatise public utilities and services, however unsuited they are to market forces
- the short-term nature of British investment, motivated by the requirement of pension-fund investors to achieve maximum short-term return on capital.[12]

The shrunken giants

Faced with these cumulative hammer blows, most UK organisations have battened down the hatches. They have adopted a strategy of cost reduction and improved productivity in order to survive. The threats have been so immediate and short-term that extensive long-term investment in innovative products and services has been out of the question for most. Their systems and structures have reflected these strategic imperatives, although some might argue that many organisations have overreacted. Certainly, the confident metaphors for organisation in the 1970s – organism or machine – have given way to such tentative analogies as 'network' or 'amoeba'.

Cost reductions have been achieved through a variety of structural changes. The most prominent of these has been downsizing – making people redundant at all levels of the organisation and not replacing them. The consequence has been that the remaining jobs have increased in size, though not necessarily in their level of responsibility. Individuals work longer hours and so, by definition, productivity per employee rises. A second structural change is de-layering – the reduction of the number of hierarchical levels or grades. We should note, however, that downsizing and de-layering have been neither universal nor always concomitant.[13] (See Table 7.1.)

Two further structural measures have also been deployed to enhance cost competitiveness. First, many functions that are not considered core to the business have been outsourced – contracted out to external suppliers of the service in question. These have included even routine personnel functions and the organisation's IT capability. Secondly, many unskilled and semi-skilled jobs have been reduced to part-time status. This allows organisations to pay for labour only at times of peak demand.

Finally we should note one other development of a structural nature that also has profound implications for careers. In order to get to market more quickly organisations increasingly use project teams.[14] Hence work is structured for many employees more in terms of a sequence of projects than in terms of a series of jobs.

Reshaped structures mean revolutionised careers. With redundancy comes loss of security; with de-layering comes a drastic reduction of promotion prospects. If your function is outsourced then you suddenly become a contractor in competition with others. If you work in project teams your moves to other teams depend on the accidents of project completion and the availability of another project. And, to cap it all, the recession and the reduction in the number of jobs make it very likely that you will have already been stuck in your present position longer than you spent in your previous one.[15]

Rhetoric and reality

Structural changes have been aimed at reducing costs. A whole range of systems has suddenly been introduced and no less suddenly discarded in an effort to boost productivity. These management fads have included performance-related pay, business process re-engineering, total quality management, and many other effectively marketed 'solutions'. They have been

Table 7.1
DOWNSIZING AND DE-LAYERING

Percentage of managers reporting various combinations of managers and levels in 1992 in comparison with 1987.[13]			
Levels	**Number of managers employed**		
	Fewer	Same	More
Fewer	31	2	8
Same	13	15	11
More	3	1	16

supported by a rhetoric which seeks to disarm by assuming various supposedly self-obvious truths.[16] 'Flexibility', 'lean and mean', 'empowerment', 'self-development', and even the ubiquitous term 'human resources' itself are all items from this rhetorical lexicon. If we take the phrase 'human resources' by way of example we can clearly see that anyone using it is making a whole set of assumptions. The speaker is challenging the listener to deny that people working in organisations are human capital – another form of economic asset. They are there to be used up, conserved, discarded, developed – whatever helps the organisation achieve its business objectives. Or consider the term 'empowerment'. The rhetoric assumes that everyone gets more power, when the reality is that the real power is with top management. They have the power to download much of their responsibility for achieving budget but to withhold the resources necessary for their subordinate to succeed.

After stripping away the rhetoric surrounding management fads, we find a wide range of career management practices, characterised mostly by the constantly reiterated need to 'respond to change'. For example, young managers are rapidly moved across a range of functions so that they can join a pool of those who are sufficiently developed to make the major qualitative jump to the next level of management. Such moves may not however enhance the individual's external employability. Furthermore, they may in the longer run deprive the organisation of functional expertise it will need. However, they do provide a cadre of versatile middle managers capable of riding the next wave of change.

As a footnote, one of the success stories of the 1990s is the growth of outplacement services. Here is a process that is capable both of helping those made redundant with their career planning and also of ensuring that those who remain do not feel a burning sense of injustice on behalf of their departing colleagues.[17] Yet it is surely symptomatic of the current fluidity of organisational careers that the greatest development effort has been expended on a system designed to help employees leave!

Get safe, get out, or get even

To the outside observer, the structural and systematic changes in organisations appear both radical and arbitrary. To employees caught up in the midst of them, their effects feel profound.[18] Returning to the theme of the psychological contract, mature employees of the 1990s find themselves with a rather different deal from that which they enjoyed in the 1970s. Instead of receiving security, promotion, and care they find themselves offered a job that they are fortunate to have and a salary somewhat higher in real terms than they would have received in the 1970s. Loyalty, conformity, and good citizenship are still desired in return. But they are nowhere near enough. Today's employees are expected to be accountable for reaching budget targets; to learn new skills while maintaining their present expertise; and to work the longest hours in Europe.

The comparison of the two deals is painful in the extreme. Employees' sense of inequity is compounded by the sight of those they hold responsible receiving obscenely large golden handshakes. However, perhaps even stronger than the feeling of inequity is that of powerlessness. Employees had no say in the breaking of the old contract of the 1970s, nor in the introduction of the new. Nor could they argue when a two-yearly sequence of management fads was introduced and responsibility for their implementation was passed down to them. Given the depressed state of the labour market, they hadn't even the option of voting with their feet. They felt powerless.

These feelings are especially typical of middle managers and professionals. After all, the idea of a career in the sense of a steady and predictable progress up a corporate hierarchy is a peculiarly middle-class phenomenon. The workforce has lived for a long time with a degree of insecurity. Their deal was always more concerned with the immediate rewards for their work than with any longer-term expectations. Middle management, on the other hand, constructed its lifestyle, and indeed its very identity, on the basis of career progression. When that prospect is removed, fundamentals are under threat. After all, the very purpose of professions in the first place was to protect their members from the vagaries of the labour market.

What options, then, *are* open to employees in the early to mid-1990s?

Perhaps the most common reaction is to *get safe*. Feeling powerless and insecure, employees keep their heads below the parapet. They take care to fulfil instructions to the letter, but they take no risks in case they give opportunity for dismissal. Rather than going the extra mile, these employees are walking the required one as gingerly as they possibly can. A second response is to *get out*. When the labour market eases, employees tell themselves, they will go where the grass is greener. Alternatively, the fortunate ones will wait until their share options mature and they become financially self-sufficient. Many are hanging on only because of financial commitments to children, parents, or a mortgage. A final response is to *get even*. There are a few cases of sabotage, but the most common reaction is quietly to even up the deal. If the organisation has reneged on the bargain and unilaterally reduced its offer, then (some employees say) we will reduce our own contribution to compensate: we will, in other words, restore the balance and make the deal a fair one again. It is hard, of course, to call this process a deal, because both parties have unilaterally reduced their offers without reference to the other; the notion of contract implies negotiation.

The consequences for organisations are also profound, however. Whereas insecurity can result in risk avoidance, perceptions of inequity can have a wide variety of outcomes.[19] Research evidence indicates that perceptions of equity are related to:

- satisfaction with pay, job, career, and promotion
- commitment to one's organisation and career
- intention to stay
- feelings of career success
- effectiveness in managing one's career
- non-alienation from work
- effort at work
- job security
- low absenteeism.

Here is an extensive armoury for any individual to choose from if they wish to get even, although they are likely to damage themselves as much as the organisation with certain selections of weapon.

It is tempting for the top managements of private-sector organisations and for the political masters of public-sector institutions to believe that our national slow-but-sure emergence from recession will herald a brilliant flowering of enterprise and innovation. If my analysis of the present state of the psychological contract is largely correct, then these are false hopes.

Enterprise and innovation are unlikely to emerge readily from an angry, exhausted, and powerless workforce.

The millennium: swords into ploughshares?

Change and decay

Looking into the future is not an activity to be undertaken lightly. In as much as forecasts and predictions may themselves affect what subsequently occurs, the crystal-ball gazer's responsibility is indeed a heavy one. However, it is hard not to conclude that present trends towards national and global social and political fragmentation will continue.

Globally, the world's population continues to increase exponentially while man's attempts to create new resources themselves carry unforeseen dangers. A growing army of 'have-nots' with nothing to lose gain ever more frequent glimpses of the lives of 'haves' with everything to lose. The break-up of empires results in the renascence of historic nationalistic or tribal allegiances and the growth of divisive fundamentalist religions. Weapons of mass destruction are becoming available to such groups. Throughout the world, a politician's is one of the least respected occupations.

At home, we see the world writ small. Most of those institutions that have served to maintain the fabric of our social and economic policy have failed to adapt to their changing context. Parliament, training and education, monarchy, local government, the City, the press — all have colluded with the assumption that the short-term pursuit of individual, sectional, and national interests has been both desirable and 'natural'. The consequence, domestically and globally, is an ever more fragmented and unpredictable context within which organisations have to survive. Neither product markets nor labour markets will act as constants in the business equation any longer; the only constants will be the constant increases in competition and change.

Fly like a butterfly

The surviving organisation of the next millennium will have to be light on its feet. This implies two characteristics — an absence of bulk, and the capacity to adapt and innovate. The first of these requirements has got under way with a vengeance over the last two decades. The various forms of restructuring that we have already seen have considerable mileage still to go. In particular, we may envisage further use of flexible (part-time) labour and the contracting-out of yet more non-core functions. It is worth noting that this growth necessitates the development of negotiating and contract management skills in the core of the organisation. The aim, of course, is to continue to maintain cost-competitiveness by reducing capital and overhead expenditure.

Yet the globalisation of business means that cost-competitiveness alone is not a sufficient strategy for survival. True, in a local market, organisations can often maintain their market share by being no more costly than their local competitors. New tiger economies are ever rising on the Eastern horizon, however, and goods and services may be produced cheaper elsewhere. In the longer term – in the next millennium, in fact – British organisations cannot hope to compete on the basis of cost-competitiveness alone. They also have to be faster to market with innovative products and services.

And there's the rub. The organisational structures and systems of the present are designed to cut costs and increase productivity. Tight budget accountabilities, demanding work schedules, individual performance-related pay, short-term contracts – all these are attempts (some of them successful) to reduce costs. Yet it could be argued that all of them are actively hostile to innovation. Take performance-related pay, for example. This system is unlikely to lead individuals to take risks or to collaborate with others in doing so – yet risk-taking and collaboration are necessary for innovation. On the contrary, each individual concentrates upon the specified approved behaviours, which are by definition unlikely to be innovative.

How, then, is it possible both to retain the benefits of the cost-competitiveness acquired with such pain and also, at the same time, stimulate innovation? Organisational structures seem to be moving inexorably towards Handy's clover-leaf formation: part-time employees, specific contractors, and the remaining core.[20] The first two will maintain cost-competitiveness whereas the last will create innovation and negotiate with, and manage, the others.

Engineering diversity

How will the core organise itself? By what processes will it not merely adapt flexibly to change but also shape change by innovation? It would be rash indeed to predict the existence of specific systems. However, we can at least foresee certain practical directions:

■ The core will be open – an external labour market. Although a certain degree of security is needed, it is more important to ensure a constant flow of fresh ideas.

■ The core will be diverse. It is vital to obtain a variety of perspectives for innovation to occur.[21] Therefore recruiters will actively seek out people different from those already employed.

■ The culture will be heterogeneous. Instead of having induction and socialisation processes aimed at homogenising culture, active steps will be taken to encourage diverse subcultures.

■ Evaluation of projects will occur during their course and after their completion. Evaluative criteria will not be limited to the achievement of timetable, budget, and task objectives. Rather, the aim will be to learn from the difficulties experienced and from unexpected outomes.

■ Projects will be treated as a sequence of learning opportunities, and personal development plans will be developed accordingly.

■ Development plans, reward packages, and employment contracts will be negotiated with employees individually.

New deals

The core, then, will have structures and systems designed for flexibility and innovation. How will those in the core perceive the deal of the new millennium? The psychological contract will have changed once again (see Table 7.2). Employees will still be expected to add value in some clear way. However, they will be expected to learn continuously, and therefore not merely to learn but to learn *how* to learn, for it is abundantly clear that organisations will not be able or willing continuously to train and develop employees. They will merely provide a context in which learning can occur (for example, they will cost the process of evaluation into all projects and expect learning-points to be circulated organisation-wide).

In exchange, organisations will offer employability. By enabling individuals to develop their knowledge and their ability to learn, organisations will make those individuals more employable externally. In other words, they will give employees the security of knowing that they can get a job elsewhere. Or will they? Perhaps one of the threats to this new deal to be enjoyed by the core is that some of their learning will be organisation-specific. Particularly if they wish to leave to become self-employed contractors, cross-functional general management skills might not be transferable.

One of the potential benefits of the deals of the next millennium is however that the varied career needs of individuals may be met as well as the

Table 7.2
THREE PSYCHOLOGICAL CONTRACTS

The individual offers:		The organisation offers:
	1970s	
loyalty		security
compliance		promotion
good citizenship		care
	1990s	
accountability		a job
flexibility		higher salary
long hours		
	2010s	
learning		employability
learning to learn		flexible contract
clear added value		individualised rewards

cost-competitive and innovative needs of the organisation. The variety of structures leads to a variety of deals which each appeal to different individuals.

The *part-time* deal, for example, offers the prospect of a specific and delimited amount of work which allows individuals to fulfil the other roles in their lives. The *contractor* deal offers the opportunity to exercise specific professional skills in the achievement of agreed objectives without all the additional problems of being employed within a large organisation. Individuals can, in principle, exercise personal and professional autonomy in terms of when they work and how they achieve their contracted objectives. The *core* deal permits a degree of security while also offering the opportunity to learn, change, and manage.

Yet, although these deals in principle permit both organisational and individual needs to be met, in practice this benign outome will not necessarily be achieved. Just as the psychological contract of the 1990s is weighted heavily in the organisation's favour because of its present power in a buyer's labour market, so too the deals of the next millennium are potentially at risk. Indeed, we are already beginning to see the abuse of the part-time and the contractor deals. Excessive requirements for flexibility in hours worked destroys the very availability of part-time workers to fulfil their non-work roles. Award of contracts invariably to the lowest bidder and constant managerial interference removes the possibility of maintaining high standards and autonomy for professionals. Requirement to range widely can deprive the core workers of their professional expertise.

What is certain is that the new millennium deals will not be a repeat of the relational contract of the 1970s. Rather, they will be explicit transactions in which parties will clearly state what their perception of the deal is and what they expect to offer and receive. The crucial task, however, is how to get from the 1990s to the millennium. Consider again the responses of many of today's employees: they feel inequitably treated, powerless, and insecure. To reconstruct these people as innovative core workers or expert autonomous contract professionals requires a prodigious leap of the imagination. How is such a transformation to occur?

From power to process

Dignity through contract

One response to this last question is to argue that many of today's employees have abandoned the idea that they have a deal with their organisation. That is, they do not feel that the notion of a 'psychological contract' describes the nature of their present relationship with their employer. This is because the idea of contract implies negotiation: the recognition of the other party's interest and a willingness to accommodate it. Instead, many employees believe that the present relationship represents simply the unilateral use of labour market power. Such a belief reflects their own feelings of powerlessness – powerlessness to exit or to loosen the ever-tightening systems of control.

A necessary condition for the achievement of the varied deals of the next millennium is therefore to re-establish the very notion of the psychological contract itself. For, from such a re-establishment, a variety of benefits will follow. First, individuals will regain dignity and self-worth. The very idea of contracting implies that you can have an impact on what happens to you. It implies that you have something that the organisation needs and wants. It therefore suggests that the organisation depends upon you, as well as you upon them. Contracting involves bargaining and negotiating between parties who at least *act* as though they are equal, even though one or the other may in reality hold the whip hand. Secondly, contracting implies a promise or guarantee that you will fulfil your side of the bargain and that the other will fulfil theirs; such promises imply both agency and reciprocity. Thus the process of contracting may, of itself, help to heal the psychological wounds caused by the current bruising exercise of unilateral power.

Four stages of contracting

Contracting is not, however, an activity that can be switched on or off at will. The process of contracting is a complex one and requires a variety of skills from each party. We may describe the process as consisting of four stages (see Figure 7.1):

- *the exchange of information*. Each party needs to know, first, what they themselves want and can offer; and, secondly, what the other wants and can offer. Then each needs to be able to match the information they have thus obtained in order to answer two further questions:

  Can I offer what they want?

  Can they offer what I want?

- *the negotiation itself*. Here parties bargain so as to maximise their cost–benefit ratio, where cost is what they themselves offer and benefit is what the other offers. For some, cost is a difficult construct to use because they benefit from and enjoy offering their side of the bargain.

- *monitoring the deal*. At this stage, parties check that both are keeping their side of the deal. They also decide whether the needs of either party have changed in the interim, or whether changed circumstances have rendered inequitable a deal that was fair when it was made.

- *renegotiation or exit*. Depending on the outcome of the monitoring process, one or the other party may decide to seek to renegotiate the deal or to exit from it. Employment within the same organisation for any length of time nearly always implies renegotiations of the psychological contract. Indeed, one might define an organisational career as *a sequence of renegotiations of the psychological contract.*[22]

Such a complex process requires organisational initiatives and individual skills if it is to be carried through successfully. The primary task of the human resource professional for the next decade is to help both parties to learn to contract.

The exchange of information

The same information is required by both parties: individual and organisation. Both need to know what their own wants and offers are and what

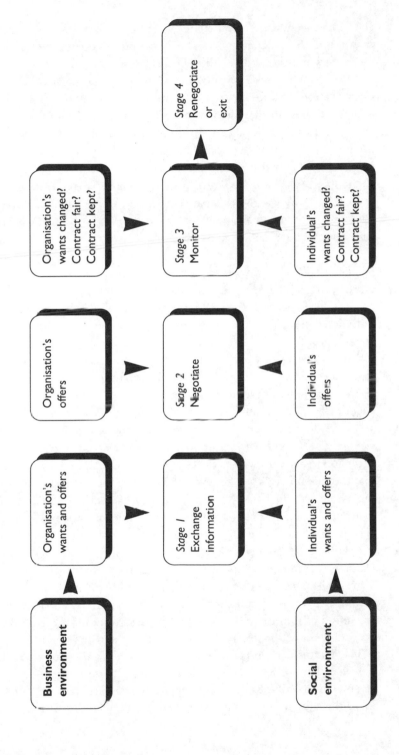

Figure 7.1
THE FOUR STAGES OF PSYCHOLOGICAL CONTRACTING

Business environment → Organisation's wants and offers → Organisation's offers → Organisation's wants changed? Contract fair? Contract kept?

Social environment → Individual's wants and offers → Individual's offers → Individual's wants changed? Contract fair? Contract kept?

Stage 1 Exchange information → *Stage 2* Negotiate → *Stage 3* Monitor → *Stage 4* Renegotiate or exit the other's wants and offers are. Only then can each decide whether their own wants are sufficiently matched by the other's offers; and whether their own offers are likely to match the other's wants.

The first and most obvious question to ask here is: do they know? Organisations will need to discover, and be explicit about, what they want and what they are prepared to offer in exchange. In an era of constant change they may want a cadre of infinitely flexible core workers, supplemented by a wide range of expert contract professionals. They will have to say so clearly, and also specify the limits within which they will negotiate their offers. Individuals, likewise, will need to spend time discovering what they really want at this particular point in their lives. They will also have to be accurately aware of the skills, knowledge and capabilities that they have to offer, and how much of their lives they are prepared to surrender to their work. Both parties will be seeking to make these discoveries. Both will need the tools to do so. There will be a growth in ways of representing knowledge resources so that organisations can specify their needs.[23] And the market will be flooded with self-help systems enabling individuals to explore their own interests and motives and to profile their own capabilities.

Once they have discovered their own wants and offers, how will the parties inform each other of them? Some of the tools and procedures are already available. Consider the recruitment stage, for example – the initial negotiation of a psychological contract. Organisations can help applicants understand what will be expected of them by means of realistic job previews.[24] They may even give applicants the opportunity to tackle samples of the job to discover whether they are suited. Organisations will also indicate the capabilities they believe are required, and request evidence about the extent to which the applicant has such capabilities. They will, furthermore, be explicit about what they will offer in return. In a climate of uncertainty and ambiguity, this may not be much, but what little it is, especially in terms of enhanced employability, will be spelled out.

Since the responsibility for managing the recruitment process rests largely with the organisation, it will take pains to ensure that applicants have the opportunity to express *their* wants and offers. Such a sequence of exchanges of information permits each party to opt out of the process at particular points, or to take steps towards the agreement of a contract.[25]

The recruitment process is a conveniently straightforward example, however. The political complexities of information exchange when the psychological contract is being *re*negotiated are far more daunting. Surviving organisations will nevertheless find a way for if they fail to do so, they will lose the highly motivated core of innovative employees on whom their future rests. Hewlett-Packard (UK) show the way forward with an effective variety of informational channels (see Table 7.3).

Table 7.3
HEWLETT-PACKARD (UK)
INFORMATION EXCHANGE

- Annual employee attitude survey
- 1995 employment relationship chosen as 'breakthrough issue'
- Employee feedback system (anonymous if preferred)
- Framework profile: key result areas and required skills
- Appraisal by superiors, peers, subordinates, and customers
- Weekly meetings to communicate current business issues
- Everything about pay and grade (except other individuals').

The negotiation itself

In order to engage in the act of negotiation, organisations will first have to abandon one of the rhetorical planks of human resource ideology – the unitarist assumption that both parties share the same interests. Rather, they will have to recognise the variety of career motivations that will be displayed by their employees.[26] Such 'career anchors' include technical competence, autonomy, security, and life-style. These motives are unlikely to feature very strongly in the personal priorities of top management, however. They are more likely to be oriented towards managerial competence or pure challenge. Thus, top management will have to stop projecting its own motives onto others.

Secondly, negotiation implies that the parties have rejected the option of the unilateral exercise of labour market power, even when the boot is on their own foot. It also implies that they are capable of adapting their own wants and offers to the needs of the other in order to achieve agreement. Such compromise by organisations to meet the needs of individuals will require considerable flexibility in making a wide range of offers – more holiday rather than more money, for example.

Finally, organisations will have to recognise that they set the scene and organise the props for the negotiation. Hence, they will have to manage the stage so as to ensure that individuals can fully act *their* part. For example, they will not leave the only opportunity for negotiation to the last 10 minutes of the annual appraisal meeting. Nor will organisational representatives use their own personal or procedural power to exercise unfair weight. In sum, they will ensure procedural equity.

As for individuals, they will learn the skills of negotiating contracts so that they become expert deal-makers. They will be able to

- estimate the strengths and weaknesses of their own and the organisation's bargaining position
- recognise the organisation's interests and concerns
- sell the benefits of the deal they want for themselves to the organisation
- develop a variety of persuasive techniques to suit different occasions.

Individuals will also have acquired enough political awareness to estimate the extent to which whoever is representing the organisation is actually empowered to do a deal. For example, the individual's immediate line manager may have little knowledge of what's available or the authority to bring it about. Individuals will need to appreciate the status of an organisation offer, and be prepared to require an explicit statement of whether the offer is a guaranteed commitment, a firm intention, or a longer-term aspiration.

Monitoring the deal

Both parties will pay careful attention to changes both in what each wants and what each can offer:

- organisations may need new skills eg international management
- individuals may develop different needs eg to spend time with their children
- organisations may make new offers eg employability rather than job security
- individuals, too, may make new offers eg broad business awareness in place of waning technical expertise.

At some point any one of these changes may become sufficient to trigger the need to renegotiate. Or perhaps one or the other party will be seen to be failing to fulfil their side of the original bargain. This is particularly likely if the balance of power has changed: 'Why worry – I can get another job/employee if I have to.' Or it can occur if one party, believing that the other has failed to fulfil their side of the deal, retaliates in kind.

Both organisations and individuals will grow skilled at periodically monitoring the psychological contract, perhaps at formal career review meetings. Such reviews will require individuals in particular to maintain high levels of insight into:

- their changing selves:
  'Are my skills getting rusty?'
  'Is my commitment to the organisation decreasing?'
  'Am I working more hours than last year?'
  'Are my value priorities changing with age?'
- the organisation:
  'Who's getting promoted these days?'
  'What sort of projects are favoured?'
  'How is performance relative to the competition?'
  'What are the perceptions of the business press?'
- the business scene:
  'What is the general business climate?'
  'What's happening in my business sector?'
  'What's the state of the labour market in my skills?'
  'Who is recruiting, and whom?'

Monitoring the deal means keeping an eye both on parties and on the environment. The career negotiators of tomorrow will keep their antennae constantly sensitive to change – in themselves, in their organisation, and in the outside world.

Renegotiation or exit

In the future, renegotiation or exit will take place at any point in the employment relationship. In the old days there were certain points at which new deals were struck – when someone reached their late 20s, for example, when a professional or more managerial direction might be negotiated, or at the point of plateauing, when further promotion became unlikely. These renegotiation points were based upon assumptions of an age–stage correspondence. In the future, a wide variety of events will precipitate a renegotiation. This is because wants and offers can change at any time, and so can the willingness to stick to the deal.

Exit will be handled differently too. Instead of a total break, exit will be regarded by organisations as the acquisition of a potential new partner, customer, client, or even subsequent re-employee. Instead of going for a better financial deal elsewhere, individuals will more often leave for the prospect of enhancing their employability. Instead of leaving in bad odour, having spoken their mind and thereby burned their boats, they will treat their present employer as a potential future client.

Or will the next millennium be so different that for the majority 'the organisation' and 'the individual' will not be the terms in which they think? Will organisational existence become so difficult to sustain that, apart from a few global companies, people will organise themselves? Will the ownership, capital, and labour distinctions become blurred? Will, in sum, the notion of the psychological contract become irrelevant? It is at least a nice idea!

References

1   ARTHUR, M, B, 'The boundaryless career: a new perspective for organisational inquiry', *Journal of Organisational Behaviour*, Vol. 15, 1994, pp295–306.

2   MORGAN, G, *Images of Organisation*, California, Sage, 1986.

3   PFEFFER, J, AND COHEN, Y, 'Determinants of internal labour markets in organisations', *Administrative Science Quarterly*, Vol. 29, 1984, pp550–72.

4   SONNENFELD, J, A, AND PEIPERL, M, A, 'Staffing policy as a strategic response: a typology of career systems', *Academy of Management Review*, Vol. 13, 1988, pp588–600.

5   LENTZ, C, W, 'Dual ladders become multiple ladders at Dow Corning', *Research Technology Management*, Vol. 33, No. 3, 1990, pp28–34.

6   HIRSH, W, *Succession Planning: Current practice and future issues*, Brighton, Institute of Manpower Studies, 1990.

7   ROUSSEAU, D, M, AND PARKS, J, M, 'The contracts of individuals and organisations', in L. L. Cummings and B. M. Staw (eds), *Research in Organisational Behaviour*, Vol. 15, Greenwich CT, JAI Press, 1993.

8   ORGAN, D, W, 'The motivational basis of organisational citizenship behaviour', in B. M. Staw and L. L. Cummings (eds), *Research in Organisational Behaviour*, Vol. 12, Greenwich CT, JAI Press, 1990.

9   LAWRENCE, B, S, 'Age grading: the implicit organisational timetable', *Journal of Occupational Behaviour*, Vol. 5, 1984, pp23–35.

10 ROSENBAUM, J, E, 'Tournament mobility: career patterns in a corporation', *Administrative Science Quarterly*, Vol. 24, 1979, pp220–41.

11 FERENCE, T, P, STONER, J, A, F, AND WARREN, E, K, 'Managing the career plateau', *Academy of Management Review*, Vol. 2, 1977, pp602–12.

12 MOORHOUSE, H, F, 'No mean city? The financial sector and the decline of manufacturing in Britain', *Work, Employment and Society*, Vol. 3, No. 1, 1989, pp105–18.

13 WHEATLEY, M, *The Future of Middle Management*, Corby, BIM Press, 1992.

14 COULSON-THOMAS, C, AND COE, T, *The Flat Organisation: Philosophy and practice*, Corby, BIM Press, 1991.

15 HERRIOT, P, PEMBERTON, C, AND HAWTIN, E, 'The career attitudes and intentions of UK managers in the finance sector', *British Journal of Management* (in press).

16 KEENOY, T, 'HRM: a case of the wolf in sheep's clothing?' *Personnel Review*, Vol. 19, No. 2, 1990, pp3–9.

17 NOER, D, M, *Healing the Wounds: Overcoming the trauma of layoffs and revitalising downsized organisations*, San Francisco, CA, Jossey-Bass, 1993.

18 HERRIOT P, AND PEMBERTON, C, *New Deals: The revolution in managerial careers*, Chichester, Wiley, 1995.

19 HERRIOT, P, AND PEMBERTON, C, 'Contracting careers', *Human Relations* (in press).

20 HANDY, C, *The Future of Work*, Oxford, Basil Blackwell, 1985.

21 HERRIOT, P, AND PEMBERTON, C, *Competitive Advantage through Diversity: Organisational learning from difference*, London, Sage, 1995.

22 HERRIOT, P, *The Career Management Challenge*, London, Sage, 1992.

23 PRAHALAD, C, K, AND HAMEL, G, 'The core competence of the corporation', *Harvard Business Review*, Vol. 90, No. 3, 1990, pp79–91.

24 PREMACK, S, AND WANOUS, J, P, 'A meta-analysis of realistic job preview experiments', *Journal of Applied Psychology*, Vol. 70, 1985, pp706–19.

25 HERRIOT, P, 'Selection as a social process', in M. Smith and I. Robertson (eds), *Advances in Assessment and Selection*, Chichester, Wiley, 1989.

26 SCHEIN, E, H, *Career Anchors: Discovering Your Real Values*, San Diego, University Associates Inc, 1985.

CHAPTER EIGHT
National Cultures and International Management

Chris Brewster

Internationalisation of business

It is not necessary to be an expert on modern-day business to know that there are few organisations entirely limited by national boundaries. The smallest independent entrepreneur in the UK will have office equipment made in Japan or the USA; the most isolated local authority will be aware of the possibility of receiving money from the European Union (EU). At the level of the larger trading organisations, many of these companies operate across the globe or are in competition with companies operating in that way. It is indeed impossible for most employing organisations to act as if their world was bounded by the national border of the country that is their home base. Across the world there is increasing extension of trading blocks, increasing development of internationally operating multinational corporations (MNCs), and increasing internationalisation of business.

The impact of current developments adds an extra dimension to this picture. The EU has developed in a series of stages (see Brewster and Teague 1989) and is going through another spurt of increasingly close co-operation. The Maastricht Treaty has had a significant impact in focusing the minds of the European governments and civil servants, and has clearly given added impetus to EU developments.

The rapid changes in Eastern Europe have been a source of constant interest to our media over the past few years; one major effect has been the opening up of increasing trade links, with companies now straddling what used to be the Iron Curtain.

This increasing internationalisation has led, inevitably, to greater interest in the subject of international HRM and a growing realisation that many of the analyses and prescriptions laid out in the standard management textbooks are, fundamentally, drawn from one particular culture: that of the USA. They may not work in many societies – often in societies more successful economically than our own – and they need therefore to be examined with a sharp eye.

This chapter therefore examines the issues raised by the internationalisation of HRM. It does this by exploring two distinct approaches: first, using the concept of national cultures as a mechanism for analysing different national and particularly managerial values; and then using the emerging models of international HRM to identify differences between HRM in an indigenous and an international setting. The first section of the chapter outlines the concept of culture and draws on the research that has addressed the topic as far as it relates to management. The briefer second section of the chapter explores some of the attempts now being made to develop international models of HRM. The concluding part of the chapter attempts the ambitious task of bringing together these currently somewhat separate approaches to international HRM. It gives examples of the challenges these ideas pose to the more straightforward 'Anglo-American' views of HRM, and argues that the evidence is unequivocal: there is no universally applicable model of HRM, and in these times of increasing internationalisation we shall have to become more modest and more wide-ranging in our attempts to understand HRM.

The concept of culture

A key factor in the increasing internationalisation of employment is that there are cultural differences between nations. We know that there are differences in national attitudes and value systems. Every manager in UK industry is aware that the Japanese, for example, do things differently, particularly in the way they manage their people. Of course most UK managers will not be very clear what the differences are in any detail, and the dangers of this form of anecdotal stereotyping are clear. It is not just that our stereotypes often come from very limited and often biased information (how much do we *really* know about Japanese culture, for example?), but more importantly it is also the case that people are all different. So despite our general stereotypes managers who operate internationally know that, although they may be atypical, it is not difficult to find brusque, time-pressured South Americans; relaxed, easygoing US executives; dictatorial Scandinavian managers – and so on. To treat any of them on the assumption that they were bound to conform to one of the national stereotypes could lead to difficulties.

We are therefore faced with a dilemma: we know that national cultures can be very important, particularly in understanding the process of doing business in different situations, but we also know that stereotypes are dangerous. The dilemma can be resolved by being clear about our definitions and our levels of analysis.

Definitions

There are many definitions of the word 'culture'. In 1952, well before the explosion of studies that has accompanied the internationalisation of world trade, researchers found, in a much-quoted study, 164 definitions of the concept (Kroeber and Kluckhohn 1963). There have been many more since.

In practice these definitions range from those which include a wide swathe of different situations to those which are more restrictive. At one extreme lies the definition of culture as 'the way we do things around here'. It is on this broad interpretation that the notion of 'organisational cultures' is generally built.

One familiar definition is given by Hofstede (1980). He argues that culture is 'the collective programming of the mind which distinguishes the members of one human group from another – the interactive aggregate of common characteristics that influences a human group's response to its environment'. Terpstra and David (1985) apply this to the international management context: 'a learned, shared, compelling, interrelated set of symbols whose meaning provides a set of orientations for members of a society.'

In this chapter, therefore, the word 'culture' will be taken to mean something that

- is shared by almost all members of a group (and generally in this chapter that will mean a nation)
- is passed on from the older or more senior members to the younger or subordinate members
- shapes our perception of the world and of people's behaviour (eg morals, laws, customs).

As such, culture is formed by and linked to a whole series of societal artefacts (see Figure 8.1).

Levels of analysis

We will need to be clear about the level of our analysis if we are to make sense of our definition and avoid some of the common errors (particularly that of stereotyping) that bedevil this subject. It is important to be cautious

Figure 8.1
THE COMPOSITION OF CULTURE

Language
spoken
written
official
linguistic
pluralism
hierarchy
international languages
mass media

Religion
sacred objects
philosophical systems
beliefs
norms
prayer
holidays
rituals
taboos

Values and attitudes
time
achievement
work
wealth
change
scientific method
risk-taking

Law
common law
codes
foreign law
international

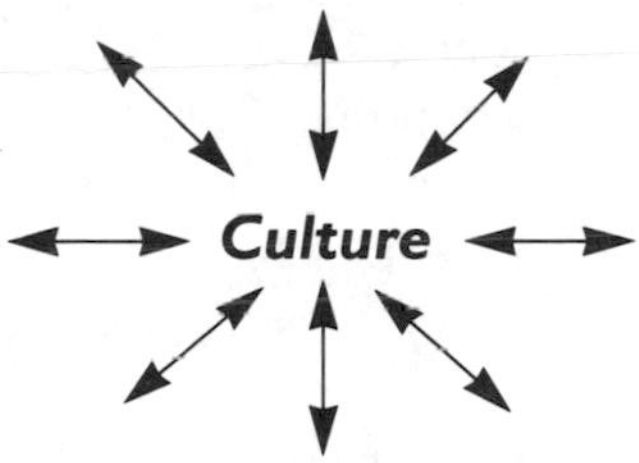

Culture

Education
formal
vocational
primary
secondary
higher
polytechnics
scientific
literary

Politics
nationalism
sovereignty
imperialism
power
national interests

Technology
transportation
energy systems
tools
communications
urbanisation
invention
science

Social organisation
kinship
social institutions
authority-structured
interest groups
social mobility
social stratification
status systems

about our sources of data and our extrapolation of it. A common error is to transpose theories at one level of analysis to another: to distinguish the societal from the individual levels, for instance.

We have also to recognise that all cultures are internally differentiated; and some may be more differentiated than others. About half the nations in the world are linguistically heterogeneous and on that basis alone are likely to be multicultural (Mendenhall *et al* 1995:85). Within any society there will be individuals who match the national-level analysis almost exactly, but also others who do not match it at all. This does not invalidate the use of this level of analysis, but warns us not to be too casual in its application.

Elements of culture

What, then, makes up these national-level cultures? The basic elements can be said to lie in the responses that nations make, or would generally accept, in relation to six fundamental questions:

- Who are we?
- How do we relate to the world?
- How do we relate to one another?
- What do we do?
- How do we think about time?
- How do we think about space?

Who are we? How does a society conceive of people's qualities as individuals? It may be generally held, for example, that people can go wrong but that they are basically good. Or the opposite. Or something in between. It may be generally considered that, in the end, people's characteristics are fixed: that however much they may be persuaded to act differently, eventually their true character will come out. Or a given society may believe that people can and do change.

If societies believe people are basically good, they will try to exercise social control through exhortation and encouragement: if people are seen as fundamentally bad, control will be exercised through a plethora of rules, laws, and policing. If societies see people as capable of being changed, they will prefer reform to punishment.

How do we relate to the world? How important is nature and the environment in our thinking? And how do we conceive of nature? Different societies have different answers to these sorts of questions. There are societies where the mark of successful people is seen as their ability to fit in with the world and to accept it. Arabic cultures frequently use the expression *inshallah* or 'God willing' to indicate their belief that there are many things over which humans have no control. In the USA, by contrast, people expect to be able to override the 'constraints' imposed by the environment: farmers are expected to 'improve' upon nature; there are research programmes aimed at controlling the weather; and, in perhaps the most radical proposal to date, there are methods of reprogramming our genes.

In a business context these last-mentioned beliefs come through strongly in the attempts to control markets, to make consumers 'need' products that they had not realised they needed, and in campaigns by organisations to win the hearts and minds of their employees.

How do we relate to others? Do we conceive of ourselves as individuals or more typically as members of a group? Do we think of everyone else in their relationship to us individually, or in relationship to the way that their group relates to our group? Societies, like individuals, do not answer these kinds of questions the same way. This has many ramifications. In the individualist, anomic societies that typify 'Western' cultures, it is quite normal for people to live far from the other members of their family; not to feel personally threatened by attacks on their organisation or social grouping; and not to expect their employer to provide work for distant relatives of theirs. In other societies it would be seen as very strange to want to leave the succour of your extended family; people would be expected to uphold the honour of the widest interpretation of 'family'; and not only would the employer be expected to reward loyalty by providing work for relatives, but this would also be seen as a sensible way for the employer to ensure that only trustworthy individuals were recruited.

In organisational and particularly HRM terms this element of culture means, for example, that some countries will be happier with concepts of individual leadership, individual responsibility, and target-setting whereas other countries will be happier with ideas of group working and shared responsibility.

What do we do? Is our purpose in life to do things, to achieve success, or is our purpose to enjoy what is happening to us? Are we people whose primary orientation is *action*, or people whose primary orientation is *being*? This differentiation will affect a large part of a particular society's approach but will certainly affect the approach to work. It is clear that managers in achievement-conscious countries ('Doing' cultures) are more likely to suffer stress. The response of managers in 'Being' cultures is more likely to involve acceptance of difficulties as the way things are – or, as one of those societies would put it, *que será será* ('what will be will be'). Managers in a Doing society who are under stress are likely to try harder, to work longer, and to place more demands on themselves; managers in a Being culture are more likely to just leave.

How do we think about space? The concept of space is also culturally determined. The amount of space we feel we need varies around the world. The further west you go in the northern hemisphere, the larger rooms and offices tend to be: very small in China, bigger in Europe, much bigger in the USA. In Japan rooms often have no walls, or only variable walls. At an individual level this is amusingly visible in meetings between British and Arab executives. The Arabs are in general comfortable being about half an arm's length away from the person they are talking to; the British prefer to be about a full arm's length away. So a sort of stately dance takes place in which the Arabs advance a step, the British move back a pace, and thus both parties proceed to circle the room.

Allied to the question of the amount of space is the privacy of that space. In Europe office doors are usually closed; even if they are not, we knock before we enter. Important meetings are held literally 'behind closed doors'. Our space is private. In Arab countries it is quite normal for people to walk freely in and out of offices, even when important business is being discussed. Space is more public.

How do we think about time? Time is perceived culturally. It has two elements: locus and speed. For the Westerner, time flows, as Western poets tell us, like a river. It moves in one direction. Time past is lost, gone. It has no importance. The locus of attention is on the future: what is still to come. In the Pacific, however, time is not seen as divisible in that way. We are located in a swirl of time with all parts connected. We are our past: the most important people for us are our ancestors and our parents. They, and our past, have shaped us. There is little point in focusing on the future: we may get killed by a runaway lorry (or rickshaw?) tomorrow.

The speed with which we feel ourselves to be 'spending' (a very Western notion) time is also culturally determined. For many Western societies time is a commodity to be 'managed' and 'used well'. Clocks are everywhere. Appointments are made, and kept (usually). Apologies are tendered if people are late. In the view of other societies, we live in time and we should focus on experiencing it; the Americans have adopted the Spanish-Mexican word *mañana* (meaning, literally, 'tomorrow') to express this more relaxed approach to the timing of things.

Research into national cultures

This outline of some of the elements of national culture (drawn mainly from Kluckholn and Strodtbeck 1961) is helpful in clarifying what we mean by that concept, but it is still fundamentally anecdotal. Researching into such a complex issue is of course difficult, and nearly all such research will be open to criticism. Nevertheless, it is only by exploring the research data and the hypotheses it generates that we will be able to move beyond the level of stories, experience, and prejudice.

In practice there is not a great deal of research in the area. By examining just a few of the more notable names it is possible to cover most of the main findings. Three European researchers have been particularly influential.

Laurent, a Frenchman, studied the responses that management students from different countries gave to a series of statements about managerial styles. He was able to show significant differences. For example, he found that some nationalities are much more likely than others to assume that a manager should have the answers to any questions that subordinates might ask; that some nationalities tend more than others to see reasons for organisational hierarchy as connected with knowing who has authority over whom; and that some nationalities are more likely than others to by-pass hierarchical structures (Laurent 1983). Laurent was able to classify the nationalities concerned according to separate theories of organisations: as political systems; as authority systems; as role-formalisation systems; and as hierarchical-relationship systems. Whichever view was taken, clear national differences emerged.

Hofstede, a Dutchman, administered a questionnaire about their values to 160,000 employees of IBM (called 'HERMES' in his work) across more than 60 countries (Hofstede 1980; 1991). He was able to analyse the results to show that there were four fundamental dimensions of difference that were correlated only with nationality. Because this is in many ways the single largest and most seminal work on the concept of culture it is worth exploring these dimensions in a little more detail.

The four dimensions that Hofstede named are: power distance, uncertainty avoidance, individualism, and masculinity.

Power distance The power distance index measures the extent to which members of a society, the less as well as the more powerful, accept that power is distributed unequally.

Uncertainty avoidance The uncertainty avoidance index measures the degree to which people feel so threatened by ambiguous situations that they create beliefs and institutions that try to avoid uncertainty.

Individualism This index measures the extent to which people believe that their primary concern in life is the well-being of themselves and their immediate family, as opposed to an orientation towards a wider grouping with more extended responsibilities and a more extended network of loyalty and support.

Masculinity This rather ineptly named index measures the extent to which achievement through such values as visible success, money, and possessions is given priority over the more caring values of nurturing and sharing.

This categorisation, taken from such an extensive piece of research, provides a discussion framework for some of the cultural differences already identified. Table 8.1 gives the resulting scores from Hofstede's work on each of these dimensions.

Table 8.1
NATIONAL DIFFERENCES: VALUES FOR HOFSTEDE'S FOUR INDICES

Country	Power distance index	Uncertainty avoidance index	Individualism index	Masculinity index
France	68	86	71	43
Great Britain	35	35	89	66
Germany (F.R.)	35	65	67	66
Italy	50	75	76	70
Japan	54	92	46	95
Spain	57	86	51	42
Sweden	31	29	71	5
USA	40	46	91	62

Trompenaars, another Dutchman, administered research questionnaires to over 15,000 managers from 28 countries. He identified seven dimensions of difference (Hampden-Turner and Trompenaars 1993:10–11):

1 *universalism v particularism:* measuring the extent to which people believe that general principles are more, or less, important than unique circumstances and relationships

2 *analysing v integrating:* similar to Lewin's (1951) distinction between specific and diffuse modes of dealing with information – how much societies prefer to deal with situations or problems by breaking them down into components, as opposed to dealing with them holistically

3 *individualism v communitarianism:* similar to Hofstede's individualism dimension

4 *inner-directed v outer-directed:* the extent to which it is seen appropriate to follow one's own views rather than adapt to the majority or to some particular reference group

5 *time as sequence v time as synchronisation:* see the discussion of time above (page 212)

6 *achievement v ascription:* how status and power are seen to be allocated in a society – whether it is given or can be gained

7 *equality v hierarchy:* similar to Hofstede's power distance dimension.

The works of Laurent, Hofstede and Trompenaars are not without their critics, who point to the narrow base of their research (management students at one business school in the first case, employees of one firm in the second, and managers the researcher had access to in the third). Indeed Hofstede himself, working with Bond (a researcher based in Hong Kong), has criticised his first four dimensions as being too heavily drawn from Western conceptions (Hofstede and Bond 1988). They argue that the uncertainty avoidance dimension ('associated . . . with man's search for Truth') may not be relevant in Eastern cultures. They find, however, another dimension, which may look odd to Western eyes but is important in the East. They call it 'Confucian dynamism'.

Confucian dynamism values

Relative importance of:	**Relative unimportance of:**
Persistence (perseverance)	Personal steadiness and stability
Ordering relationships by status and observing this order	Saving face
Thrift	Respect for tradition
Having a sense of shame.	Reciprocation of greetings, favours, and gifts.

They found high scores on this dimension to be correlated closely with the successful economies of the Pacific.

Hofstede's re-analysis of his own theories is a timely warning: none is 'right'. We have far too little data to expect the theories to have settled to any kind of accepted wisdom – and should perhaps be cautious even when they do. The value of this research lies in the fact that it is the best we have, that it gives us data against which to test our anecdotes, and that it helps to make us aware of the cultural differences and challenges that exist. If it does this in the form of theories and propositions that we can argue about, rather than in the form of established facts, this does not invalidate the research.

The challenge to management thinking

The challenges that the concept of national culture pose are seen clearly when we examine managerial theories. Management theories of the kind we use, for example, in our MBAs are generally presented as 'culture-blind' ie they are assumed to be equally applicable in all countries and cultures. If they are not being followed by managers in a particular location, it probably indicates that the country is in some ways 'backward'. Most of these theories are essentially American or Anglo-American (using 'American' here as shorthand for the USA). Such theories have come under pressure recently, because it has become apparent that countries that do not follow these theories are nonetheless equal to, or surpass, the USA in economic growth. The cultural awareness literature gives us an explanation for this. The Anglo-American way of management may fit US culture – but other approaches may fit other countries rather better. Our management theories will have to become more sophisticated and less didactic. Cultural differences will have to be recognised in such subjects as

- leadership
- organisation
- accounting.

Here are some brief examples of the challenges posed to theory in each of these topics.

Leadership Leadership theories have been developed (almost exclusively) in the USA. There have been attempts to adapt such theories to the UK and other countries, but the predominant literature is US. It reflects US culture: it is focused on individual people (the UK is high on individualism in Hofstede's data) and on a median level of power distance. The theories propound therefore a leader who will discuss with subordinates and take their views into account, but will retain the personal decision-making power. In societies that are more collectively oriented (some of those from the Pacific, for example), the model is clearly inappropriate. Leadership in these countries can be effective only if it encompasses loyalty to the group (a concept alien to US leadership literature) and group responsibility for decisions (ditto). There are no societies more individualist than that of the USA: but there are many that are very collectivist.

On the participation issue, societies can vary from the USA in either direction. If they are less participatory (higher power distance index), such as those in Arab countries, India, and Indonesia (but also France, Spain, and Belgium), leaders will be uncomfortable with the concept of allowing subordinates to get involved in decisions. And so will subordinates: 'Why are they asking me? They are the bosses – don't they know what they are doing? Is it a trap?' In countries with a lower power distance index than the USA, such as the Scandinavian, there will be forms of employee determination where managerial prerogatives of the kind laid down in US law will be challenged. The leader's decision may not always be accepted; indeed, the right to take such a decision may be disputed.

Hence many of the famous 'leadership' packages developed by US specialists, and often sold around the world for large fees, have proved unsuccessful. This includes the theories of Drucker (management by objectives), McGregor (Theory X/Theory Y), Likert (System Y), Ouchi (Theory Z), Blake-Mouton (the Managerial Grid) and Reddin (3-D Management). Although it is true that the success rate of such packages is difficult to prove or disprove, outside their own cultural base, and faced with different cultural assumptions, much of their rationale is questionable.

Organisation It has already been noted that Laurent found a link between preferred organisational models and nationality. The message is clear. Some organisational forms will work better in some cultures than in others. The clash can be seen most graphically in the subsidiaries of certain multinationals. In one German multinational operating in the UK there has been a running battle for nearly a decade between the Frankfurt headquarters and the London base over how to respond to an increasingly competitive and cut-throat business environment. Headquarter's response is to issue new regulations and subregulations to take account of the need for increased flexibility and discounting, and to expand departments with a 'rule-maintenance' function. The UK response is to ignore the rules, cut staff from the centre, expand the selling operation and, in short, do whatever is necessary to retain market share and profitability. That means, for them, ignoring headquarter's demands for data and statistics in favour of getting on with the job. The continuing, and sometimes acrimonious, debate between the two groups – both trying to respond in the best possible way for the good of the organisation – is a microcosm of the culturally different approach to organisations.

Accounting Even the hard-numbers end of management theory is culturally bound. At bottom, what we measure and how we count reflect our views of what is important. The need to balance the columns of figures is undisputed; but do we need to do that on a month-by-month or year-by-year basis? We do if we have short-term horizons. But in Japan and other countries in the Far East they expect to lend and invest for far longer before they see a return, and their accounting systems reflect that. To take another question: is money spent on training an expense or an investment? Is a new machine a cost, an asset, a depreciating asset (at what rate?), and so on? It is no wonder that accounting systems throughout the world vary markedly. They reflect deep-lying local values. Even at the hard, financial end of management, cultural awareness challenges our assumptions.

International human resource strategies

We turn now to a different approach to the internationalisation of the management of people: one drawn, in most cases, from the rather different context of managerial practice rather than of a critical psychology. It is argued that all international organisations will have to develop international HRM policies and practices. This will manifestly not be easy. On the other hand, it will be crucial to the success of the international business. Schuler *et al* (1993:721) define the field as covering

> human resource management issues, functions and policies and practices that result from the strategic activities of multinational enterprises and the impact on the international concerns and goals of those enterprises.

Most international businesses employ both locals and expatriates; most have overall strategies and try to be culturally aware in each country; they aim to be successful in each location, and successful overall. If they are to achieve this they will need to have clearly thought-out, well-integrated human resource strategies that are part of, and contribute to, their overall international strategy.

Attempts have been made to link HRM strategies to life-cycle models (Kerr 1982; Fombrun and Tichy 1983; Kochan and Capelli 1984; Kochan and Barocci 1985; Schuler 1989); to Porter's models for achieving competitive advantage in different industry conditions (Schuler and Jackson 1987; Schuler 1989); to markets (Baird *et al* 1983: Dertouzos *et al* 1989); and to groups within organisational levels (Lorange and Murphy 1984). The 1990s have been characterised by a growing realisation that nationality and international operations are at least as central a feature of modern HRM as any of these other factors.

The literature on the role of HRM in international operations is now expanding fast. Hendry (1994) has analysed the importance of human resource strategies for international growth, and there is now an increasing number of attempts to develop a theory of international HRM. Amongst other significant contributions the work of Schuler and his colleagues has perhaps been in the forefront (Schuler *et al* 1993). In particular, they go beyond the approach that international HRM is just HRM writ large, to stress the need to focus on inter-unit linkages and the likelihood of co-ordination and differentiation between headquarters and the subsidiary and between the subsidiaries themselves.

Some aspects of the Schuler approach are controversial. In particular, there have been challenges to the familiar categorisation, initiated by Perlmutter in the 1970s, of the way that international organisations develop (Mayrhofer and Brewster 1995) and also challenges to the resultant expatriation strategies (Edwards and Brewster 1995). However, the need to develop a coherent and testable framework for the analysis of international HRM is beyond dispute and this is, at the very least, a valuable starting-point.

Expatriation policies

One benefit of these types of analysis is to bridge the gap between the strategic management literature, which has tended to look at reified MNCs almost apart from any discussion of national boundaries, and the HRM literature on these organisations, which has tended to focus on the international transfers of key employees. Much of the debate about the management of these expatriates, even within MNCs, is still conducted in terms of assessments of how well the structures and systems for managing them are handled (Brewster 1991; Scullion 1995). However, in some companies the issues are being seen in a more strategic light. For these organisations the key issue is now one of 'value added': in other words, what can we do to ensure that these, our most expensive (and in many cases crucial) employees, are generating real additional value over and above that we could get from other staffing arrangements? Essentially this means assessment of the alternatives to expatriation as one approach to decreasing the cost side of the equation; assessment of ways of managing the systems and processes better as one approach to improving the value side of the equation; and a strategic assessment of the balance.

There are now, particularly within the EU, a range of alternatives to expatriation. These would include: using locals; using third-country nationals; short-term assignments; Eurocommuting; employing expatriates on local terms; and the employment of temporaries.

Where expatriates are used the pressure is to ensure more effective expatriation. This implies doing better the things that MNCs currently do to manage this group: going through the expatriation cycle of selection; contract determination; settling in; adaptation; monitoring of performance and repatriation (Dowling et al 1994; Black et al 1991; Brewster 1991; Scullion 1995).

Conclusions

The task for international organisations and scholars is therefore to reconcile the cultural and the IHRM approaches to HRM in international organisations. As a tentative attempt at this, it is worth summarising the impact of the two approaches and then drawing out the links between them. At that point we can look, briefly, to future developments.

·As we have seen, an awareness of national culture poses a challenge to management theory in many areas. Of course, it is where people are concerned directly that the most direct challenges arise: in other words, in the HRM arena. To pull the discussion in this chapter together it is worth examining some examples:

- motivation
- employee appraisal
- careers
- reward systems
- management development and careers
- employee relations.

Motivation

Hofstede has pointed out the way that most motivation theories rely on a (US-type) pattern of uncertainty avoidance, individualism, and masculinity. They imply, for example, taking risks to get a result. That is acceptable in low uncertainty avoidance cultures such as those of the UK or the USA, but it fits less well in Germany or Japan. As Hofstede put it (Hofstede 1983:80):

> Interestingly, these security-seeking countries seem to have been doing better economically . . . than the risk takers, but the management theories that tell us that risk taking is a good thing were made in the US or Great Britain, not in Japan or Germany.

Employee appraisal

In the USA and most of Europe, employee appraisal is seen as a sophisticated way of ensuring either that people's performance is monitored or that their potential is identified (or both). Performance appraisal is however largely unknown in the Pacific, and indeed certain economies there seem to have managed quite well without it. Its proper context is a society where individuals are held accountable, rather than groups; where power distances are not so great that all responsibility rests at the top, or so small that the opinion of a subordinate is just one amongst many; where time horizons are short and deadlines matter; and where the need to formalise opinion at regular intervals is unquestioned. Few societies have this combination of values and it is therefore unsurprising that many adopt the process of employee appraisal grudgingly or not at all.

This is, amongst other things, a considerable problem for multinational companies trying to assess the performance of their managerial cadre – their expatriates – in different countries. It is even less easy if the process of appraisal is conducted half-heartedly or 'adapted' to fit local mores. More and more, MNCs are tending to adopt a 'multiple' approach to appraisal, recognising the weakness of any attempt to impose one, 'best' system and using instead a battery of methods, amongst them assessment of financial results, reports, visits, and formal appraisal systems.

Reward systems

Clearly some cultures (those with a high uncertainty avoidance index) will be happier with laid-down, stable pay systems; others will prefer more flexibility. Cultural differences may also help to explain why some of the stability-preferring countries tend to include a substantial element of employee benefits in the reward package. Equally, some cultures (those with a high individualism index) will prefer individually based systems, whereas others will find that uncomfortable. There may be here too an explanation of why some countries (including the most economically successful) have tended to have pay set at the national level, whereas other countries have developed decentralised bargaining systems.

Management development and careers

Cultural assumptions of status, career, appraisal, and reward will all influence management development. The responsibility that the organisation is expected to take for someone's development and career will vary, as will the individual's expectations. In societies that have an 'ascriptive' culture, where it is believed that their position is the result of eg the caste they are born into or the decision of a deity, there will be little drive for development. The perceived status of the management teacher will also vary (a 'guru' in some societies, 'another bloody academic' in others), and the national culture will also have a profound influence on the local education system from childhood to adulthood. There will also be influences on the status and success of development methods: a bigger job and 'sink or swim' philosophy will be acceptable in some cultures but not in others; students in the UK will challenge their lecturers and debate with them, but students in China are less likely to do so.

Concepts of careers, of career planning, and of career management depend upon underlying ideas about our ability to influence the world, our individual or collective orientation, and our approaches to achievement (Evans *et al* 1989). If, like many Arabs, we believe *inshallah* ('God willing'), or like many Africans, that our extended family comes before any personal or work objectives, or like many Scandinavians, that personal ambition and competitiveness are unpleasant traits, then a UK approach to careers will be inappropriate.

'Typical' career paths vary from country to country. In the UK individuals often change employer, but more rarely occupation. In Japan employees far more frequently change their occupation or function, but may well remain with the same employing organisation throughout their working lives.

In Europe many women have careers; in many Pacific countries women are not expected to have a career at all. And within Europe the kinds of jobs in which women will find it easy to succeed are different in different countries.

Employee relations

Employee relations are also affected by culture. It is not just a matter of whether a society tends to be more or less formal or legalistic, more or less individually or collectively oriented, or higher or lower on a power distance index, and whether that in turn affects the nature and role of trade unions and employment laws in that society. It is also a question of the ways in which employees are thought of and behave. All employees are individuals *and* group members, occupy some position in a hierarchy, and have some degree of information and knowledge. How these issues are handled, however, varies considerably from society to society. In some, collective representative organisations will have the right to challenge managerial action formulated in law, and their ability to play a central role in the relationship between managers and employees will be unchallenged. The concept of 'industrial relations' is an essentially Anglo-Saxon one. In continental Europe employee representative organisations are often granted more power by law than in the UK, and are also more responsive to organisational demands. In other societies all relationships may be individually based, representative organisations may be illegal, and superiors' prerogative of having power but also responsibility for all aspects of subordinates' lives will be clear.

Attempts by international organisations to impose common approaches to HRM in different countries are therefore going to be problematic. In some cases where such attempts have been made HRM specialists at corporate headquarters have been able to convince themselves that they were successful. However, a closer look showed that although the subsidiaries were able to send back appraisal forms, for example, they barely resembled any similar process carried out at headquarters; the results were not comparable.

In reality, of course, few international organisations are so naïve. In general they stay within the range of practices acceptable in each society in which they operate. MNCs are more likely to operate like the majority of organisations in the host country than they are to operate in the way that they do in the headquarters country.

HRM practices within Europe

Organisations across Europe are now developing Europe-wide strategies for HRM. These are in many cases aimed at developing a lobbying influence within the EU and are not available for public inspection. A similar shroud tends to cover the policies for attracting lower-grade employees from southern into more expensive northern countries. Much more widely discussed are the attempts made to create strategic approaches to European HRM and, in particular, to develop 'Euromanagers'.

There are arguably two developments here that are relevant. One is the attempts now being made to develop a European model of HRM that can be distinguished from traditional US models (Brewster 1995; Brewster and Hegewisch 1994; Sparrow and Hiltrop 1994). The second development concerns the practical issue of employment strategies within Europe. This has two elements: the identification of those areas where Euro-wide policies are important, as against those where local policies are more appropriate; and the development of policies in those areas.

This is not a straightforward proposition for MNCs. Few of them, for example, have a definition of Europe that matches the boundaries of the EU – without Switzerland or Norway. Many do not have a definition that matches the European Economic Area. It is by no means unknown for MNCs to include areas as far away as the eastern fringes of Russia, or even North Africa, within their 'European' region. The identification of subject areas in which it would make sense to develop region-wide human resource policies is therefore one that has to be taken on a case-by-case basis.

In terms of actual policies, one issue that has attracted significant attention is training and development for a European cadre of management. There is evidence that this need is being increasingly recognised in UK organisations (Scullion 1994) and that steps are being taken to address the complex of problems associated with the different forms of alliance and joint venture that are spreading in Europe (Bournois 1992; Bournois and Chauchat 1990). It is however also worth noting that, following discussions with managers who deal with these topics, Storey (1992) refers to the 'myth' of the Euromanager.

International HRM in the future

This chapter has shown that discussions of HRM that assume they are addressing a universally understood topic are inevitably limited. The facts are unequivocal: not only that practice (and the underlying values which give rise to that practice) varies from nation to nation, but also that our understanding of HRM itself varies – in particular, what 'good' or even 'effective' HRM is.

On the other hand, our analysis of international HRM has shown that organisations operating internationally have to develop international HRM strategies that can, if necessary, be applied globally. We are perhaps at too early a stage in our understanding to attempt a definitive reconciliation of the two perspectives here – and trite and misleading aphorisms ('think globally; act locally') are of little value. It has been argued elsewhere (Mayrhofer and Brewster 1995) that the national culture of the country of origin of most MNCs is a valuable co-ordinating 'glue' which it is dangerous to risk in some trendy attempt to become truly 'global', as some gurus recommend. Companies are not free to develop any corporate culture that they choose (Johnson and Scholes 1993): they operate within the limitations of their home and, if different, their current dominant culture. They are to a substantial degree bound by their national culture and it is within those limits that they can attempt to develop their own corporate culture.

There seems little doubt that the influence of international factors on HRM will continue to grow. The UK is already a multicultural society, with class, regional, gender, and racial differences. UK managers will have to be ever more aware of these cultural differences in order to have the most effective workforces. At the European level, the different cultures and national patterns are manifest in many areas: most of all, perhaps, in HRM (Brewster and Hegewisch 1994). An awareness of these differences is a necessity for the increasing numbers of organisations operating across Europe, indeed for anyone who wants to understand developments in the EU's social policy.

Internationally, the UK has a major advantage, and a major problem, because of the English language. At a conservative estimate English is the mother tongue of around 300 million people and is an official language for 1,400 million people in over 60 countries. It is the language most likely to be learned as a 'business' language when people come to develop their linguistic abilities. Three-quarters of the world's mail and four-fifths of the world's electronic data is in English. Many international businesses – air transport, for example – have English as their official language of communication (Crystal 1987:358). The obvious advantages that this gives us in certain situations have to be set against our poor language skills and the problem these create in trying to appreciate other cultures. Paradoxically, if the UK is to get the greatest benefit from the widespread use of English, Britons will have to develop their own ability to speak other languages.

Organisations that operate internationally face different problems. Some are experienced international operators. Most of these are facing problems of cost control and pressures for localisation; they are having to manage a consequent reduction in the number of international employees. Others are new to the game and are having to work hard to get themselves up to a higher level of sophistication, even though they may not be in a position to copy the methods of the more experienced international operators. Over the next few years the latter group are likely to predominate in the EU. Both groups are going to have to pay more attention to their international human resource strategies. This means making careful judgements between the need to be sensitive to national cultures and the need to control human resources across international boundaries.

References

BAIRD, L, MESHOULAM, L, DeGIVE, G, (1983), 'Meshing human resource planning with strategic business planning, a model approach', *Personnel*, Vol.60, No. 5, pp14–25.

BLACK, J, S, MENDENHALL, M, AND ODDOU, G, (1991), 'Toward a comprehensive model of international adjustment: an integration of multiple theoretical perspectives', *Academy of Management Review*, 16, pp291–317.

BOURNOIS, F, (1992), 'The impact of 1993 on management development in Europe', *International Studies of Management and Organization*, Vol.22:3, pp7–29.

BOURNOIS, F, AND CHAUCHAT, J-H, (1990), 'Managing managers in Europe', *European Management Journal*, Vol.6:1, pp3–18.

BREWSTER, C, (1991), *The Management of Expatriates*, London, Kogan Page.

BREWSTER, C, (1995), 'Towards a "European" model of human resource management', *Journal of International Business Studies*, 26(2), pp1–21.

BREWSTER, C, AND HEGEWISCH, A, (1994), *Policy and Practice in European Human Resource Management*, London, Routledge.

BREWSTER, C, AND TEAGUE, P, (1989), *European Community Social Policy*, London, IPM.

CRYSTAL, D, (1987), *The Cambridge Encyclopedia of Language*, Cambridge, Cambridge University Press.

DERTOUZOS, M, L, LESTER, R, K, AND SOLOW, R, M, (1989), *Made in America: Regaining the productive edge*, Cambridge, Mass., MIT Press.

DOWLING, P, SCHULER, R, AND WELCH, D, (1994), *Human Resource Management*, 2nd edn, USA, Wadsworth INC.

EDWARDS, C, AND BREWSTER, C, (1995), 'Do you need expatriates?', Cranfield School of Management working paper.

EVANS, P, LANK, E, AND FARQUAR, A, (1989), 'Managing human resources in the international firm: lessons from practice', in P. Evans, Y. Doz and A. Laurent (eds), *Human Resource Management in International Firms: Change, globalisation, innovation*, London, Macmillan.

FOMBRUN, C, AND TICHY, N, M, (1983), 'Strategic planning and human resource management: at rainbow's end', in R. Lamb (ed), *Recent Advances in Strategic Planning*, New York, McGraw-Hill.

HAMPDEN-TURNER, C, AND TROMPENAARS, F, (1993), *The Seven Cultures of Capitalism*, New York, Doubleday.

HENDRY, C, (1994), *Human Resource Strategies for International Growth*, London, Routledge.

HOFSTEDE, G, (1980), *Cultures' Consequences*, London, Sage Publications.

HOFSTEDE, G, (1983), 'The cultural relativity of organisational practices and theories, *Journal of International Business Studies*, Vol.13,3, pp75–90.

HOFSTEDE, G, (1991), *Culture and Organisations: Software of the mind*, Maidenhead, McGraw-Hill.

HOFSTEDE, G, AND BOND, M, (1988), 'The Confucius connection: from cultural roots to economic growth', *Organisational Dynamics*, spring, pp5–21.

JOHNSON, G, AND SCHOLES, K, (1993), *Exploring Corporate Strategy*, Hemel Hempstead, Prentice Hall.

KERR, J, (1982), 'Assigning managers on the basis of the life cycle', *Journal of Business Strategy*, Vol.2:4, pp58–65.

KLUCKHOLN, F, AND STODTBECK, F, (1961), *Variations in Value Orientations*, New York, Row Peterson & Co.

KOCHAN, T, A, AND BAROCCI, T, A, (1985), *Human Resource Management and Industrial Relations*, Boston, Little Brown.

KOCHAN, T, A, AND CAPELLI, P, (1984), 'The transformation of industrial relations and the personnel function', in P. Osterman (ed.), *Internal Labour Markets*, Cambridge, Mass., MIT Press.

KROEBER, A, L, AND KLUCKHOLN, F, (1963), *Culture: A critical review of concepts and definitions*, New York, Vintage/Random House.

LAURENT, A, (1983), 'The cultural diversity of Western conceptions of management', *International Studies of Management and Organisation*, Vol.XIII, No.1–2, spring–summer, pp75–96.

LEWIN, K, (1951), *Field Theory and Social Science*, New York, Harper and Row.

LORANGE, P, AND MURPHY, D, (1984), 'Bringing human resources into strategic planning: systems design considerations', in C. J. Fombrun *et al* (eds), *Strategic Human Resource Management*, New York, John Wiley.

MAYRHOFER, W, AND BREWSTER, C, (1995), 'In praise of ethnocentricity: expatriate policies in European MNCs', Cranfield School of Management working paper.

MENDENHALL, M, PUNNETT, B, J, AND RICKS, D, (1995), *Global Management*, Cambridge, Mass., Blackwell.

SCULLION, H, (1994), 'Staffing policies and strategic control in British multinationals', *International Studies of Management & Organization*, Vol.24, p3.

SCULLION, H, (1995), 'International human resource management', in J. Storey (ed.), *Human Resource Management: A critical text*, London, Routledge.

SCHULER, R, S, (1989), 'Human resource strategy: focusing on issues and actions', *Organisational Dynamics*, Vol.19(1), pp4–20.

SCHULER, R, S, DOWLING, P, J, AND DE CIERI, H, (1993), 'An integrative framework of strategic international human resource management', *International Journal of Human Resource Management*, 4(4):717–64.

SCHULER, R, S, AND JACKSON, S, E, (1987), 'Linking competitive strategies with human resource practices', *Academy of Management Executive*, Vol.1, p3.

SPARROW, P, R, AND HILTROP, J-M, (1994), *European Human Resource Management in Transition*, Hemel Hempstead, Prentice Hall.

STOREY, J, (1992), *Developments in the Management of Human Resources*, Oxford, Blackwell.

TERPSTRA, V, AND DAVID, K, (1985), *The Cultural Environment of International Business*, Dallas, South-western Publishing.

Further reading

ADLER, N, (1986), *International Dimensions of Organisational Behaviour*, The Kent International Business Series.

ADLER, N, AND JELINEK, M, (1986), 'Is "Organisation Culture" culture bound?', *Human Resource Management*, spring, Vol.25, No.1, pp73–90.

DOWLING, P, J, AND SCHULER, R, S, (1993), *International Dimensions of Human Resource Management*, PWS-Kent.

HARRIS, P, AND MORAN, R, (1979), *Managing Cultural Differences*, Gulf Publications.

HOFSTEDE, G, (1980), 'Motivation, leadership and organisations: do American theories apply abroad?', *Organisational Dynamics*, summer, pp42–63.

ONDRACK, D, A, (1985), 'International human resource management in European and North-American firms', *International Studies of Management and Organisation*, Vol.15, No.1, pp6–32.

PERLMUTTER H, V, (1969, 'The tortuous evolution of the multinational corporation', *Columbia Journal of World Business*, January–February, pp9–18.

TAYEB, M, H, (1992), *The Global Business Environment: An introduction*, London, Sage.

TROMPENAARS, F, (1993), *Riding the Waves of Culture*, London, Nicholas Brealey Publishing.

CHAPTER NINE

Economic Indicators
of HRM

Andrew Mayo

Introduction

Ever since the days when Robert Townsend (1970) advocated getting rid of the personnel department, organisations have questioned the economic value of human resource departments. As an overhead they become easy victims of cost-cutting programmes or candidates for outsourcing. All too often the function is the butt of jokes in the organisation, causing those who work in human resources to be understandably defensive and often to go to extraordinary lengths to appear helpful. At the same time, organisational leaders are the first to acknowledge that people are their 'prime asset' or 'most critical resource'. Two questions for organisations are:

- Is HRM valued as an essential and integral contribution to business success, rather than being seen as just a new name for traditional personnel departments?
- Is the contribution from human resources a net positive or negative on the 'bottom line'?

If we go back some years, personnel was concerned with the welfare and administration of people, whereas their contribution to results was more the province of work study engineers. This lingers on: Fitz-Enz (1990) quotes results from his survey of over 1,500 human resource professionals world-wide to the effect that the top two arguments for their existence were 'keeping the company out of court' and 'providing standards, consistency and equity'. A parallel survey of line managers indicated a general image of human resource departments as too costly, constraining, and delivering little value.

The heavy focus on individual productivity exemplified by Taylorism has become less appropriate as the percentage of knowledge workers has increased. Organisations need to maximise potential and decision-making capability at all levels. A more complex set of skills and parameters contributes to effectiveness than before, in every area. The IBM/Towers-Perrin report of 1992 surveyed 2,961 firms to discover what different interest groups identified as the key human resource issues for the year 2000. Human resource people and line colleagues agreed closely on the top five, which were: productivity, management development, teamwork, workforce planning, and skills development.

It seems reasonable to start with the premiss that in any competitive sector the organisation that can achieve the maximum utilisation of the potential capability and accumulated learning of its people will have a distinct and lasting advantage. This leads into many areas that are a long way from administrative systems and processes, even though they can play a major part in helping or hindering effectiveness. In this chapter we shall look at both

- measures of effectiveness that concern the contribution of people to results
- the effect that dedicated and/or specialist HRM resources may have in enhancing those measures.

In 1993 the (former) Institute of Personnel Management (now the Institute of Personnel and Development) published a consultative document, *Managing People: The changing frontiers*. It recognised the irreversible economic forces that were making the deployment of people so critical, and at the same time required a different role for human resource practitioners. There is no space in tomorrow's organisations for individuals or functions that do not add value towards organisational goals. Fitz-Enz (1990) introduced the concept of 'human value management', and subtitled his book 'The value-adding human resource management strategy for the 1990s'. He describes this simply as *'creating value through and with people'*, categorising value in three ways:

- *human* eg motivation, satisfaction, development, co-operation
- *financial* eg revenues, costs, margins, waste
- *production* eg efficiency, productivity, quality.

Clearly people contribute to all of these. Organisational culture and processes are heavily influenced by whether the underlying attitude is that people are a *cost* or whether they are seen as an *investment*. Likewise we may ask whether the human resource function is seen as primarily a cost to be minimised or as a creative, proactive value-adding contribution.

The 'bottom line'

The concept of the 'bottom line', meaning the profitability of an enterprise (and much beloved of macho executives), has come in for a very necessary review. As Hampden-Turner (1994) shows, this has been a peculiarly Anglo-American concept of capitalism, particularly in its short-termism. It is encouraging therefore that it is from the USA that the reassessment comes – from the work of Robert Kaplan and David Norton (1992) in explaining the concept of the 'balanced score card'. This recognises that financial achievement is the result of achieving success on a range of measures in four areas:

- *customer perspective* – how do customers perceive us?
- *internal perspective* – what must we excel at?
- *innovation and learning perspective* – can we continue to improve and create value?
- *financial perspective* – how do we look to the shareholders?

Goals and measures can be defined under each of these headings. Following on from this principle of balance, organisations have different sets of *stakeholders*. The most common core set in a commercial organisation includes: customers, employees, shareholders, and the community. Setting the areas of measurement is a key task for organisations.

Professor Robert Eccles of Harvard argues that one starts with a model of the organisation showing the key variables by which it is managed and the relationship between them. He argues that there should not be more than six or seven of these. Understanding and reaching a consensus about these variables ensures that all stakeholders will be satisfied. An example

Figure 9.1
KEY VARIABLES IN A MANUFACTURING ORGANISATION

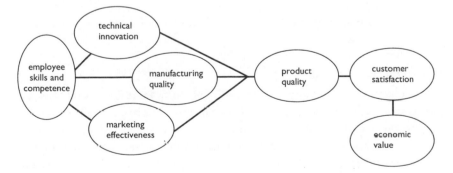

for a manufacturing organisation is depicted in Figure 9.1. For each of these areas measurement methodologies are devised and goals set.

Hewlett-Packard is one of many companies seeking a balanced approach to results, goals and measurements. They deploy a company-wide executive performance review system, the measures being adjusted each year. In 1995 they used the following:

Customer satisfaction	People productivity
Market competitiveness	Employee opinion
	Organisation diversity
Revenue growth	
Financial competitiveness	Future success
	credibility
Profitability	
Inventory management	Teamwork

Rank Xerox concentrate on four main areas – market share, return on assets, people satisfaction, and customer satisfaction. At least 40 per cent of an executive's goals concern the satisfaction of people and customers.

The balanced scorecard approach needs a range of non-financial measures complementing financial ones. In this chapter we shall concentrate on establishing the links between HRM and economic results, rather than focus on the 'softer' measures (which normally take the form of focused survey data).

Measures of people effectiveness

Working hard is not necessarily an indication of working effectively. So a distinction needs to be made between *efficiency* – achieving greater outputs from the level of inputs made – and *effectiveness* – achieving for a given input a better return in its output.

The two major concepts used to evaluate these factors are *productivity* and *added value*.

Productivity

The general definition of productivity is very simple: it is the *level of output* generated by a *given level of input*. It is common to use people costs as the input, but clearly it can be applied to any type of cost in an organisation. Such measures are important for interfirm comparison and for tracking increases in effectiveness, data often being in the public domain. Constant improvement is necessary for sustaining a competitive position.

Many firms focus on output/head as a measure. The output measured may be sales, profit, added value, production volume, design successes, and so on. However, at the enterprise level it is an imperfect measure, for a number of reasons. Using 'headcount' as a base implies that each head has the same average cost. They clearly do not, especially in an international corporation. Many quite illogical decisions in resourcing may result from instructions and budgets related to 'headcount'. Some reductions can be achieved with very little change in actual cost to the organisation. Taking an extreme example, for the price of one chief executive officer (CEO) in Switzerland one can employ several hundred workers in a developing country! Yet it is not unknown for US corporations to structure around 'Europe, the Middle East and Africa' and supply headcount targets to the appropriate vice-president to implement in his or her area!

The other flaw in this approach is the assumption that employees who are counted as permanent 'headcount' are the only input into the costs of labour services when organisations increasingly have a range of human resources contributing to their goals and outputs. How often has a head-count restriction been circumvented by the use of temporary staff!

We need therefore a cost measure, as the input, and if we are measuring labour productivity it should be the total cost of the contributing labour. This would typically be the direct salary costs of employees, plus 'on-costs' such as benefits, social security, and pensions, together with the cost of bought-in labour services contributing to the output measure. Thus, measures such as total sales/total people cost are useful.

Added value

Added value is perhaps the most useful approach to measuring the contribution and productivity of people. It may be defined as 'the wealth created through the efforts of the enterprise and its people'.

It can be calculated as a *residual* ie as the difference between the revenue streams and the costs of bought-in materials and services. Alternatively it can be calculated as an *aggregate* of compensation and capital costs with operational profit. There are different accounting interpretations of capital and profit items, so the first definition is usually the better to take.

Quinn (1992) cites statistical data from the USA indicating that the added value from the manufacturing sector is about the same as the private services sector – about $40,000 per head. The more profit and loss (P&L) summaries can be devolved to smaller units, the closer we can come to assessing the added value of teams within the organisation. For service providers, the price that a customer is prepared to pay for an individual or a team, less the (usually low) costs associated with providing the service, gives a figure for added value that can be taken down even to individual contributors. For overhead employees, a measure of their value is what the organisation would have to pay to an outside provider. However, it should be financially higher than this because of the value of 'inside knowledge' – of knowing what can be realistically achieved within the culture.

This is tested in harsh commercial reality with the trend for outsourcing managed services and competitive tendering of public services. The further one goes from the 'sharp end', the less easy it is to evaluate the added value of an individual. A senior manager may make a decision one day that has a very large impact, but for considerable periods be just supporting and developing the added value from others.

The US giant ITT advocated the use of value added/total people cost, which they called the 'compensation recovery factor' and regarded as the best enterprise-level measure of effectiveness in utilising people.

Spencer (1986) discusses a number of measures. He advocates three. The first is value added/employee. The second is comparative staff system ratios: the ratio of overhead people to total employees, or to revenue-earning staff. This is otherwise referred to as the 'direct to indirect ratio'. The third measure is the average span of control: the number of employees under each manager or supervisor. De-layering in organisations has changed this considerably.

Just as businesses discuss the value chain in their operations, so the question of the added-value chain of management should be addressed. The old premise was that the scheduling, monitoring, and control of people were essential activities. A new premise, however, states that if people are given five essential elements – direction, resources, performance measures, training, and confidence – then they will be able to organise tasks themselves. Thus the only justification for each level of management is that it adds value in its own right. Organisations implementing de-layering and empowerment have not always provided all these five essentials.

Staff utilisation rates Firms whose livelihood is based on their staff personally earning revenue have timesheets as a way of life. Where physical products are the output, utilisation of people and capital assets can be turned into a variety of local productivity ratios. Measuring the productivity of overhead staff is, however, much more difficult. Spencer (1986) advocates the concept of 'applied rate'. This is the number of hours billed to specific projects divided by the number of hours paid (gross applied rate) or worked (net applied rate). Standard gross applied rates in professional firms would be between 60 per cent and 75 per cent ie between 156 and 195 days billable in a year. A manager of a staff department may need to utilise up to 50 per cent of his or her personal time for management and administration. This should distinguish between added value management activity (which would include setting and giving direction, adding ideas and experience to the projects of subordinates, communication of what is happening, and time spent coaching and developing) and routine activity. Clearly the first should be maximised and the second minimised, as far as is consistent with maintaining optimal efficiency.

The balance sheet – people as assets

The balance sheet is about the state of health of a business, and indicates its present and future viability. *Assets* typically include fixed assets such as plant and buildings as well as liquid assets such as debtors and bank balances. Unfortunately, the problem of finding a satisfactory method of accounting for people (human asset accounting) has never been solved in a way that leads to its widespread use. We can regard human resources as a largely variable cost on the P&L account; indeed the expenditure incurred in paying for them appears there. At the same time we can regard them as an asset that appreciates with experience and investment in continuing learning.

Can these assets be valued? They may be a significant competitive advantage, particularly if specialised and scarce. Capitalising 'non-tangible' assets is a constant difficulty. Information technology companies have to decide whether to capitalise investments in software; if they do, they normally depreciate each year's investment over a period. Should 'brands' be capitalised, as the food and drinks company Grand Metropolitan suddenly decided to do in the late 1980s? Should the same be done for training investment? The problem with this is that it is very difficult to relate revenue streams to a specific investment.

The best indicator of an *individual's* relative value is probably the gross remuneration they can command as a full-time employee, or a proportion of their free market value if they had to sell their capability. The latter is nearly always a higher sum. This is to compensate for the lack of continuous employment and for associated benefit packages. On the other hand, whether reflected in the remuneration paid or not there may be a premium asset value arising from the specialised knowledge and experience that the person has of the organisation, its history, and its people; their ability to understand and work with the culture and the politics; or the 'intellectual property' value that they personally hold.

Likert (1967) attempted a system of human asset accounting which was applied in practice in the R. G. Barry Corporation of Columbus, Ohio. A human capital balance sheet was used, where investments in replacements and development were balanced with losses through attrition and an amortisation based on expected future service. The basis was a cumulative historical cost–asset valuation ie recruitment and development. The assumption was that if $x was invested in an individual's development, then his or her asset value increased by $x. Such an assumption does of course raise a number of questions as to the effectiveness of the development spend.

Flamholtz, a major contributor to the field of human asset accounting, asserts that the aim of HRM is to optimise human resource value. He derives a complex model for the measurement of individual value (Flamholtz 1985). An individual's *conditional value* is the present worth of the *potential* services that could be rendered if the individual stayed with the organisation for x years. The conditional value is a combination of productivity (performance), transferability (flexible skills), and promotability. The last two are heavily influenced by the first element. This needs to be multiplied by a probability factor that he or she will stay for x years. This gives the *expected realisable value*, which is a measure of the person's value. One way to calculate the effect from a learning programme would be to estimate the change in value resulting from the change in productivity, transferability, or promotability.

Few will have the patience to do this rigorously, but from time to time it may help to understand the value of investing in people to do so. Flamholtz quotes the example of the increase in individual value of people attending a particular management development programme, where the value of those who attended against those who had not rose from $81K to $93.5K a rise of (15 per cent). The cost of the programme is not stated, but probably it was about $3,000. Such calculations are loaded with assumptions, but the important question is: 'Does this proposed investment in our human assets give an acceptable rate of return?' Many training programmes do not, because they do not address any defined learning needs of the individuals or the group attending.

Value normally increases as an individual becomes more mature. In the early years investment in learning may be for a long-term return. This is true for graduate trainee programmes and apprenticeships, for example. ICL has a 'Eurograduate' training programme, hiring graduates from various

European countries and training them together. Much of the 10 months' training takes the form of work assignments, but it is essentially a vehicle for learning. It costs about £30,000 per person. The return from this investment is some years away through the creation of a group of cross-national friends who will use their network and cross-cultural experiences in leadership roles.

Giles and Robinson (1972), in a joint IPM and ICMA paper, proposed the 'human asset multiplier'. This represents a number of years' capitalisation of annual remuneration. This is described in the following steps:

1   Distinguish the break-up value of the total assets and the value as 'a going concern'. The difference measures the value of the management and employees.

2   The human asset value should be less than, or equal to, the going concern value (say, 7 × profits), less the net assets (due allowance being made for other goodwill elements).

3   Relate the result to the gross payroll to arrive at the average multiplier.

4   This is weighted for different categories of employees by assessing their personal value as part of the total asset value. The weighting, or multiplier, reflects:

    qualifications/expertise   experience
    attitudes   promotion capability
    loyalty   replacement scarcity

    and estimates of expected future service.

5   Apply the multiplier to gross remuneration.

As an example, in one case to which the method was applied, they evaluated the multipliers as:

senior management   2.5+
middle management   1.5–3
supervisors   1–2
clerical/operative   0–1.5

When does an asset become a liability?

Most fixed assets depreciate but do not normally become a liability ie have negative value. Human assets *can* become liabilities, however. Their knowledge and skills can depreciate in value and relevance with time and, although it is often recognised far too late, their 'portfolio' may have fallen behind competitive levels.

Figure 9.2
THE IMPORTANCE OF CONTINUOUS LEARNING

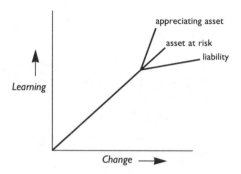

Figure 9.2 is another way to express the formula that the rate of learning needs to be greater than, or equal to, the rate of change. If individuals, teams, and organisations keep along, or above, the 45° line then they remain assets. However, once they fall below they run the risk of becoming a liability, in that their skills become obsolete and there may no longer be a place for them. If termination has to be evoked, the cost may be up to two or three years' salary, depending on the country, the organisation's policies, and the person's years of service. There is a mutual role *and* interest here in the continuous benchmarking of an individual's capability profile against the needs of the organisation and its customers.

The difficulties in putting numbers on our human assets should not deflect us from the principles involved. Even though a method may be imprecise, if at least we use it at regular periods it enables us to see the *trends* taking place. Thus, calculating 'shareholder value' and matching against the asset value on the balance sheet on a regular basis is one way to track progress.

The premium between the *market value* and the *net asset value* according to the balance sheet is normally described as *goodwill*. The value of human assets, of advantageous systems and processes, of brand image(s), and of 'intellectual property' may all be generally or specifically included. Quinn (1992) refers to 'Tobin's Q' as a ratio of market value as a percentage of asset value. He quotes Tom Watson Jr of IBM as saying:

All the value of this company is in its people. If you burned down all our plants, and we just kept our people and our information files, we would soon be as strong as ever. Take away our people and we might never recover.

This premium may be quite substantial. Quinn cites some acquisitions in the USA between 1987 and 1990 with premiums from 55 per cent to 1,720 per cent over the physical assets. These premiums represent the value of people, databases, organisational capability, systems, alliances, and Intellectual Property Rights (IPRs).

The effects of competence, learning and development

A chief executive of Motorola is credited with the statement, 'If you think training is expensive, try ignorance.' Today we would go further, and see learning as the most pervasive and critical influence on competitive advantage or disadvantage. Learning is the key to increasing value at every level – for the individual, for business teams, and for the organisation as a whole.

The commonest system of evaluation (Kirkpatrick 1975) of formal learning programmes goes as follows:

Level 1 Programme satisfaction (where 'programme' may be a series of learning experiences). This assesses how people *feel* about a programme.

Level 2 Measurable increase in knowledge, skills, attitudes, or experience.

Level 3 Measurable impact on the results of the person's role: whether he or she *does* anything differently as a result of the programme.

Level 4 Measurable impact on the organisation's objectives.

The last level is one that causes much difficulty. To come to qualitative conclusions regarding links between specific learning and increased customer satisfaction, innovation, or image improvement, for example, can seem quite credible. The difficulty is always to relate investment to bottom-line measures.

This is however lessened if we take the trouble to define the learning needs as precisely as possible in the first place; the better this is done, the easier evaluation is afterwards. (See Figure 9.3.)

The Saratoga Institute (Fitz-Enz 1995) has developed a seven-step approach to evaluation, as follows:

1   Specify as programme objectives the desired capability change in event delegates.

Figure 9.3
DEFINING LEARNING NEEDS

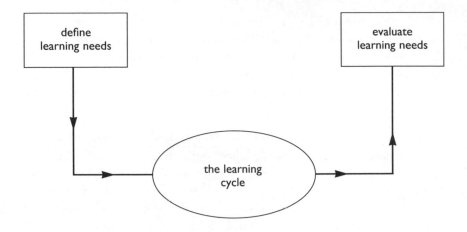

2   Design programme to meet objectives using appropriate learning methodologies.

3   Collect Level-3 measures appropriate to the group before attending (and, if possible, identify a control group of employees against which the delegates can be compared). Design capability diagnostics where possible.

4   Implement learning. Use pre/post-diagnostics wherever appropriate.

5   Collect Level-3 data two to three months after end of event.

6   Compare data with control group, if available; assess effects of other variables on data.

7   Provide follow-up event to check maintenance of capability change, and reset new needs.

In a 1994 study on strategic HRM the Boston Consulting Group asserted that they believed 25 to 40 per cent of training spend was misspent or redundant, as matched against well-defined needs derived from a business requirement. They discovered also that although 80 per cent of companies did spend on training, fewer than 20 per cent of these did any evaluation, and only 1 per cent could claim rigorous cost–benefit assessments. As mentioned earlier, the benefits often become clearer if we think of the effects of *not* spending.

The connection between the continuous generation of fresh revenues as a direct result of effective organisational learning is easy to make. It includes:

- learning about what is happening in the market-place and in the environment and being able to respond speedily through bringing more innovative products and services to the market faster than others
- having the knowledge and skills that gives customers confidence in the products and services offered
- increasing the market value of teams or individuals in their ability to earn revenue through their expertise.

Other valuable returns might include increased

- capability to lead or motivate employees/teams to better results
- flexibility in the range of roles a person is able to perform
- opportunity for innovation through broader thinking, contacts, or basic knowledge
- personal performance against objectives and measures of the role
- competitive knowledge or appreciation of best practice.

Cost avoidance is the other side of this coin.

Poor or inadequate investment in learning results in an enormous waste of people-time, the great invisible cost of organisations that is rarely measured. Costs due to mistakes, ignorance, and personal agendas lead to wasted expenditures on every cost line. For example:

- duplicating the same work in different parts of the organisation, because we have not invested in the disciplines and systems of knowledge management
- solving the same problems more than once
- being locked into inappropriate processes and not being able to 'unlearn' old ways of doing things
- power games and political agendas gaining precedence over what is right for the organisation as a whole; unwillingness to share knowledge across the organisation
- spending on 'rationalisation' by paying people to leave the organisation when forethought on retraining them in new skills would have prevented both this cost and the hiring of the needed skill
- spending on training and education without thinking systematically about the learning benefits or the alternative solutions
- lost productivity and long learning curves in times of change
- spending inappropriately through lack of knowledge, skill, or experience – or through a 'not-invented-here' attitude to previous, or other's,

work (for example, money spent on consultants to solve problems already solved elsewhere)

■ people not being encouraged to take ownership of their learning and waiting for things 'to be done for them' – many opportunities are wasted because accountability is shifted away from where it rightly belongs.

It may not be easy to calculate actual figures for a particular increase in learning. However, it is often helpful to make estimates of a percentage change in productivity, added value, or competence.

Fitz-Enz (1995) quotes an example of cost-cutting that reduced a customer service programme by 50 per cent. This yielded considerable savings. However, a study of the effect of this on performance showed that the cost savings were eaten up in 45 days through mistakes made and lower productivity.

Expenditure

Expenditure in learning is normally measured only in terms of the costs of *formal* training – the sum of internal and external provision. Spencer (1986) lists in great detail all the costs that contribute to the provision of training events, including the opportunity costs of the time taken out for normal productive activity. There are of course many other learning activities, mostly involving time and therefore opportunity costs of those involved. On the other hand, if we believe in risk-taking and experimentation as allowable learning, then we need to be prepared for some unpredictable costs!

The most common measures used include:

absolute expenditure
average days per person
expenditure as a percentage of payroll
expenditure as a percentage of revenues
expenditure as a percentage of gross margin
expenditure as a percentage of spend on research and development.

(The last one compares the expenditure on people development as contrasted with product development.)

These measures can be used for comparative benchmarking (an increasingly important area) but only with care. Different sectors have different needs: younger people would be expected to score higher than the average; high-technology or rapid-change companies need heavier investment.

Typical spend rates in information technology, for example, are:

Percentage of turnover 1
Percentage of payroll 5

Market leaders typically spend at higher rates, and there is a general correlation between spend and business success over time.

The Industrial Society Training Trends (October 1993) reported an average for UK industry of about 2.5 per cent of paycost, equivalent to 4.2 days per person.

Measures of individual learning

The most direct way to measure a return for individual learning is where the additional expertise immediately merits an increased market value for the services of an individual. This is the clear justification for the intensive training given to staff by the major consultancies.

This is becoming more and more important as organisations look for ways of paying people for personal value. The philosophy is a logical extension of the new approach to HRM that is called for by empowered, learning organisations. However, it is not easy to do, especially if we want to avoid the kind of bureaucracy that job evaluation created. The techniques available are discussed elsewhere, but the description of the competence level needs to be accompanied by indicators of *output* at the same time.

For the individual, the personal portfolio of capability (in knowledge, skills, attitudes, and experience) increases, and the equation is simple (see Figure 9.4). Where a sensible measure can be made, the expression of delta C/C_1 gives a percentage increase that may be useful in assessing the effectiveness of programmes or other learning initiatives.

It is in this area that the two traditional 'halves' of HRM – compensation and people development – come closely together in a common strategic intent. The resulting focus encourages greater precision in the

Figure 9.4
CAPABILITY GAIN

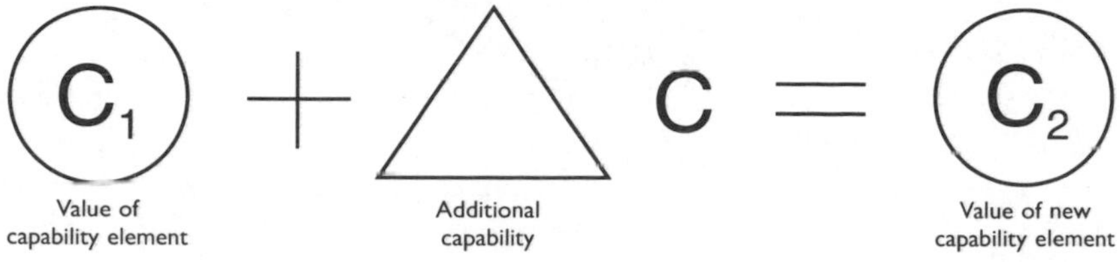

$$C_1 + \triangle C = C_2$$

Value of capability element | Additional capability | Value of new capability element

definition of learning needs, which in turn helps achieve more direct value from the chosen learning solution.

In an organisation where the ownership of personal learning plans becomes a key HRM process we would expect three of the measures of HRM effectiveness to be:

1   percentage of learning plans completed
2   percentage of learning plans realised
3   average increase in competence levels in key skill areas/person.

The cost of learning curves

An organisation is a network of learning curves. Both individuals and groups are either on natural or programmed curves (the latter term being normally used for *planned* changes in role, or role holder, or in organisation structure). We have noted above that the learning curve of young entrants is very long; of newly promoted senior executives the expectation is often that it will be almost negligible. Every change causes loss of momentum and productivity, often forgotten in change planning. This applies when individuals change jobs, new teams are formed, new subsidiaries are created, or mergers and acquisitions take place. If we look broadly at output versus cost, the graph goes like the one in Figure 9.5.

We could argue that the shaded area in Figure 9.5 represents the avoidable loss in effectiveness if we took a disciplined approach to the new learning needed. In turbulent, fast-changing organisations this is a very significant problem. In ICL we studied the business success of country operations against the stability of their management teams, and found an unmistakable positive correlation, even though those teams did not

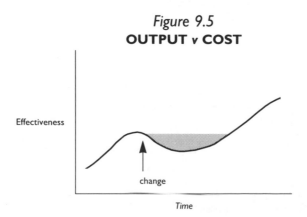

Figure 9.5
OUTPUT v COST

necessarily have 'world-class people' in them. It makes sense to have as a key measure of HRM effectiveness the time taken v time planned to achieve defined competence levels in situations of individual or team change.

Learning curves can of course be costed in absolute terms by looking at training, lost productivity, and lost opportunity costs.

The economic effectiveness of the HR function itself

The organisation of the 1990s and beyond cannot afford to have resources and activities that do not add value. We have looked at how people in general should add value and be effective, but what does this mean for a specialised and dedicated human resource department? Many of the economic influences that human resources has are not overtly visible in traditional accounts: *invisible* costs and *lost* revenues are often overlooked. They are there, nonetheless. A classic case is the cost of attrition, as discussed below.

The question that is usually answered inadequately by human resource practitioners is, 'What is the relationship between human resource processes, programmes, and initiatives with *any* level of economic measures?' Spencer (1986) gives five reasons why human resource people show little attention to this area:

- They do not know how.
- They fear that evaluation will give an unpalatable answer.
- They believe that cost–benefit figures do not mean very much.
- They believe that the effort is not worth the time – that qualitative judgements and common sense are enough.
- They find little incentive or encouragement to do it.

We can consider a hierarchy of effectiveness measures in people deployment based on the immediacy of impact and to be considered under the following headings.

Local effect – has a positive influence on measures related to a local or departmental operation eg a team-based incentive scheme, productivity improvements, motivational programmes, and learning initiatives.

Intermediate effect – direct link to a wider or longer-term set of measures, beyond the short term or local.

Ultimate effect – direct contribution to the key bottom-line organisational goals (such as those outlined above).

Long-term effect – has a positive influence in shaping future results beyond this year's goals. This may be more an act of faith than actually measurable eg investments in individual development culture change programmes, and career management initiatives.

The same distinction between *efficiency* and *effectiveness* made earlier is important. It is easy to be consumed by activity, and to do so efficiently. For example, we may have a well-oiled system of job evaluation and consequent salary grading, and yet not ask what it is contributing to human resource strategy; or a really efficient graduate application and selection machine, and yet be missing out on the quality and characteristics the future organisation will need. Again, we may have a wonderful succession-planning process, but in practice we may find ourselves short of the necessary skills. *Effectiveness* relates to strategies and goals, and moves the organisation forward and contributes real added value. All HQ departments – and quality and personnel functions are prime examples – often fail to distinguish between the excellence of their processes and what they actually achieve for the organisation.

There are two popular truisms regarding measurement:

[handwritten note: Good quote]

- You cannot manage what you do not measure.
- Anything you measure improves.

However, Harrison (1992) points out the dangers of attempting to measure the unmeasurable, and of a focus on ratios and figures that drives out managerial judgement and common sense. As the guardian of values and ethics, and the frequent owner of longer-term change processes, the senior human resource practitioner must hold a balance. Schumacher (1989) said that

> It [cost–benefit analysis] is a procedure by which the higher is reduced to the level of the lower and the priceless is given a price. It can therefore never serve to clarify the situation and lead to an enlightened decision. All it can do is to lead to self-deception or the deception of others; for to undertake to measure the immeasurable is absurd . . .

Nevertheless, if a human resource function ignores a sound range of measurements it is vulnerable to decisions made only on costs. It will lack the means of defending its roles and contribution. It also risks complacency, both in blindness as to whether its activities and priorities are what is needed at a given point in time, and in relation to its effectiveness compared to that of similar functions in competitors.

It must therefore address itself to the *outcomes* of its efforts. Services provided need measures of value and client satisfaction. Processes may be subjected to the disciplines of Total Quality Management (TQM) and re-engineering. Projects and programmes such as a recruitment assignment, introducing a new consultative system, or a new benefits policy need criteria of success and milestones of achievement. These should be precise and the function should be monitored against them. Often human resources is involved in programmes that have a long-term benefit, such as culture change. Here the organisation has a direction and some objectives, but will be learning as it progresses and may modify the endpoints through that learning. The use of diagnostic tools and opinion or evaluation surveys on a regular basis will be very helpful in such programmes.

Benchmarking, meanwhile, should be a way of life for the human resource function that wants to be in the lead. Partners for this purpose are chosen because of their similarity to the sector of the organisation, or for their reputation for best practice. 'Industrial curiosity' may of course yield information but no action; so benchmarking must be translated into targets and programmes when the results are understood. Areas for doing this fall into the hard measures, such as ratios and financial figures, and the softer comparators. These would include policies, values, functional structure and roles, survey data, and programme designs. Many organisations form opinion survey clubs where some common questions are used for cross-company comparison. Major consultants in this field also offer services of comparison with national or sector averages.

In the hard cost area there are many factual costs that can be compared. Cannon (1979) and others list comprehensive breakdowns of the people costs that are the result of human resource department decisions or are incurred by them in administration. However in comparing the function as a whole the two commonest hard measures are:

- the costs of the human resource function relative to total costs
- the ratio of total personnel staff and/or professional human resource people to total staff in an organisation (or subpart of it).

Note that there is always difficulty in defining the scope of professionals included – does it include trainers, the salary payments department, personnel, IT, or security functions, for example? Harrison (1992) reports from his study that ratios varied between 1:75 and 1:100 for total human resource functions, although the upper end could be considerably extended owing to automation of administrative processes, or devolution to line managers or teams. An internal study in British Telecom showed a variation of from five times to one-fifth of the median, depending on the nature of the site or unit. Thus some caution is needed in focusing on a *standard* target ratio, because it will depend on the rate of change that the unit is going through.

Burn and Thompson (1993) describe a system called APAC – the Audit of Personnel Activities – which is an approach to assessing the performance of the human resource function and around which they have built a national human resource database. Module one gathers fundamental data about the operation of the function and about corporate statistics. It looks at the time spent on seven major human resource activities (subdivided into 42 elements); the costs associated with the in-house human resource function; the costs of externally provided services; and time spent on human resource-related functions such as recruitment by line managers. The second module focuses on the level of satisfaction with the services provided and the needs of user departments. Module 3 audits policies and procedures against legal requirements and published codes of practice. Statistical comparisons from over 200 organisations are available. Compiled since 1989, figures quoted in February 1995 (with some from March 1991 in parentheses) included:

- personnel staff to full-time employees: 1:95 (1:84)
- human resource function costs as percentage of total: 1.7% (1.5%)
- recruitment costs per new recruit: £950
  (but varying considerably between large/small and public/private sectors)
- training costs per employee per year: £207 (£79)
- average days lost through absenteeism, all firms: 3.8%
- labour turnover, all firms: 15% (18.6%).

It is interesting to note that in four years the *number* of people in the function has gone down, but not the cost – a reflection perhaps of a greater number of higher added-value roles. There is also an interesting rise in training spend, as firms moved out of a recession and more towards the realisation of the competitive-edge factor in skills.

Jac Fitz-Enz, a prolific writer in this field, created the Saratoga Institute in California to provide a highly comprehensive database of human resource effectiveness measures, both in people deployment areas and in the function itself. The Institute has expanded considerably around the world, and participants have access to a software package that looks at over 60 preprogrammed benchmarks. The aim of the Institute is to enable benchmarking against best practice as far as possible with comparative organisations. Surveys are submitted every six months.

Service level agreements

Service level agreements are becoming common for that part of the human resource function that concerns itself with providing cost-effective, quality services. Especially in devolved organisations, where local financial accountability is given, imposing HQ costs without question is a cause of conflict. Agreements between service providers and users may cover such areas as:

- payroll management
- medical services
- graduate recruitment
- pension management
- in-placement services
- recruitment advertising
- young entrant induction
- general personnel administration
- psychological testing
- personnel information systems
- potential assessment
- international assignment contracts.

A service level agreement simply lays down the level of service that will be undertaken for a given cost. Services will be those that are economic to provide from one point. For example, an in-placement service that helps find positions for otherwise redundant employees may save literally millions of pounds for the cost of one person's dedicated efforts. Some services may be provided and paid for on an as-needed basis. The benefits of this approach are several:

- It forces an identification of the costs associated with each activity.
- It enables external benchmarking to take place objectively.
- It enables outsourcing decisions to be made easily.
- It removes argument and subjective impressions and puts the value of the service on a commercial basis.
- It enables simple auditing to be carried out of satisfaction with service levels.

Of course it means 'no hiding-place' for the providers of the services, but that is the world of the 1990s.

There are also risks involved. Users may feel free to choose other sup-pliers. They may do this for either sound or unsound reasons, and the human resource function may be left with too much cost to provide the service to those who have not opted out. Organisations may insist users take a minimum of a year's contracting at a time, or else that a minimum notice period of withdrawal applies. This enables restructuring of resources, and may also give time for negotiation. It may also be deemed undesirable to allow withdrawal – for example, on graduate recruitment where a common company image needs to be portrayed. And yet, the ser-vice level agreement still provides a helpful basis for defining the service.

Specific aspects of the human resource function's contribution

Policies and strategies for HRM

It is only one step of logic to realise that the goals and strategies of any organisation are dependent on its people and their skills, and therefore that the first and foremost function of HRM is to ensure policies, processes and programmes support them. Not doing so can have a very serious effect on the bottom line, leading for example to failure to:

- achieve the degree of flexible working practices needed to be competi-tive
- have reward systems that encourage behaviours and results that are key for success
- be wary of 'global' processes that conflict with a need for fast organisa-tional responsiveness
- put in place international remuneration or assignment policies to sup-port planned growth
- achieve succession capability through inadequate selection and devel-opment policies
- design and implement an organisational structure that meets business needs and that works effectively.

However much we devolve and simplify, some initiatives and changes can be made only at the co-ordinating level. The greatest contribution that human resource functions make to the bottom line is to be in close touch with business needs and to be able to translate them into the changes needed in people management.

Human resource initiatives and cost–benefit analysis

Human resource people initiate many programmes designed to yield improvements to their organisation, yet many lack the ability to evaluate the costs and resulting benefits beyond the strict compensation and benefits arena. In addition, professionals are easily tempted to solve the problems *they* want to solve – ones which may be of great interest but not a high priority for the business. For example, extending a job evaluation scheme into a developing country for the sake of global consistency may be far less important for that country than effort spent on developing local capability.

Cost–benefit decisions often rest on some very subjective data and are, in the end, made using common sense and judgement. Financial data has to be balanced with the costs or benefits to other stakeholders such as customers, employees, or the community. As we have observed in discussing structural change, many of the costs are hidden. Losses (or increases) of productivity or motivation may be hard to foresee in figures. There are costs of gathering information, of controlling and monitoring, and of learning curves. If we already have a measurement culture in human resources, then we are better placed to do the necessary analysis.

Human resource people should have knowledge and capability in techniques such as investment appraisal, discounted cash flow, sensitivity analysis, probability analysis, decision trees, risk assessment and so on – or at least they should know when these techniques need to be employed and who can help them. Some of these are helpfully described in Cannon (1979), and details are widely available in their own right. Some useful disciplines to remember are:

- Always understand the exact nature of the problem you are trying to solve, preferably in terms of hard cost or disadvantages to be eliminated or reduced.
- Generate alternative solutions to the problem.
- Cost each solution and value the benefits using all the techniques available.
- Make a balanced choice on the information then available.

Organisational effectiveness – structure and operation

People should add value as individuals. They do this in a number of ways. Whereas they bring unique sets of capabilities, when put together in teams the sum of their individual added value should be enhanced. The *structural design* of organisations should maximise the overall contribution of both the individuals and the teams that make up the whole.

Unfortunately this may not be the case. Some of the considerations are as follows:

- The number of business units will affect the devolution of accountability and the distribution of overhead functions. Units should be such that internal discussion and trading are minimised. The balance of overhead between HQ and units must be weighed up carefully, otherwise one can end up in devolution with more overheads overall as each unit seeks to become more self-sufficient.

- The number of layers clearly affects the overall cost, the principle being to spread accountability and ensure value is added at every level. Fewer layers means greater spans of control and less attention to individuals from communication, coaching, and performance management. The processes in use may need to be redesigned to ensure they continue to produce value.

- In matrix structures the balance between each constituent must be defined in terms of clear accountabilities. Failure to do so can produce disruption and argument, with a loss of focus on the stakeholder's interests.

- The balance between horizontal and vertical structures – processes v functions – also requires careful thought. Again, confusion and loss of productivity result if people are unclear about their roles.

- Skills and capabilities at all levels need to be assessed and gaps scheduled to be closed at the right time. A lot of confusion in new structures results from people not *understanding* why changes are necessary, and from people not being *capable* to deal with the new scenario.

These are only some examples. Often organisational redesign has cost-cutting as one driver. Time after time, the inevitable loss of productivity and learning that results is underestimated. The human resource function can make an immense difference by the design and management of an effective change programme supporting the redesign.

Effectiveness of career management and succession planning

Individuals must own their own careers, and yet organisations will continue to have an interest in the development of talent. Although not economic *per se*, a number of useful measures can be applied that provide the means of assessing and tracking organisational health. The following are suggested:

■ *the percentage of people identified as having significant upwards potential as a proportion of the total population.* (By 'upwards' we do not mean grades or layers, but the ability to take greater accountability.) At the lower end of an organisation one would expect a higher figure than in the senior tranche. A 'healthy' figure depends on the general rate of movement in the organisation, but typically might average 5 to 10 per cent.

■ *the percentage of technical/professional populations classified as 'expert' in their field as a proportion of the desired number* The desired number of experts will depend on the core competences of the organisation and the strategy for maintaining them competitively.

In an international organisation some measures of increasing international capability may be helpful. These might include:

■ the percentage of senior managers with international experience
■ the percentage of top-level managers who do not come from the home-base country
■ the number of international project teams
■ the percentage of international assignments for planned career development purposes rather than expediency. (Studies have shown (eg Conference Board, Europe, 1992) that this is rarely more than 25 per cent in organisations.)

Rewards for performance

Remuneration and benefits are major costs for organisations. Human resources influence them considerably in often being the arbiters of the relevant policies. Most organisations have a base pay status that is conditioned more by their history than deliberate positioning. In the area of variable pay, such as bonus schemes and incentives, they may have much more freedom to initiate. An IPM survey in 1992 showed 74 per cent of organisations surveyed had some form of performance-related pay.

Increases in base pay are increasingly related to the performance of the individual or to his or her level of competence. The transition from rigid pay scales based on seniority and service, increased by an agreed inflation rate annually has opened the door to managerial judgement, flexibility and innovation.

The process of individualised pay increases begins with setting individual performance objectives, then assessing performance against these, formulating a performance rating as a summary, and relating this to a scale of pay increases. But there are dangerous assumptions here – for example that the distribution of objectives is equitable; that the judgements of managers on overall ratings is consistent (even assuming the person concerned had the same manager over the year); and that managers tend towards averaging in order to reduce conflict. In times of low inflation the ability to distinguish pay rises may in any case be minimal and lose meaning.

Such schemes have been used to break away from centralised uniform bargaining, and to give more flexibility to managements. In this they have undoubtedly succeeded in creating a culture where the individual counts more than in an impersonal reward system. The influence on actual performance and bottom-line results is hard to prove, but the principle of individual targets and achievement must be positive, and other benefits are found to accrue.

This approach is under question in the 1990s for two reasons linked to organisational transformation:

■ the trend to focus on team-based structures, whether 'horizontal' or 'vertical'

■ the emphasis on individual value through accumulated learning and skill, rather than the job they do at a given point in time.

It is nevertheless probably a phase that organisations need to go through in order to establish the importance of the individual and distinguish between the contribution of one person and the next. The second phase is to see base pay as a measure of market value, and look at the whole person and his or her accumulated capability.

Variable pay is, however, different. This is pay devoted to the achievement of results, and may be pitched at any level. Individual bonuses may relate to preset objectives or to outputs. Activity-related incentives such as the 'payment-by-results' schemes of the 1970s have declined heavily. Salespersons' commission schemes thrive, however, being linked directly to bottom-line measures.

Managers may have a mix of personal targets, team results, and organisational results. The challenge is to maintain a relationship between effort and reward. As one goes further down the organisation, company results feel more and more remote. The question is then whether the variable pay is a shared reward or an incentive. A typical pay policy might consist of base pay, related to the value of the person, with a variable element based on achievement of good performance, budgets, or objectives (individual, team, or organisation-wide) and an incentive element based on exceptional achievement related to a key bottom-line measure (individual and/or team). In measuring pay against market rates, the first two elements comprise 'on-target earnings' as the comparator.

Incentive elements should be constructed in such a way that the benefits are shared between the organisation and the contributors. This is typically done for the financial measures, but increasingly the importance of other key stakeholder measures is being considered. This is a highly important area of HRM. Poorly designed or soft schemes can cost a lot of money, with no clear return to the organisation. In particular the distinction between variable remuneration and incentives for overachievement can make all the difference to motivation. An incentive element exists only if the individual or team can see a real link between their effort and the reward, and if the targets they are working to are accepted as realistic and challenging.

Share/stock option schemes are also popular in large private-sector organisations (mainly Anglo-American) for all levels of employees, and in smaller ones, for executives. The aim is to distribute the benefits of achieving capital growth and to align employee rewards with those of shareholders. At a senior level large sums can be involved, and the desire to achieve share growth is high. At lower levels schemes are more about sharing and commitment to the company. Because benefits are normally lost when employees leave, large options can be a powerful incentive to stay. In some US corporations shares may be given as an alternative to salary up to a certain percentage.

Share prices are in reality subject to many factors, and whether share option schemes are a real influence on business results may be doubted. Certainly they serve as a retainer. But probably more executives have found themselves rich owing to changes in organisational ownership than for reasons of exceptional organic growth. Many would question, also, whether such schemes do focus companies on the right balance of measures for long-term success for all stakeholders. Sadly, an announcement of significant redundancies is likely to result in a boost of the share price, for example.

Attrition and recruitment

The measurement of attrition, or labour turnover, is perhaps one of the most common measures used in HRM. It is usually calculated on an annualised basis from:

$$\frac{Number\ of\ leavers\ in\ a\ time\ period}{Average\ number\ of\ people\ over\ the\ time\ period}$$

This calculation may be done monthly or quarterly, then annualised, but should also be done on a rolling basis over the preceding six months. This is because the *trend* is as important to understand as the absolute figure. The bald calculation may be quite misleading, and it should be broken down between (for example) the following headings:

- voluntary and involuntary leavers
- leavers for reasons of dissatisfaction with the company (as opposed to personal or other reasons)
- specific categories of skill
- location/business unit.

Thus a unit may show a relatively low overall figure, but if the majority are skilled people dissatisfied with their rewards voting with their feet, there is a clear message that must be heeded.

It is fashionable today in the wake of the turbulence that organisations are going through for some to say that frequent movement between companies is to be encouraged. This is a strange thing to set against the economics of *investing* in people. Boston Consulting Group estimate that the average employee in the UK has 29 per cent of annual salary costs as human asset value derived from training investment. This assumes a 10-year depreciation of the training (which would be generous in industries where the pace of change is high). The report states that the total wage bill in the UK is £350 billion, and therefore the asset stock from training is some £100 billion. Losing good people is a real asset loss. This is particularly true for graduate trainees, where the ratio of investment to return is particularly high in the early years.

The unsung cost of organisations is the replacement cost. There is no doubt that the effort made to reduce undesirable elements of turnover is likely to yield rich returns, to all stakeholders. For example, customers like continuity of relationships. Some elements to consider are:

- loss of productivity once decision to leave is made
- loss of knowledge and experience
- preparation of job specification
- recruitment costs
- selection costs

- induction costs
- learning curve
- lost opportunity costs owing to handovers etc
- cost of temporary cover.

The final sum for professional or managerial employees is likely to be at least equivalent to one year's salary; Fair (1992) estimates between six months and two years, depending on the role. We saw above from the APAC studies that average turnover runs at about 15 per cent across all sectors. Let us say that at least 5 per cent is unplanned and undesired. This means that for an organisation of 1,000 people, 50 are going to be replaced. If the average is one year's salary per person, then the firm's pay-bill has effectively been increased by 5 per cent. Total cost might be £1 million, at an average compensation package of £20,000 per head. The cost of reducing this by even 1 per cent is very easily justified. Exit interviews are some of the most important interactions with employees that we can have, and even better if followed up three months after they have left (when they will usually be more honest).

There are a number of measures of recruitment efficiency and effectiveness that can be used. For many organisations young entrant recruitment is the major task in this area through the year, regardless of the economic situation.

The following are some examples from the *efficiency* side of this equation:

- average cost per recruit
- average time elapsed between various process stages
- percentage of offers made to candidates attending final selection procedure
- offer-acceptance rate.

On the *effectiveness* side there are these factors to consider:

- retention rate after three to five years. 'Stability factors', are calculated as follows (Fitz-Enz 1990):

$$\frac{\textit{Original employees remaining}}{\textit{Total number of original employees}} \times 100$$

- percentage perceived as high potential after three to five years
- promotion rate profiles.

Useful proformas for calculating the actual costs involved can be found in several of the reference texts (eg Fair 1992; Fitz-Enz 1995).

Absenteeism, and manpower- and skills-planning

Along with labour turnover, absenteeism has been the other main traditional measure that is regularly reported – with good reason, for many working environments see it as a major cost. Fitz-Enz (1995) provides comprehensive formulae for calculating the costs, although what he calls 'miscellaneous' – the effects of disruption to expected work programmes and searching for acceptable alternatives – may be as much as the overt measured costs. Cannon (1979) reported absenteeism as a rising and major problem in the UK; however APAC report an average in 1995 of 3.8 per cent. It is nonetheless becoming increasingly difficult to monitor absenteeism in many areas because timeclocking gives way to trust, and activity/time served to results achieved. Added to this, the increasing spans of control in de-layered organisations make monitoring difficult. Is the issue becoming less important?

In environments where a unit of labour must be replaced if it is not present when needed it remains a key parameter to be monitored. Such environments are decreasing all the time. It is well known that the rate of absenteeism is directly inversely proportional to job satisfaction. Thus, challenging roles, empowered space, and objectives based on achievement generally lead to people *wanting* to be at work. In such an atmosphere monitoring and recording becomes unnecessary.

Turning to manpower, traditional manpower-planning models are ceasing to be helpful as we move away from the paradigm of human resources as a discrete number of permanently contracted employees. The fixed job set within a grading and salary structure is being replaced with roles built around skills and flexibility. Traditional manpower-planning becomes less easy and less needed as resourcing becomes more pragmatic. One of the challenges for the human resource function is to help their organisations evaluate those skills that need to be core and developed for competitive advantage, as opposed to those that can be bought in when needed. Predictions of the changes in the UK workforce vary, but all point to an increase in the ratio of 'contract services' to 'full-time employees' – even as far as 50:50.

The savings in liability and employment costs are substantial, and in efforts to reduce the costs of redundancies many organisations have offered transitions that include one or more of the options below. ICL, for example, offers employees over the age of 50 the option of taking a lower job, or going part-time in the same job, whilst maintaining pension contributions at the full-time salary of the current job. Some of the options that need to be balanced include:

- job-sharing
- flexible hours
- career breaks
- teleworking
- associate status (used frequently but not permanently contracted)
- freelance hire
- fixed-term contracts.

The coming decade will see a lot of attention to these options. In particular the cost of employment *space* will be balanced with that of home-working or teleworking. Changes in management and organisational structures encourage these questions to be asked, and they lead to a completely new paradigm of the employment, reward, and development of people.

Skills-planning derived from business plans is becoming a higher priority for many firms than the planning of headcount. Each business strategy or programme has demands for knowledge and skill, today and tomorrow, and these need to be defined. They must then be benchmarked against the current capability level and the learning capability of existing people must then be assessed for any changes required. We are finally in a position to decide whether and how much to buy, train, or subcontract.

Again, we see the importance of human resources being closely aligned and responsive to business priorities. A failure *to have the right people in the right place at the right time with the right capability* can destroy business effectiveness. Indeed, this is as good a mission statement for a human resource function as any!

There is also the question of human resource audits. Matthewman (1993) and others advocate the value of total human resource audits, done either by internal or external consultants. These should cover four areas:

- quality of procedures and practice
- cost analysis and the effectiveness of use of time and resource
- capability profiles of staff in relation to role needs
- client satisfaction and expectations.

The first stage in such audits is to understand the organisational goals and objectives against which to benchmark the contribution of HRM (or the lack of it).

The future impact of HRM on organisational success

It would be helpful to all concerned if a satisfactory formal way could be found of accounting for human assets. This would help human resource functions both to quantify their contribution and to improve it. In the winter 1994–95 edition of *Transformation* (the journal of Gemini Consulting) Alan Dunn dreams he is the director of the Financial Accounting Standards Board of the USA, and that he issues some new directives. Two of them are:

> The sum of all costs associated with the hiring and development of employees will be capitalised as a year end general ledger entry. Accounts normally period-expensed, such as training, employee development, and hiring costs, will be credited and a new account, called Capitalised Human Assets, will be debited.
>
> Each year, all employees will be evaluated for competency and the results will be compared with scores from the previous evaluation. The book value of the capitalised human assets will be increased by improved scores, and scores that decline will be a charge on a contra-asset account called 'Accumulated Capitalised Human Asset Depreciation'. The Capitalised Human Asset Expense account will receive the offsetting entry.

This would help investors to look at companies in a new way, he says, and help companies to invest in the talent available to them. If an employee's book value were to reach zero, it would be advantageous to replace him or her.

As we have looked at some of the work of the human resource function it has been possible to note that the bottom-line returns are potentially very high in some areas. When a young personnel manager going through a crisis of self-questioning on the value of what I was doing, I once tried to list the cost/benefits of all the areas I worked in. Way ahead in the list was effective recruitment: the benefit of getting it right *and* the cost of getting it wrong were far and away the most significant. Yet how many functions assign recruitment work to the junior members?

Working in some of these areas may not seem very attractive to the modern human resource specialist. However, a functional leader concerned to be making a positive bottom-line impact will ensure that resources and efforts are in proportion to the results that might be achieved.

The focus of people management will change over the next few years to be quite different from what it has been over the last quarter-century. The organisation that wants to be flexible and competitive must build its cultural development on a platform of learning, which it must see as the bloodstream keeping the organisation alive and thriving. Rigid systems designed to pigeonhole people are incompatible with this. Whereas there seems little business sense in telling employees that we do not mind if they leave us (an illogical extension of the end of the jobs-for-life expectation), we *do* want them to feel ownership for their performance, learning, development, and careers. We need systems that encourage this approach – and not just to rely on de-layered, flatter organisations to force it.

The link between 'learning' as we have described it and the 'bottom line' has been developed in the arguments above. Organisations will want not only heavily to encourage learning on the understanding that it leads to competitive advantage, but they will also look for stronger relationships between specific activities and results.

The need to justify the contribution of the human resource function against service levels provided or added value to organisational goals must only increase. This will necessitate a review of the roles that form part of the function. Tyson and Fell (1986) proposed three models of a personnel function: the 'clerk of works' (essentially an administrative service); the 'contracts manager' (technically expert in eg industrial realtions, where needed); and the 'architect' (proactive and business-oriented). A team from IMD and Manchester concluded their study of HRM in Europe (Hiltrop *et al* 1995) with four models of future human resource functions:

- the in-house cost centre
- the internal consultancy, paid for as needed
- the business unit, selling services both internally and externally
- the external consultancy, being outsourced.

Most human resource departments will be a combination of these, and cost considerations will be balanced with the added value that is provided. The following is suggested as a vision of tomorrow's human resource department:

- A small but significant number of senior human resource professionals are 'business partners' as members of business teams.
- They are concerned with the minimum number of human resource policies necessary to safeguard the organisation's legal integrity and to

support its values – plus the translation of business goals and strategies into human resource strategies and programmes.

- Other roles become service providers or added-value consultants.

- Consultants do not pursue their own agendas, but respond to problems, issues, or needs in various parts of the organisation, and are expected to add value – through their professionalism and through activities that can be related to organisational goals. They will be paid for by units on the basis of work commissioned (HQ may also pay for projects).

- Service providers are measured against cost and quality parameters according to a service level agreement with operational units.

In terms of outsourcing decisions, the roles described above form a hierarchy, as follows:

Role	Core value	Basis of outsourcing
Business partner	Strategic	None
Human resource consultant	Organisational knowledge	Value added
Service provider	Cost/quality	Regular review

Thus, if one accepts the importance of HRM at a strategic level, one would not consider outsourcing a senior member of the business team. Not all businesses are large enough to support a member devoted to human resources; depending on the industry and rate of change, a guideline to size might be 'any business above £20 million p.a. turnover or employing 200–300 people'. At the second level, a significant part of the value added by the internal consultant may be due to his or her knowledge of the culture, the history, and the people in the organisation.

What is in any case certain is that human resource departments will be continually scrutinised to see whether they are sufficiently adaptable and responsive in terms of their own structure and contribution. Measurement of their activity will be vitally important in order to make the necessary decisions. However, over the coming years the professionalism and overview of HRM will be needed more than ever before. The economic potential for both benefit and waste is significant in

- organisational structuring

- the management of learning and knowledge
- flexible pay and reward systems
- manpower resourcing
- employee motivation
- non-employee motivation.

Figure 9.6
SCALE OF HR CREDIBILITY

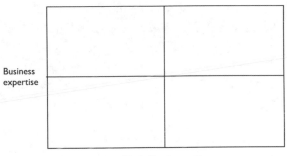

Traditional measures such as turnover and absenteeism will need to be reassessed as organisations change. Where more and more work is contracted and results-based, either internally or externally, measures based on contracted people being present at a place of work will be less applicable.

The human resource function has too often been seen as insular, bureaucratic, reactive, and process-driven. It can no longer exist 'by right', but only by being business-oriented, flexible, responsive, and focused on the value it is adding. Credibility will not be earned by just being efficient and helpful: the function must be seen as part of the decision-making process, and that implies a sound understanding of the business of the organisation. The scale of credibility can be depicted as in Figure 9.6. The top right-hand quadrant is the only place for those human resource practitioners who want to be real partners in the organisation's decision-taking.

Meanwhile it will greatly help human resource functions to place more focus on quantitative evaluation of both visible and invisible costs, and to help operational units to see the effects of their decisions. Likewise the ability to quantify investments in learning options, and the effects of *not* investing, can have a huge influence.

The winning organisation today is the one that has the right skills available at the right time to be able to seize business opportunities of all kinds.

References

ARMSTRONG, M, (1989), *Personnel and the Bottom Line*, London, IPM.

BOSTON CONSULTING GROUP, (1994), *Strategic Human Resource Development*, London, Boston Consulting Group.

BURNS, D, AND THOMPSON, L, (1993), 'When personnel call in the auditors', *Personnel Management*, January.

CANNON, J, (1979), *Cost-Effective Personnel Decisions*, London, IPM.

ER CONSULTANTS, (1994), *Performance-Related Pay*, Topics Issue 1.

FAIR, H, (1992), *Personnel and Profit*, London, IPM.

FITZ-ENZ, J, (1990), *Human Value Management*, San Franciso, CA, Jossey-Bass.

FITZ-ENZ, J, (1995), *How to Measure Human Resources Management*, 2nd ed, Maidenhead, McGraw Hill.

FLAMHOLTZ, E, (1985), *Human Resource Accounting*, San Francisco, CA, Jossey-Bass.

GILES, W, J, AND ROBINSON, D, F, (1972), *Human Asset Accounting*, IPM/ICMA.

HAMPDEN-TURNER, C, AND TROMPENAARS, F, (1994), *The Seven Cultures of Capitalism*, London, Piatkus.

HARRISON, F, W, (1992), *Measuring the Effectiveness of the HR Function*, Consultant Report.

HILTROP, J-M, DESPRES, C, AND SPARROW, P, (1995), 'The changing role of HR managers in Europe', *European Management Journal*, March.

INSTITUTE OF PERSONNEL MANAGEMENT, (1993), *Managing People: The changing frontiers*, October, London, IPM.

KAPLAN, R, S, AND NORTON, D, P, (1992), 'The balanced scorecard', *Harvard Business Review*, Vol.70, No.1, January–February, pp71–9.

KIRKPATRICK, D, C, *Evaluating Training Programs*, (1975), Madison: American Society for Training & Development.

LIKERT, R, (1967), *The Human Organisation – Its management and value*, Maidenhead, McGraw Hill.

MATTHEWMAN, J, (1993), *HR Effectiveness*, London, IPM.

MITCHELL, D, J, B, AND ZAIDI, M, A, (1990), *The Economics of Human Resource Management*, Oxford, Basil Blackwell.

QUINN, J, B, (1992), *The Intelligent Enterprise*, Oxford, The Free Press.

SCHUMACHER, E, F, (1989), *Small is Beautiful*, London, HarperCollins.

SPENCER LYLE, M, JNR, (1986), *Calculating Human Resource Costs and Benefits*, Chichester, John Wiley.

STEWART, T, A, (1994), *Your Company's Most Valuable Asset: Intellectual capital*, London, Fortune.

TOWNSEND, R, (1970), *Up the Organisation*, London, Coronet Books.

TYSON, S, AND FELL, A, (1986), *Evaluating the Personnel Function*, London, Hutchinson.

CHAPTER TEN
Looking Ahead

Shaun Tyson and Alan Fell

What will the future bring? From time immemorial this question has occupied men's minds, though not always to the same degree. Historically, it is chiefly in times of physical, political, economic and spiritual distress that men's eyes turn with anxious hope to the future, and when anticipations, utopias, and apocalyptic visions multiply.

Collected Works, C. G. Jung (1957).

This book set out to explore the present state and the way ahead for HRM as a strategic activity. What should we conclude from this examination of HRM at the end of the twentieth century? The various contributors have painted a picture of complexity and diversity. Existing models of HRM remain varied; there is no one general model of which to make a critique; and whereas we can identify themes and issues, each organisation has its own priorities and strategic responses. Industrial relations in the UK has been shown to be characterised by diversity in Mick Marchington's chapter (Chapter 4). The trends in organisation structure are towards decentralisation and divisionalisation. As Keith Sisson explained in Chapter 3, companies are in a state of continuous change: merging, downsizing, entering into joint ventures, acquiring and being acquired. These changes now occur on a global scale where corporate cultures are tempered by national cultures and, as Chris Brewster reminded us in Chapter 8, this prompts us both to look at the links between organisation units and also to explore culture as a human construct within HRM theorising.

Alternative scenarios

The effects of the worst recession in the UK since 1945 inevitably pervade all accounts of the key areas in HRM discussed in this book. Two extreme scenarios could be set out: a pessimistic total-change scenario, and a buoyant gradualist scenario. As Jung suggested, when faced with unpredictable change most people are fearful, and it would be difficult to find an unboundedly optimistic forecast for our society into the next century. The contributors here have provided a balanced account, neither toppling over into despair nor becoming euphoric at the way ahead; they have seen and evaluated the current trends but have looked at what seem the most probable outcomes and themes for the future. There is a consistency, however, in each extreme scenario, and we can see elements from each 'worst' and 'best' case in the previous chapters.

Total change

The pessimistic total-change scenario forecasts continuing political and institutional uncertainty. Parallel to this period of deconstruction and re-examination, and along with the accompanying 'anxious hopes' for the future, come some of the social disorders associated with the apocalypse. If not Death riding a Pale Horse, such a view beholds the disintegration of family life, the rise in crime, and the end to social consensus and common values as threats to social cohesion. The free movement of capital around the globe encourages rapid change; new technology de-skills; and both these forces result in obsolete working people.

According to this scenario new organisation structures, instead of providing opportunities for leadership and flair, produce stunted careers; 'empowerment' becomes a one-way exchange without any commitment from the company to employment security in return for the extra responsibility shouldered by working people, whilst 'downsizing' produces stress and fear. As redundancies take hold, the survivors find themselves working harder amongst mounting chaos whilst the jobs around them are outsourced or converted into merely part-time tasks, or ones carried out by casual labour. In such a scenario the psychological contract based on mutuality is replaced with either a one-sided bargain with an instrumental response or a negotiated hard contract, which offers flexibility only in the short-term, all subsequent change being at a price. In these circumstances there seems little room for HRM as a separate strategic function. Assuming the trade unions continue to decline in membership and influence, some of the current trends towards 'balkanising' the function into a range of subspecialisms will be reinforced, and the strategic role will be invariably centred on senior line management.

Buoyant gradualism

The buoyant gradualist scenario envisions a slowly improving future. Those taking this stance see some of the more pessimistic trends as phases through which our society must pass in order to solve its problems:

management is a process, and the underlying notion is that the system will right itself. Political and economic changes in the past encouraged a belief in the doctrine of progress, after all. Changes in the nineteenth century – the factory system, urban living, a more secular society, and the move towards democracy – were all painful and slow, and there were winners and losers. The romantic tendency to hark back to some golden age has always been a habit in human society, but such golden ages never existed. Whereas there are features of the past to which we might wish to return, we are highly selective in our collective memory, as Alistair Mant reminds us (see Chapter 2). The English rural idyll, for example, still has a powerful affect on the imagination – a cottage in the country, rolling parklands, village life, and so on – but no one would really wish to live in a plaster-and-daub building with no proper heating, water, or sewage system, with an irregular supply of simple food in an unvarying diet, working six days a week on the land for a pittance. Progress consists, it is argued, in giving up some things in order to achieve a better overall standard of living.

According to this stance, therefore, new technological advances will improve living conditions, and any unemployment caused by these advances will ultimately result in fairer ways to redistribute wealth. The collapse of old industries leads to the creation of new industries. The increasing pace of change produces a more developmental approach to work: intelligence and the capacity to learn are interdependent, so learning organisations need intelligent knowledge workers, whose creativity and adaptability will be the main source of competitive advantage. Management's role is thus facilitatory, its sole purpose being to aid those interfacing with customers – or making the product. Empowerment has real meaning in lean organisations, where there are few overheads. Employees may have to take some risks, but they also have the exhilaration of making decisions relating to their own work. Empowerment is only possible if there is also some involvement of employees in strategic decision-making. Trade unions, recognising the value of efficiency and competitiveness will work increasingly as social partners within a broad European legal framework which will extend more rights to employees, along with the associated responsibilities.

The contributors to this book have argued for some elements of the pessimistic scenario whilst looking forward realistically to a more gradualist vision of change in the future. Taking each in turn, we can see how logically each position has been derived.

The contributors' analysis

Peter Herriot (Chapter 7) shows how the competition typical of the 1990s has produced sourcing strategies that have had major consequences for careers. General uncertainty and lack of job security have made employers continually negotiate and renegotiate the psychological contract. In spite of the so-called end to careers, employers still demand loyalty, conformity, and commitment from their staff. This rather pessimistic future scenario predicts that in the next decade the management of people will be largely about striking deals with individual employees who may be working in a variety of contractual relationships.

Similarly, Alistair Mant (Chapter 2) forecasts changes to work roles, which he sees emerging from new technology applications where highly specialised knowledge-workers will require new management approaches, with the manager acting more and more as a co-ordinator and negotiator. The implications from Mant's evidence on the growth of non-profit organisations also suggests that there will be a greater normative attachment to work and that the psychological need for work will be met by people taking up different roles, including more and more home-working, job-sharing, and part-time work. This contrasts vividly with the 'anxious class' of managers working long hours and seeking visibility as good corporate citizens as a self-protecting response to the fear of redundancy. This vision of the future sees both alternative scenarios available, but hints that ultimately the negative perspective may prevail.

Taking a sceptical view, Keith Sisson (Chapter 3) questions whether it will be possible to meet the demands for greater efficiency and to improve the quality of working life, given the four trends he identifies of a changing corporate portfolio, internationalisation, privatisation, and externalisation. Restructuring is set to continue as companies become 'extended' organisations operating within highly flexible structures. For HRM, the strategic responses of the 1990s which have invariably resulted in 'cost-cutting' exercises will need to be re-examined in the light of any new corporate governance arrangements in the following decade. A new type of organisation seems to be needed where stakeholders have a real place and a voice in the way the company is run.

The possibilities for 'partnership', 'mutuality', or 'jointism', with the unions working with employers at workplace level, are explored by Mick Marchington (Chapter 4), who demonstrates the diverse character of UK industrial relations where there is the whole gamut of industrial relations strategies and collective bargaining on display, from edging out the unions, direct employee involvement, forms of representative participation and communication techniques, single-table bargaining, decentralised bargaining, through to increased width-of-bargaining units and to multi-employer bargaining. Industrial relations trends are difficult to predict against this backcloth of diversity. The optimistic scenario is based on the notion that there will be a move towards social partnership, perhaps even a 'European' model of industrial relations. The more pessimistic scenario would see the ascendancy of labour, perhaps supported by a future Labour government, with conflict and disputes increasing through the absence of a coherent industrial relations system. However, the labour market effects and the factors that produced such a diverse industrial relations system are such that neither of the extreme scenarios seems probable, rather a more patchy shift towards partnership (whilst trade unions also rethink their role), and a continuing diversity in collective bargaining arrangements.

Chris Brewster (Chapter 8) argues that companies operating internationally have to develop international strategies that are effective globally. He demonstrates how understanding cultural diversity is facilitated by appreciating the norms and values underlying cultural preferences. Because, as he explains, the influence of international factors on HRM will continue to grow, we need to re-examine our culture-bound management theories, not least because of the multicultural character of UK society.

The evidence from the Cranfield European Executive Competencies study conducted by Andrew Kakabadse and his researchers (Chapter 6) shows how general global trends towards stakeholder value are moderating traditionally derived cultural assumptions. The geographical map does not represent the cultural map. In addition, there are considerable differences in strategic behaviour amongst executives – differences that have significant implications for international management and for management development policies, especially in career planning, leadership experience, and general management training.

These results also inform the answer to the questions posed by Cooper and White (Chapter 5): how can the study of organisational behaviour improve competitive advantage, facilitate the roles of line managers, and help to generate effective cultures in organisations? Cooper and White see the main answer to these questions as the need to put the people back into HRM. They illustrate this theme by showing how the study of organisational behaviour informs current issues such as stress management, equal opportunities, and organisational politics, suggesting that only from a return to social science knowledge as the basis for HRM can we expect to produce solutions to problems and to understand the key issues of the 1990s and beyond.

Andrew Mayo (Chapter 9) takes up the theme of the significance of learning and of improving productivity if we are to stay competitive. This requires HRM to be at the forefront in finding, keeping, and developing the skills needed for high-level performance. Paradoxically, as this viewpoint becomes more widely accepted as a truism, so the contribution of HRM is thrown into greater doubt – hence the increasing attention to evaluation, both as an aspect of the value-for-money philosophy and also as all managers become more aware of what can be achieved in the field of human resources. That there are different models for HRM is now accepted. What seems to be occurring at present is a debate on the mechanisms for delivering the service – for example, whether as an internal or external consultancy. This debate places a question mark over the future of the more traditional models of personnel management, however, so peripheral has the old vision of personnel management as a separate profession now become to the crucial issues faced by organisations. The chapters by Cooper and White and by Mayo are not necessarily contradictory. Whereas a return to social science knowledge and research is essential if we are to tackle the problems of the twenty-first century, these issues are not the sole property of a particular professional specialism – rather they are issues for all managers.

Economic, social, and organisational change

On the whole, the contributors take a cautiously optimistic view of the strategic prospects for HRM. However, the caution derives from more than a mere, if natural, reluctance to make long-term predictions on human affairs. Economic trends in Western Europe, North America, and in Japan and the Pacific are critical determinants of what will happen to labour markets, pay, industrial relations, and training and development. How can we forecast the future when there are still massive uncertainties which might have very different outcomes?

Following the end of the cold war, with the breakdown of the old borders and the ideologies that supported them, capitalism now seems to be the unchallenged mode of creating wealth through production and services, and the main method by which goods and money are exchanged. The spectre of communism to which Marx gave theoretical shape and to which the Russian and Chinese states sought to give corporeal presence has been exorcised. In his account of the end of ideology, Herbert Marcuse foresaw the closing of the political universe (Marcuse 1964). According to him society is controlled by vested interests which manipulate the social needs of the population through the very institutions established ostensibly to protect the people's freedom:

> Its supreme promise is an even-more-comfortable life for an ever-growing number of people who, in a strict sense, cannot imagine a qualitatively different universe of discourse and action, for the capacity to contain and manipulate subversive imagination and effort is an integral part of the given society.
>
> Marcuse (1964:35).

Now that the broad defining positions set out in the nineteenth century no longer constitute viable positions – neither the capitalist owner nor the wage labourer dependent for all aspects of survival on the employer or his representative are to be ascendant – it is argued that we should be looking at different forms of capitalism, for example changed stakeholder roles for institutional shareholders, for some form of 'ethical' capitalism built upon sound environmental principles, or perhaps we should look at postcapitalism. Drucker (1993:38) believes that we have now moved to such a society, which is based upon knowledge, and that management is the 'generic organ' of the knowledge society: 'knowledge is the only meaningful resource today.'

The new 'knowledge' workers signal the change from muscle power to brain power, and increasingly to computer-aided brain power. There is no reason to suppose that this trend will cease; on the contrary, it is accelerating. In Drucker's phrase, 'knowledge is now being applied to knowledge.' New occupations and changes to existing occupations cause uncertainty and, as a process, require new ways for people to work with others. For example, the changes to roles in the health service – hospital consultants, technicians, administrators, nurses and all the specialists in health care – now have to combine in new ways, to work in various teams, which demonstrates how flexibility has assumed a new importance in regard to knowledge: it is a necessary precondition for knowledge to be used effectively.

This flexibility of task is accompanied by a different approach to careers, which have now virtually disappeared within organisations, 'company man' being, in Anthony Sampson's words, as 'extinct as an eighteenth-century clergyman' (1995:307). Instead we can see the growth of portfolio careers. These give people the chance to spread the redundancy risk, and to provide variety and a balanced lifestyle with more choice. The number of part-time jobs has increased in the UK by 2.6 million since 1971, the proportion rising from 15 per cent of all jobs in 1971 to 28 per cent in

1994. According to the Industrial Relations Law Bulletin, 73 per cent of part-time employees work part time because they want to (IRS July 1995); only 13 per cent do so because they are unable to find a full-time job.

One reason for changes to occupations, and to a changed approach to HRM as a consequence, are changes to production systems. The move to a 'post-Fordist' organisation through, for example, 'lean' production methods has major consequences for HRM. In contrast to the Fordist mass-producer, 'the lean producer combines the advantages of craft and mass production, while avoiding the high cost of the former and the rigidity of the latter. Towards this end, lean producers employ teams of multi-skilled workers at all levels of the organisation and use highly flexible, increasingly auto-mated machines to produce volumes of products in enormous variety' (Wormack et al 1990:13). Customers are also becoming more demanding for a variety of goods customised, and at lower prices. There is also the question of 'ethical' buying. High standards of service are demanded in all services. In the public sector, and in some private-sector corporations, the response has been to develop codes of practice ('customer charters') and to benchmark quality more conscientiously.

Organisational reactions to these new demands have come in the form of new structures which seek to be more responsive. The 'learning organ-isation' concept is often said to be the pioneering idea behind flexible approaches to organisation design. The idea of the learning organisation seems to be predicated upon a philosophy of learning that links policy-making with operational and individual thinking, where there is a flow back and forth of ideas, experience, and information (Burgoyne, et al 1994). Learning, it is said, must move from 'double loop', which inte-grates the strategic and operational levels, to transformational ie to take employees into new approaches to problem-solving and decision-making. In his research into four large corporations, Nevis concluded that all organisations are learning organisations and that there are stylistic varia-tions in learning systems, but that certain generic features facilitate learn-ing, such as the climate of openness, an experimental mindset, and an involved leadership (Nevis et al 1995). These ideas support the view that what successful corporations can do is to create a process of continuous renewal so that they can transform themselves in response to market chal-lenges.

As organisations 'downsize' and reorganise, the social costs of change rise. These costs are already considerable and it is now clear that GDP can and does increase year on year without necessarily resulting in improved employment levels. If we are to live with permanently high levels of unemployment, then the mechanisms for redistributing wealth will need to be improved in order to maintain social cohesion. Already massive unemployment throughout Europe threatens social order. In the USA violence at work is the second most common cause of work fatalities. These issues reflecting social disorder are part of a wider social agenda and include the problems of stress and mental illness, sexual politics in the workplace, elder care, child care, and alienation.

The economic and political climate in which social adjustment is taking place is itself uncertain. Thatcherite experiments with the market economy may have moved all political platforms to the right, but there is no new philosophy being clearly articulated to cope with the consequences of this shift. Ideas such as an institutionalised community spirit or greater individual responsibility are not capable of being turned into operational plans. The strategic use of a flexible labour market that has attracted much inward investment into the UK is at odds with the ideas of central planning and European-wide regulation. Future conflicts may tend to occur more between a central European bureaucracy and transnational corporations.

As companies become more global and organise as markets rather than hierarchies they shift capital around with less and less regard for old ideas such as 'loyalty', 'career', and 'hierarchy'. In contradistinction the EU seeks integration. For example, in commenting on future approaches to planning, a commissioner states:

> The basic theme which runs through *Europe 2000+* is that as the European Union prepares to enter the 21st century, growing interdependence between the regions which make up the Union and the increasing relations with other parts of Europe call for closer and more systematic cooperation over territorial planning across Europe as a whole.
>
> (Bruce Millan, *Europe 2000+ Report* 1995:3).

The report goes on to consider trends in the spatial distribution of population and employment, recent changes in the regional distribution of foreign investments, and the regional effects of transEuropean networks. The European co-operation required is cross-border in regions such as the Atlantic Arc, the Mediterranean Arc, the Northern Seaboard, the Pyrenees, the Benelux area, and so on. It is instructive about the trend. The report recommends more transnational programmes and solutions, as well as raising the question of what new planning roles should be in the revised treaty of 1996. Given the infrastructure networks, the way data movement and transportation are more and more rapid, and shared environmental issues, this seems logical. However, one cannot escape the conclusion that the next millennium will witness on the one hand the sidelining of the nation state, and on the other the advancement of a European identity to a point where the old nationalisms of the twentieth century will seem strangely anachronistic, part of long-forgotten dreams of empire which were themselves attempts to create a confederation of countries.

People management in the future seems destined to be at the forefront of handling change. The new corporation – smaller, networked, transnational, trading globally, recruiting and developing people with many different cultural, educational, and linguistic traditions – will operate in a more fragmented society. It will have to withstand and respond to enormous social pressures and to compete in an ever more demanding market-place. What then is the future of HRM in the UK? How well prepared are managers to cope with the challenges to come?

The effects of change on HRM

We have argued previously for an analytical approach employing contingency theory (Tyson and Fell 1986). The deconstruction of HRM in the UK context at least, over the last 10 to 15 years vindicates that argument.

Personnel management, or HRM, is the management activity most severely altered over the past decade. To say 'altered' is perhaps to baulk at directly confronting the sea change that has taken place. Several forces have been at play, including: the deployment of global capital (which includes the effect of new centres of cheap manufacture – Eastern Europe and northern and eastern Asia for example); distributed intelligence management (still in some quarters rather quaintly called 'IT'); and the accelerated internationalisation of labour markets. These forces are played out in the contemporary great game called long ago by behavioural science the 'organisation'. Such is the non-linear rate of change around the entity 'organisation' that we are now seriously in need of a more up-to-date shorthand descriptor. There is a great legacy of meaning bound up in the universal construct 'organisation' – not least, the entire edifice of HRM. What are the strategic prospects for HRM when many of the props now sustaining the 'organisation' are being kicked away (Flood et al 1995)? Each of these themes – the globalisation of capital, the impact on organisation design through distributed intelligence, the internationalisation of labour markets (which has as its metaphor 'flexibility') – will affect HRM immeasurably into the next century.

Flexibility – whether of job or worker, or of social, labour, and legal institutions – is part of a constellation of approaches to improving the position of the firm in its product market, coupled with the desire to improve the firm's competitive position by greater control over labour costs and utilisation. Flexibility is therefore, profoundly, a managerial ideology.

The UK – and Europe – is viewed by many as having an industrial base that is not competitive in global terms. The origin of this in the UK case, and the recitation of a catalogue of missed opportunities, has been provided by a number of commentators, the most intellectually satisfying being perhaps Barnett (1986). OECD reports and (of growing stature) Bank of England industrial surveys have added to the database. The argument became, in crude terms, whether enhanced competitiveness could be achieved through cost-reducing strategies. This is a narrow argument, parochial even, but it is nonetheless the basis of the flexibility debate.

At the heart of the argument is the view that the labour market in the UK suffers from too many inflexibilities and rigidities, causing poor employment performance and economic and industrial readjustment which is too slow. This interpretation became the basis of the neo-liberal approach, rather than the need for industrial investment, subsidy, nurturing of advanced sectors or industries for the twenty-first century, a comprehensive UK Regional Policy, or other interventionist policies.

Teague (1991) fleshes out the rigidity argument: wages are both too high and too rigid, resulting in workers being priced out of jobs; wage differentials are too small, impeding labour mobility; legally based labour rights and employment protection schemes have gone too far, resulting in high labour costs causing redundancies and discouraging hiring; social security systems encourage voluntary unemployment and act as a disincentive to work. These became a *cri de cœur*, the rhetoric of the debate of the 1980s and early 1990s. The thesis was given additional official endorsement recently:

> There is a high degree of agreement among EU member states about the cause [*sic*] of Europe's unemployment problems. Increasingly they recognise that, while the recession has an effect, there are more deep-seated structural problems in Europe's labour markets: a lack of flexibility in the operation of labour markets partly as a result of excessive or misdirected regulation, high labour costs, particularly social contribution; inadequate incentives to work; a lack of the skills among significant parts of the labour force needed to compete in a fast-changing world.
>
> Hunt (1993).

These sentiments can be set in a broader context.

Beardwell (1991) puts the notion of 'flexibility' firmly within the lexicon of 1980s' industrial relations vocabulary, alongside 'flexible firm', 'derecognition', 'business unionism', and 'New Industrial Relations', the last-mentioned being the more generic description. The

New Industrial Relations is primarily concerned with system-reform and efficiency . . . with making the existing system work in a different way, so that persistent problems with union job control, bargainised wage systems and managerial workplace authority are mitigated or overcome.

Beardwell (1991:4).

The argument can be run on: 'New Industrial Relations' is the final phase of implementing Donovan, the juridical phase of Donovan having already been traversed. The 'New Industrial Relations' also extols the centrality of individual v collective rights, contract and representation. It posits an alternative model to the pluralist tradition of UK industrial relations. There are now as many actors in the workplace drama as there are employees, so the argument goes.

The 'New Industrial Relations', or variants of it, is not confined to the UK experience. One dimension is however heightened in the UK debate: an avowed aim of altering significantly the role and power exercised by trade unions. The Annual Report of the Certification Officer (February 1994) bears witness to the decline of the unions' mass membership (down from 13.2 million in 1979 to 8.7 million in 1993). The decline of manufacturing during the decade from the end of the 1970s to the end of the 1980s has ensured that the unions will never again achieve the density in the economy with which they were once associated. The 1960s and 1970s leitmotif of UK industry has all but disappeared: in 1992 the Department of Employment reported that the UK incidence rate for days lost through strikes over the five years 1987–91 was 70 per cent lower than in the previous five-year period.

Underlying the flexibility argument is a debate about the nature of work, its organisation, and the problem of 'unemployment climbing towards the 35 million mark amongst the West's industrial nations' (The *Guardian*, 15th December 1993), with the skill shortages and undertrained UK workforce persisting. It is certain that the nature of the firm will change in the twenty-first century.

In a seminal article Kiechel (1993) reviews the work of the theorists at the forefront of information technology and its attendant social organisation. It is as profound as Weber's writing was in his epoch. The six factors that, it is argued, will reshape the workplace are as follows:

■ the average company will become smaller, employing fewer people (IBM is *shedding* the equivalent of a multitude of companies)

- the traditional hierarchical organisation will give way to a variety of organisation forms, the network of specialists being foremost among these (the spiderweb organisation, so named for the lightness yet completeness of their interconnections)
- the technician will replace the manufacturing operative as the worker élite (the accumulated knowledge of the organisation is in the heads of its people, working as teams)
- the vertical division of labour will be replaced by a horizontal division (the 'radically flat organisation')
- doing business will shift from making a product to providing a service (quality is internalised)

Work itself will be redefined: it will become a matter of constant learning, of higher-order thinking (the paradigm of the 'learning organisation').

Hastings (1993) has recently addressed the so-called *software* that may bind such organisations together to enable them to deliver their purpose and act in a cohesive manner. For Hastings, such organisations will be characterised by

- radical decentralisation
- intense interdependence
- demanding expectations
- transparent performance standards
- distributed leadership
- boundary-busting
- networking and reciprocity.

Hastings is the latest to offer a typology of the 'New Organisation', or a postmodernist approach to organisation forms. But where does all this leave HRM?

The answer perhaps lies in the extension of Hasting's argument by Hinterhuber and Levin (1994). Their article reminds us that distributed intelligence has turned *time* into a strategic weapon of competitive advantage:

> . . . The time advantage is achieved by rethinking established business processes and rebuilding the organisation in the form of smaller business units with clear goals and benchmarks letting those units operate with a large degree of independence and linking them with other units in the organisations to form a flexible network.
>   Hinterhuber and Levin (1994:50).

The management guru Tom Peters is reported to have said that hierarchies are dead: successful organisations will not be structured as pyramids but instead on the 'blueberry pancake model' – all being level and all equal. In the nanosecond-1990s effective companies are structured in small groups geared to agility and to matching solutions to customers' needs, using human imagination as their chief resource. It is not a great leap of imagination in turn to envisage these units being set up anywhere on the globe. Flexibility of labour is at the heart of this model, and what many on the political right see as fetters on labour market forces (eg minimum wage, health and safety observance, the Social Charter provisions of the Maastricht Treaty and, at the most extreme, an abhorrence of child labour) do not sit comfortably with the flexibility ideology.

Building on the value-added work of Kay (1993) and amending Porter's (1985) schematic, Hinterhuber and Levin (1994) boil these arguments

Figure 10.1

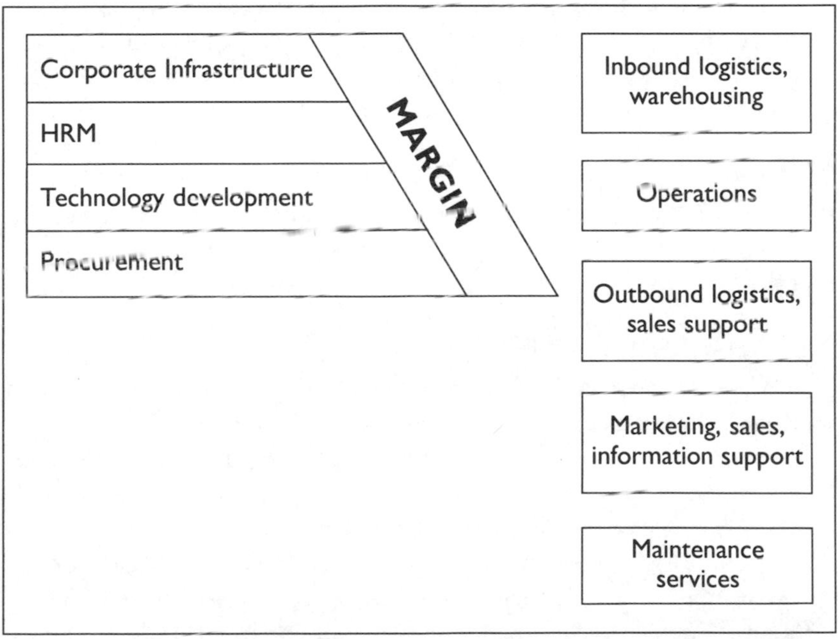

Value chain as a collection of different units supplying their competencies to the 'server' (adapted from Porter).

Reprinted from Long Range Planning, Vol. 27, No. 3, H Hinterhuber and B Levin, 'Strategic networks', p.46, © 1994, with kind permission from Elsevier Science Ltd, The Boulevard, Langford Lane, Kidlington, OX5 1GB, UK.

down to the issue of 'process'. The key props are logistics, operations, and sales support (including information and maintenance). Procurement, technology development, corporate infrastructure, and HRM are all at the margin; not unimportant, but not drivers. Hinterhuber and Levin adapt a Porter schematic to illustrate the 'value chain' as a collection of different units supplying their competencies to the 'server'. The server is simply the unit co-ordinating a given project that can and will change with the next project – the server 'co-ordinating the chaos (within the enterprise)'. (See Figure 10.1.)

As an explanation of how complex organisations can be configured and that 'an intelligently set-up network between smaller or mid-size firms can very well be superior in most regards to a larger competitor' (Hinterhuber and Levin 1994:46) is an argument finding a broad resonance. It is also, along with Hastings', an encapsulating explanation of how globalised capital, distributed intelligence, international labour markets, and new forms of physical distribution are radically affecting organisation design.

Furthermore it serves as an explanation of the forces affecting the public sector or, more precisely, the notion of central government. The 'server' now is the diminished state, focusing on a narrower remit than was traditionally accorded to all post-war governments. We are in an age when managerial ideology is concerned with 'reinventing government'. Even the language is apposite, with such phrases as 'the contract with America', as if the democratic process of the secret ballot were secondary to the contractual – and by definition the potential is implied here of a breach of contract (ie the relationship between the elected and their electors). Private-sector contracts are superior to public rights and obligations. Conveniently, contracts can exclude noncontracting parties – there are no obligations to them – whereas democrats are supposed to govern both those who elected them and those who chose the losing candidate.

The 'new organisation' in government is not about public service but rather empowerment. It is about the efficient 'delivery' of solutions to local needs: 'what Americans do hunger for is more control over matters that directly affect their lives: public safety, their children's schools, the developers who want to change their neighbourhoods . . .' (Osborne and Gaebler 1992:74). To achieve this they will inject an entrepreneurial spirit into transforming the public sector. The advocates of this ideology will extol the benefits of 'teamwork', invest in employees, praise innovation, etc (Osborne and Gaebler 1992:270–71). What they will not be concerned with is a comprehensive human resource strategy for the public sector. Rather, the concern will be about 'paying for performance', and therefore measuring performance and limited-service agreements between the public servant and the agency of government. They are concerned with transforming rule-driven organisations, the quintessential Weberian model, into 'businesses-*manqués*', ruled by expediency. We have, according to US politician Newt Gingrich, 'an absolute obligation to minimise damage to the natural world', a 'moral obligation to take care of the eco-system', but, because this collides with his wish to lift the 'ridiculous burden' of 'environmental regulations hatched in Washington', the fulfilment of our moral obligation to take care of the eco-system is left to a constituent in Gingrich's district, Linda Bavaro, who turns two-litre Coca Cola bottles into T-shirts which she sells at Disney World. 'Linda', Gingrich notes, 'has a good chance of doing well financially by doing good environmentally. That is how a healthy free market in a free market country ought to work' (*New York Review*, 10 August 1995, p8).

Nevertheless, the deconstruction of HRM is not the same thing as its demise, judged at any rate by the membership level and commercial buoyancy of the UK's Institute of Personnel Management (now the Institute of Personnel and Development). In the four years immediately prior to combining with the Institute of Training and Development, the IPM had in 1990 a membership of 40,262 and in 1994 54,333. (Membership of the merged IPD stands at over 75,000.) So how do we reconcile the shift to new organisational forms and a reduction in the perceived centrality of HRM (historically labelled 'personnel management'), and the relatively steady-state nature of the vocation of HRM? There were perhaps two distinct avenues of enquiry: the technician role and the strategic contributor to organisational effectiveness.

Armstrong (1991) posits the view that 'decision making on human resources in most of Britain's large companies takes place at levels considerably subordinate to budgetary planning and control'. He goes on:

> the 'line manager' in the present-day large company is becoming, before all else, a *budget holder* . . . the delivery of human resource management *practice* into the hands of managers controlled in such a fashion [through being primarily evaluated in terms of budgetary or return on investment, targets], whatever the rhetoric behind it, promises to turn the treatment of human resources into an instrument for the achievement of short-run accounting targets. Taken in this sense, then, human resource management, far from providing a strategic treatment of human resources, is actually likely to subordinate itself still further to budgetary control.
>
> Armstrong (1991:164).

The role of human resources is polarising in one direction towards our 'clerk of works' model (Tyson and Fell 1986): a technically proficient group of people serving the needs of their employer of the moment but working at an operational or administrative rather than strategic level. No statistics are possible, but we can surmise that much 'personnel management' currently being undertaken is, at best, high-level and tactical in nature and not strategic in content, complexity, or time margins.

This operational role is eminently suitable for competency-driven models of development and accreditation against benchmarks of work undertaken through inter-firm comparison. It sits comfortably with new organisation theories of the enterprise and project-driven cultures. European personnel managements have recently been suitably warned: 'we will see a lot more project-based companies, which open like the circus or musicals and close down when they've finished' (Akio 1995). Personnel managers will be valued – and there is no evidence they are not being acceptably rewarded – at the level of the enterprise and all that implies as being part of the management control structure. Their administrative skills will be necessary to the functioning of the servers, to rendering effective the new organisations characterised by Hastings (1993) and to enrolling the needs of the server, with the workforce having the characteristics described by Mant (see Chapter 2).

The alternative role we have elsewhere called 'the architect' (Tyson and Fell 1986). Purcell (1995), although not detracting from the argument of Armstrong (1991), asserts that there are four major areas of action in personnel to make decentralisation a success. These are:

- reconfiguring the internal labour market and contracts of employment
- managing the decentralisation of collective bargaining and building new relationships with staff generally
- working out a revised role for the personnel department and line managers
- deciding what sort of management style would be the most appropriate.

To bring this into being, Purcell argues, the first requirement is leadership 'from the top', but this is often frustrated by the top's limited imagination of what personnel can do. In one role at least this support from the top is forthcoming: a strategic role for HRM is acknowledged and the strategic prospects are rosy. Whatever the extent of the decentralisation of the enterprise, the forming of networked organisations, or the extent of

Kiechel's view of the future, the management of 'top talent' – executive resourcing – is the new meaning to the hallowed dictum, 'people are our most important asset'. At the macro level, the HRM role is concerned with organisation design and development, and with securing for the enterprise the top tier of talent to manage it. Not an easy mandate: Kakabadse reminds us that the 'business drivers' (those more likely to hold senior managing director, executive director, or directors' roles) are likely to have been employed in the same company for a limited period (see Chapter 6). They have to be continuously renewed and motivated. The continuous renewal and motivation of 'business drivers' may soon be a prominent feature of the UK employee relations landscape as an inevitable consequence of a proposal to set notice or contract periods for one year or less (Greenbury 1995).

Is the strategic prospect for HRM 'limited' to this arena? In reality, it is being polarised between two clusters of activity. The first is that of providing a high level of tactical support for employment relationships determined at the enterprise level. This is an important contribution to the *efficiency* of the enterprise. But HRM is here not a main player in the *effectiveness* of the business. The second activity is that of a group of high-level, strategic HRM practitioners concerned with business effectiveness and advising on appropriate organisational design without constraint of traditional thinking; this will most likely be a group with operational, business, or line management experience. Understanding the subtleties of what makes for organisational success and perhaps, more importantly, being credible in the eyes of peers to advise on organisation form and the selection and development of key management – having 'been there, done that' – becomes a selection criterion in its own right for joining the 'strategic HRM set'. This group will know clearly the distinction between *efficient* and *effective*.

This bifurcation of HRM mirrors our earlier argument and that of others in earlier chapters of this book. Organisations are themselves polarising into distinct groups. Whereas many of these organisations may be characterised by structures typified by Hastings (1993) and others, there is a connection with the core–periphery debate of a decade ago (Atkinson 1986). Although that debate revolved around labour forces and not organisations, is it not the case that, in the non-public sector, enterprises are adjusting to the determinants of global capital, distributed intelligence, and the internationalisation of labour markets, and that these enterprises provide the dominant international 'brands', and dictate the mode and cost of production? This goes against, perhaps, a Porter thesis of the

Table 10.1
TOP 10 CITY TAKE-OVERS 1989–95

Target	Acquirer	Date
Morgan Grenfell	Deutsche Bank	1989
Standard Charter Merchant Bank	Westdeutsche	1989
Gartmore	Banque Indosuez	1990
Midland Bank	HSBC	1992
Charterhouse	BHF/CC de F	1993
Barings	ING	1995
Jupiter Tyndall	Commerzbank	1995
Kleinwort Benson	Dresden Bank	1995
S G Warburg	SBC	1995
Smith New Court	Merryll Lynch	1995

'competitive advantage' (ie that each industrialised country has a few major industries through which, historically, such factors as creativity, natural reserves of raw materials, and diversity have been concentrated in the hands of a few who seek competitive advantage). In the UK industrial case, for example, we have been able to see since 1989 the transfer of ownership of a substantial part of one UK knowledge industry – merchant and investment banking – to seek greater global reserves in capitalisation and the exploitation of information technology. 'Take-overs', since 1989, have been prodigious (see Table 10.1). The dominant acquiring businesses of Table 10.1 will be complemented by a plethora of (national) peripheral entities which will enjoy a symbiotic relationship, for example as a supplier, franchisee, customer, outsourcer, cross-seller etc.

HRM is consequently affected. Human resource strategy passes to the new corporate centres where the remit is the long-term resourcing of the enterprise and the tactical issues that support that – for example, international mobility, performance and reward, and the present fashion to concentrate top-team development within the enterprise's own 'university' where a global cadre of management can be formed, cultured, and so on. HRM concerns, in a nutshell, are the creation of a homogeneous set of organisational values and performance standards, applied in this instance to white-collar knowledge workers. This is undoubtedly an idealised notion of the perfect corporation, but that does not inhibit many companies from striving for it. In any event, the central objective is the same: compliance. The conundrum in managing knowledge workers is how to avoid limiting human creativity while also ensuring non-deviant behaviour. We can see in the collapse of Barings the degree to which there were 'systems' failures and the extent to which distributed intelligence and wide spans of control enabled the deviant behaviour to appear.

Broader tactical levels are also becoming clearer, such as alternative means of supply (eg the agency provision of skilled labour), the relinquishment of certain business activities (eg 10-year service contracts for IT provision) and, through the continuing revision of modes of supply, of human resource services. This includes the development of new providers of human resource services, for example, public relations firms entering employee communications, and banks or building societies assuming the contract management of relocation.

The logical extension of these developments is the transformation of the human resource function into profit centres. In passing, one could remark that it is difficult to fathom a longer path being trodden from the *welfarism* of early UK personnel management to the frequently encountered contemporary model of human resource services being judged against a benchmark of value-for-money to line management. One case known to the authors, the technical training department of a large chemical 'works', is an aggressive profit centre 'trading' within the site, the division, and the group world-wide to UK and international third parties both in the private sector and with foreign governments. Although essentially a subdivision of the human resource function, this training department is a substantial business in its own right and has a trading profit and loss account greater than the divisional human resource budget.

The deconstruction of human resources does not represent its demise, as we have already stated. But what is evolving at considerable pace is a profession that is witnessing the acceptance of its own credo ('people are our most important asset') being taken up by the line, and the line is proving willing to take responsibility for managing 'the people'. They wish to be supported from above (not least because this includes the management of their personnel affairs) and from below by a range of services and professional support. Whether it is in-house or a bought-in service concerns them not a jot.

The human resource profession has not avoided the *fin de siècle* introspection generously applied to other professional groupings. But in the case of human resources there is more to it than that. In the UK there has been evolution in the profession virtually from its inception; it has not been characterised by permanency in the roles that human resource professionals undertake. If the current 'split model' continues to find favour with line management at the end of the century, or at least by 2010, this may result in a distinct separation of the two parts. The 'architects' may be appointed from a wide pool of non-human resource careerists, whereas the technicians will be better-educated (though not necessarily better trained), well-rewarded individuals, meeting comfortably a set of external competencies defining their role.

We have also illustrated the degree of change embodied in the very construct *organisation*. We have alluded to the extent to which organisations and society will co-mingle, reminiscent perhaps of the benevolent employers of the past. Employers will assume duties that have been considered over the past 60 years or so to be the responsibility of the state. The 'extended enterprise' is not only about supplier management but also community enrichment. It is private enterprise bolstering what it perceives as the shortcomings of the state: increasing the educational standards of employees, promoting continuous learning, counselling for addiction, encouraging voluntary activity, and so on. It is doing so in part altruistically, but also to ensure stability in the general environment in which it has to operate.

Conclusions

Our discussion in this chapter has taken the form of a debate upon the trends in management and organisation. Paradoxically, the best-case scenario – with the management of people at the top of the CEO agenda, a co-operative trade union movement, and a committed workforce – is arguably less likely to sustain the human resource specialist as an important functionary in the hierarchy. The specialist occupation grew from conflict, worker exploitation, and heavy state involvement in industrial relations. It has been argued by some academics that HRM is personnel management come of age. According to this view of HRM, people at work are now regarded as being so important to the process of making money and delivering quality products and services that *all* senior managers want to focus on people management. HRM is too important to be left to the specialists, therefore.

Whether or not we have yet reached such a situation is debatable. The rhetoric flowing in management journals and at conferences is so thick that we can but surmise that there may turn out to be some truth behind the claims. The literature (as we showed in Chapter 1) does offer some evidence of this, although frequently it is the same group of large companies and international businesses that are cited as exemplars of HRM. One suspects that there is some trickle-down effect to smaller employers, and again there is some evidence from the work of organisations such as 'Investors in People' that human resource development (HRD) is not just a large-scale organisation phenomenon. The prediction here is that, as the connections between business success and HRD become more clearly established, so the rhetoric will be turned more into a reality.

We have suggested here that the degree of change affecting organisations has grown to the point where, whatever the changes to management ideologies, the human resource function is itself a victim as well as a source of change. One effect is to force a split in the roles: at one end of the spectrum a high-level change agent role, specialising either as an external or internal consultant on the management of change; and at the other, basic administrative roles, applying the rules, and servicing line-management demands. A further result is found in the way the occupation has become 'balkanised' – a trend which we believe is likely to continue. Public relations and communications policy are driven together by the common need to manage meanings when faced with the mixture of internal and external organisation stakeholders in the modern organisation. The growth of business school providers linking into corporate training functions is a further example. As more specialist and technical advice is required, whether from lawyers or video producers, so the human resource role becomes more one of managing teams of consultants rather than managing a large department of internal resources. This balkanised version of HRM is consistent with the profit-centre approach, which seems destined to continue, and is equally in keeping with a broader organisation trend towards the autonomy of the subunits.

We have also examined the societal role for HRM. Societal pressures have always been a significant source of legitimacy for HRM. In this sense it takes on a societal role: adapting what happens in organisations to wider governmental, societal, and cultural needs. This role, if fulfilled, is quickly influenced by social change. The more pessimistic scenario delineated at the start of this chapter seems, on track record at least, to be closer to the reality we are likely to experience in the next century. We expect that the challenge for human resource managers will be to reconcile organisational efficiency needs with societal demands for employment, fairness, justice, and democratic values. The possibility exists that there will also be heavier burdens placed upon organisations in extra costs for elder care for employees relatives and for pension and social welfare provision.

At least if we accept that HRM thrives in adversity, this aspect of its role will henceforward guarantee a place in the sun for the function. The demands for expertise in coping with the stresses of change are set to increase. Human reactions to uncertainty can now be seen in the anxious 1990s. There are constant threats to personal and family welfare from the unpredictable business environment. Labour market, organisation, and industrial relations changes result in the kinds of responses discussed in this book. International pressure and global trading will bring managing diversity to a priority place in management. European-style industrial relations based on partnership rather than adversity, combined with new economic and social threats, will require new leadership responses. Personal development, organisation change, flexible employment patterns, and changed career structures are not new, but the long-term consequences of these and the other trends described here are. In this book we have attempted our best estimate of the effects of these consequences.

The strategic prospects for HRM are encouraging. But they are very different now from what they were before 'New Industrial Relations', before unitary models of UK industrial relations, before post-war reconstruction, the emergency war years and the central direction of labour, and the pre-war social and political upheaval of the 1930s. HRM is an evolutionary profession, compounded in this era by a fundamental redefinition of the *playing-field* of the human resource operator: the organisation. The role has evolved in the past but the construct of the organisation has remained by and large untouched. This will not remain so in the twenty-first century.

References

MIRYABAYASHI, A, (1995), quoted in *People Management*, 13 July.

ANNUAL REPORT OF THE CERTIFICATION OFFICER, (February 1994), London, HMSO.

ARMSTRONG, P, (1991), 'Limits and possibilities for HRM in an age of management accountancy', in *New Perspectives on Human Resource Management*, edited by J. Storey, London, Routledge.

ATKINSON, J, AND MEAGER, N, (1986), *Changing the Patterns of Work – How companies introduce flexibility to meet new needs*, Falmer, IMS/OECD.

BARNETT, C, (1986), *The Audit of War*, Macmillan.

BEARDWELL, I, (1991), 'The "new industrial relations?" A review of the debate,' *Human Resource Management Journal*, Vol. 2, No. 2, December.

BURGOYNE, J, PEDLER, M, AND BOYDELL, T, (1994), Towards the Learning Company, Maidenhead, McGraw Hill.

DRUCKER, P, (1993), *Post Capitalist Society*, Oxford, Butterworth-Heinemann.

EUROPEAN COMMISSION, (1994), *Europe 2000+ Cooperation for European Territorial Development*, EC Regional Policies, Brussels, ECSC. EC. EAEC.

FLOOD, P, C, GANNON, M, J, PAAUWE, J, (1995), *Managing without Traditional Methods Strategic International Innovations in Human Resource Management*, London, McGraw Hill.

GREENBURY, SIR R, (1995), *Directors' Remuneration*, Report of a Study Group, Denbigh, Gee Publishing Ltd.

HASTINGS, C, (1993), *The New Organisation: Growing the culture of organisational networking*, Maidenhead, McGraw Hill.

HINTERHUBER, H, AND LEVIN, B, (1994), 'Strategic networks – the organisation of the future', *Long-Range Planning*, Vol. 27, No. 3, June.

HUNT, D, (1993), 'Flexibility is a friend of the jobless', *Financial Times*, 9 December.

INDUSTRIAL RELATIONS LAW BULLETIN, (July 1995), London, IRS.

JUNG, C, (1957), *The Undiscovered Self (Present and Future)*, Collected Works 10, para. 488, Princeton, Princeton University Press.

KAY, J, (1993), *Foundations of Corporate Success*, Oxford, Oxford University Press.

KIECHEL, (1993), 'How we will work in the year 2000', *Fortune*, 17 May.

MARCUSE, H, (1964), *One-Dimensional Man*, London, Routledge and Kegan Paul.

NEVIS, E, G, GOULD, J, M, AND RAU, H, (1995), 'Organisations as learning systems', in D. Ready (ed.), *In Charge of Change*, Lexington, International Consortium for Executive Development Research.

OSBORNE, D, AND GAEBLER, T, (1992), *Reinventing Government*, London, Penguin Books.

PORTER, M, (1985), *The Competitive Advantage of Nations*, New York, Free Press.

PURCELL, J, (1995), 'Be a uniting force in a divided firm', *People Management*, 6 April.

SAMPSON, A, (1995), *Company Man – The Rise and Fall of Corporate Life*, Glasgow, HarperCollins.

TEAGUE, P, (1991), 'Human resource management, labour market institutions and European integration', *Human Resource Management Journal*, Vol. 2, No. 1, autumn.

TYSON, S, AND FELL, A, (1986), *Evaluating the Personnel Function*, London, Hutchinson.

WORMACK, J, P, JONES, D, T, AND ROOS, D, (1990), *The Machine that Changed the World*, New York, Macmillan.

Index